Eagan,
So glad we got to … Agile …
meet through th…
Summit. Hope …
May it inspire …

SHIFT: FROM PRODUCT TO PEOPLE

Eagan,
What a privilege to have you buy ~~my~~ our book! :-D
May you find inspiration and several "aha" moments with the content. Write notes, dog-ear pages, use sticky notes and have a few laughs!
We are not worthy!
Solid Snake

By PETE OLIVER-KRUEGER
and MICHAEL DOUGHERTY

Shift: from Product to People

Publisher: Oikosofy Series, www.oikosofyseries.com

Layout: Muuks Creative, www.muuks.com
Cover illustration: Pauli Salmi

TABLE OF CONTENTS

Acknowledgments by Pete Oliver-Krueger

This book was a joy to write, but also really, really difficult. I would not have gotten through it without partnering on this project with Michael "the Mad Dog" Dougherty. His drive, dedication, and cajoling kept us moving in the right direction. You could not call it "quick" movement, but moving nonetheless. I extend my heartfelt thanks to Michael for believing in this work and driving it along. He kept me going through three downsizings (and hence starting three new jobs), COVID, and the passing of my mom. He was always supportive, even when (understandably) impatient, gave me time when I needed it, and kept our collective feet to the fire when we needed that.

My thanks to Ali Oliver-Krueger for her patience with early days, late days, and weekends spent living in the world of the book. Also special thanks to Max and Jack (may he rest in peace) for giving me many opportunities to test out ideas with them, even when their responses were limited to just a few barks, curious head tilts, and lots of tail wagging.

And, of course, appreciation to all of the clients over the years, especially those who let me test out new techniques with them. You will probably recognize some of the techniques in this book that we did together, and your real world testing really helped to make these ideas realistic and practical. Thank you!

Acknowledgments by Michael Dougherty

Michael would like to thank his wife for her 100% support through all the days and nights working on the book as opposed to spending time without me without any complaints ever!

This book would not have been possible without her!

Michael wishes to acknowledge his co-writer, Pete Oliver-Krueger for the initial idea all the way back in January 2020 and for making it through the ups and downs (especially the summer of 2022) where the book had a time disruption nearly as bad as any comic book character or time lord.

To Vasco Duarte, you were our savior in 2020 when we had trouble finding an editor and publisher who would appreciate our book. As a "one-stop shop", you have provided all the missing parts we needed!

Michael's heartfelt gratitude goes to Jason Little for supporting us and guiding us to our publisher Vasco Duarte, the "toolbox" master in so many ways, and glad to have them show us the way!

Finally, Michael wishes to thank his mother, whom has always supported him, during his good times and especially the bad times.

Foreword by Jason Little

Author, Lean Change Management

It's 2024 and it's not a stretch to say that big-A Agile, and agile coaches, have been getting beat up for the last year and a bit.

This book will restore your faith in both if you follow this simple rule:

Don't skim this book. Immerse yourself in it.

Michael and Pete have crafted a story (based on real events) filled with situations we've all experienced. I know I've been in a few of them, and I wish I could have handled them as elegantly as Angela did.

It's a business fable, not unlike 5 Dysfunctions of a Team, and some of the lessons and techniques are laid out clear as day, while others are more subtle. Perhaps the best part is how masterfully the techniques are woven in and out of the story so you don't feel like you're reading a book about leadership and coaching.

Angela gives us a masterclass in agile coaching and congruence as she wades her way through an impossible situation with grace. She isn't the hero of the story – in fact, the story isn't about heroes at all – she's simply doing what a coach does: she helps people make sense of their context so they can make better decisions.

Along for the ride are characters you've all worked with like the control freak, and the Spock-like character who's always right, even when they're wrong. I found myself rooting for Roy many times, rolling my eyes at Naomi, then immediately regretted doing that, wishing I could help Linda, and wanting to dropkick the CEO a couple of times.

This story is about as real as it gets, and the tension is something we've all experienced. I guarantee if you've worked in a medium-sized or larger group, you'll be able to plunk yourself into the story and feel what it's like to be unheard, or thought of as the brilliant jerk, or praised as the savior even though you know that's not true, and not what you want.

But don't think of this book as a manual that will help you overcome resistance to agile from "those people". And don't think of this book as a how-to guide to become an agile savior. This book reiterated something Esther Derby told me at AYE many years ago when I was a new coach: "Jason, it isn't about you", and that's the mantra Angela lives by.

Instead, think of it as a bag of Agile coaching goodies wrapped in a story filled with triumph, tears, and laughs that will give you clues about which technique to pull out of your Agile coaching goodie bag when the time is right.

Bravo Michael and Pete for bucking the trend of a book filled with context-less easy-answers and fancy process diagrams that state how to fix your organization.

Real transformation is the hardest thing any organization will ever do, and it takes a team who argues, debates, but ultimately listens to each other guided by a coach who knows how to stay out of the way.

PART 1

OPENING THE CAN OF WORMS

Chapter 1

Naomi – A Sense of Urgency

Authors' Note:

We have condensed timelines within the book that happen much quicker than normally possible in order to accelerate the learning points and keep the story at an interesting and engaging pace.

DISRUPTED

"Naomi, are you alright?" It took a few seconds before Evah's words registered in Naomi's mind. "Naomi? Should I call somebody?"

"What?" said Naomi, finally. She noticed that she was still holding the phone in her hand, even though she obviously wasn't talking with anyone any more.

"Ok. Good," said Evah. "You're back. Are you alright?"

"Sure," Naomi replied, putting the phone back into its cradle, "Why?" Evah looked concerned, so Naomi quickly followed, "What's that look for?"

"I've actually been standing here for a couple minutes already," Evah said with care in her voice. "I'm guessing you've seen this article, then? I was afraid something like this would happen."

Naomi was battling the urge to go get another latte. A "Two-Latte Morning" was never a good morning, and this was definitely not going to be a good morning, or day, or sprint, or quarter — or life, probably. "Let's go to the lobby," she told Evah.

"So you have seen it," Evah confirmed. "I can't believe they would do this to us! I mean, we just talked with them last month about joining our network, and then they go and steal our idea! How did they get it built so fast!?"

"Yeah, I just got off the phone with Legal," Naomi responded. "They said that they already have plans to go after Intuition Bank for breaking the non-disclosure agreements, but they also said that any legal action would take a long time and may not be successful."

Naomi had been talking with Intuition Bank for months now, trying to bring them on board as an early adopter for their personal banking app, 'Breeze'. "They seemed so interested, but it was all a ruse," she said to Evah. "Those traitors were just stealing valuable information for their competing product. How dare they steal my product!!! They even stole the name! 'Cynch'? Really? All they did was probably just open a thesaurus to the page for 'breeze' and grab the first word that they could spell!!"

This set Evah off on her own rant. She was one of those friends that, no matter what the topic, would immediately rally to your side and join the protest. Evah's rants always gave Naomi a burst of much-needed hope, but not this time. Naomi wasn't really listening. At this moment, Evah was a wall of background noise. It was a terrible thing to think, Naomi knew, but still true. Evah always repeated herself enough that catching up with the conversation wouldn't be a problem. And, as a bonus, with Evah talking, no one else walking by was stopping in with their own version of "I told you so." She could see in their faces that they wanted to.

"Well, I'm not going to let Intuition get away with this," Naomi said, interrupting Evah's train of thought. "I am going to make them pay!"

Evah switched gears without missing a step. "Should we pay? Maybe we should just buy Intuition?" Evah asked.

"No," Naomi replied. "We already explored that but hit two obstacles. Intuition doesn't need money and is protected by wealthy investors, and they already made it publicly clear that they didn't want to be bought by an 'old and stodgy' firm like her company. Our only option would be a hostile takeover."

"Ohh! I like it!" said Evah, encouragingly, as she punched the button for the elevator.

"We're beyond that now," Naomi replied as they got on. "Breeze is already the premiere app for peer-to-peer transactions over ten thousand dollars. We were first to market, and we can hold that position! And we have the best product! Intuition Bank can take their new Cynch app and go..." DING!!! The elevator doors opened into the lobby.

"Good morning, Naomi! Hi Evah!" said Linda, the new Program Manager for the delivery teams, standing in front of them with a cup of coffee in each hand.

Linda's nervously-smiling face was always genuinely friendly, and that put a smile on Naomi's face. She definitely needed allies right now. But she also needed to stay focused. "Good is not the word I'd use today," muttered Naomi as she briskly exited the elevator and headed directly for the coffee line.

"So she's not taking it well?" Linda asked Evah before calling after Naomi. "Naomi, I got you this grande half-caf latte with three pumps of pumpkin. 'Pumps of pumpkin.' I always chuckle when I say that," she grinned.

"Thank you, Linda," answered Naomi without stopping, "but I think this calls for a double espresso shot."

"Oof, I hear ya!" puffed Linda in agreement as she fell in step with Naomi and Evah.

"Can I have the extra coffee?" asked Evah.

"Sure!" smiled Linda and handed her the cup.

Three of the programmers were standing in line as Naomi strode up. They respectfully stepped back and offered to let her go ahead. Naomi continued strategizing, "With the new security features we can now fully onboard new users even if they're not our existing customers. This will allow us to go viral. Imagine all of our thousands of existing users now able to add customers for us. We'll dominate the market, and Intuition Bank's copycat Cynch app will fade off into obscurity."

"The usual?" asked the barista.

"No. I'm going with a venti double-shot with white mocha," countered Naomi.

"Ok, that's one large latte with two shots of espresso and four pumps of white mocha syrup," recorded the barista.

"Wait." Naomi couldn't make up her mind. "How can I lead a team if I can't even make a decision about coffee," she thought. "Go with your gut," she told herself.

"No, I'll stick with that," she decided out loud.

The barista followed up, "Ok. Anything else?"

"Nope, that's it," said Naomi, followed by a long, audible exhale.

"Good choice," she heard from a male voice to her right. She knew that voice, and she shuddered internally, her eyes rolling back in her head slightly. The barista gracefully made her exit to start the drink as Naomi turned to face Don. He continued, "Did you hear about Intuition Bank? God, that sucks!"

"Yes, Don," replied Naomi. "I did. What happened? I thought you said they were 'locked and loaded', that they were 'definitely in the game'. Well, it definitely seems like they're in the game, but they're locked and loaded and pointing the gun at us!" she retorted with frustration.

"Woah, that's a pretty violent game you've got going there," chortled Don, having a little too much fun at Naomi's expense for her taste.

A muffled scream escaped Naomi's lips. "Well," Naomi asserted, "you were in charge of the negotiations with Intuition Bank." No attempts at humor were going to work on her this morning.

"This is how the sales game is played, Naomi," interjected Don. "You know this."

Naomi rolled her eyes and stewed quietly. Even more than the failure of losing Intuition as a customer, Naomi was also just really tired of all of Don's sports analogies.

Don continued, "Intuition was using us for research. They're jerks. They're the ones you should be angry with. You were there in those meetings. They were soooo interested. They thought we were 'really onto something.' They would 'love to get into the game.' But they were just planning to start their own team. No! I say screw them! They can eat our dust."

Naomi calmed herself. *"No need to be mad at Don,"* she thought. *"You're going to need all the allies that you can get."*

"Besides," Don added, "we're going to smoke them now that we can add new users entirely through the app! Everybody I've been talking to has lit up when I've told them that," he said, smiling broadly.

Naomi was startled. "Oh, no. Who have you been telling about the onboarding features? We haven't released them yet! Did you tell Intuition?"

Don started to back-peddle, "Hey, it's on the Roadmap, and all of my customers are talking about how none of their friends can create an account from within the app. Of course I'm going to tell people that that pain point is going away *real soon*... But... I didn't talk about it with Intuition."

"Naomi!" called the other barista, "Order for Naomi!"

Evah inserted herself, "How about we take this party back upstairs?"

Naomi started to look around. *"Oh, god,"* she thought. *"Everybody is staring at me."* The programmers were whispering, probably about her. The security guards were giving her the side-eye. Even the latte machine was steaming in concert. She gathered herself, "Come on, Don. Let's go upstairs and strategize. We've got this. Let's figure out how to blow Intuition out of the water!" Naomi led the vanguard back to the elevator, four warriors with their four lattes.

"That's right!" agreed Evah.

"Yeah!" added Linda. "This is so exciting...like a war! It's like Earth versus Mars! Breeze team, assemble!"

"What are you talking about, Linda?" asked Evah.

"That book I was telling you about," replied Linda. "Remember? 'The Expanse' by... it's two authors but they combined their names... Corey... James! James S.A. Corey. They made it into a TV show. It's set in the future, after we've colonized Mars. The planets are at war..."

Naomi also had no idea what Linda was talking about, but the conversation filled up the elevator which gave her time to think as they ascended back to the ninth floor. It would not be easy, but it was doable. This was just going to require changes. And big moves. And an idea was already forming. She'd have to kill Roy's project, and Roy was going to hate her for it, but Roy already hated her. But if she could get Tim on board, then with the backing of a VP she could probably make it happen. Tim had always respected her decisions. He was the one that put her in charge of the project in the first place. Naomi had made a lot of money for Tim in her previous job, and she was pretty sure that was why he got his Executive VP job.

In the background, Linda was still going, "You really should watch it. I think your son would love it! It's very smart...and educational. The authors really try to make sure that all the details are completely accurate. They, like, talk to NASA scientists and physicists and all. Read it, watch it, whatever. Just check it out. In this last chapter that 'proto-molecule' I was talking about escapes and starts wreaking havoc..."

WE ARE PHOENIX!

"Why do we have to drop everything for another all-hands meeting?" Naomi heard one of the programmers saying to a friend as they entered the room. "We're going to have our next one in two weeks anyway."

"Yeah," replied the other programmer, "She's probably going to change it again."

"That's right," thought Naomi, *"change is definitely coming."* She was starting to get that feeling back, that feeling of the early days of the Ares Innovation Center, when they felt like a real startup.

When she had originally joined American Banking Systems, it was a culture shock. ABS was a juggernaut in the financial industry. And there she was, a former banker, who had failed at running her own consulting company. But she got the job because she knew how to solve ABS's problems.

ABS had been seeing their market share dwindle. They needed fresh ideas, and she had plenty of those. A couple years in, Ahmed, the CEO, decided to start the Ares Innovation Center, and Naomi jumped at the chance. She wanted to get back to that feeling of running her own company.

It was thrilling! She brought her whole team with her, including Evah the best tester she had ever had; Jayson, her star programmer; and Zach who was just an intern at the time but who showed real promise. Now they were all managers and heading up their own teams, growing from eight people to a thriving team of teams, now totaling seventy-three. Evah had built one of the best testing units. Jayson, it turns out, was a natural manager of techie types, gentle and understanding, but always able to deliver when needed. Zach had surprised everyone by building a top-notch Customer Service Desk.

Those were the days, and all thanks to their app, "Breeze". They had tapped into a new market, almost accidentally. They had figured out how to make the secure transfer of large sums of money "a breeze," by automating all the mundane details that wealthy people hated. It had been the "victory march" for Ahmed, and ABS.

Those early years were rough, but they were also fun. And things were about to get fun again. Now, with Intuition Bank and their copycat app "Cynch", Naomi was starting to feel the thrill of the fight again.

An elbow poked Naomi in the ribs, jolting her out of her daydream. "Of course Roy waltzes in...what?...nine minutes late?" whispered Evah to Naomi. Tim, the Vice President in charge of the Ares Innovation Center, had insisted that their Data Scientist, Roy, needed to be there, and he had finally decided to grace them with his presence. And he had brought his ego, which was ten times bigger than his database.

Naomi smirked in agreement. "And without even a hint of an apology," she added. She turned and called out to Tim, "Tim! Roy's here. Shall we kick this thing off?"

"Oh, good," added Tim, "We can't have this conversation without him." Tim walked to the front of the room and a chorus of "shh" started to spread throughout the room. "Thank you," he began. "Thank you for dropping your work and being willing to go with the flow. As you may have heard, Intuition Bank launched a competing product of ours called 'Cynch'." An advertisement for Intuition Bank's new app popped up on the screen behind him.

Tim continued, "You may be wondering what that means for us? I'm here to tell you that it means nothing. Why? Because you all are awesome. You're the best programming team anybody could want. You've set yourselves apart here at the Ares Innovation Center, which is why you were chosen for this assignment. When we started this group two years ago we only had one team. Now there are over seventy of you. We started with a handful of users, zero revenue and increased that by millions of dollars and thousands of wealthy users. I have complete confidence in your abilities to rise to the challenge. And I have complete confidence in our fearless leader, Naomi. I'm going to turn it over to her to fill you in on our response strategy."

Naomi stood up and strode confidently to stand beside Tim. "Thank you, Tim. A round of applause for Tim, everybody!" Everybody gave Tim a hearty, although quick, round of applause. She continued, "I agree with Tim. You all are awesome! You can do anything! Let's have a round of applause for everybody." They all clapped politely.

"It was a Breeze!" yelled one of the guys from the back, which brought a loud groan from the other corner. A bubble of laughter swept through the chairs, the couches, the loveseats, and the bean bags, which nicely broke the tension.

"Intuition may have launched a competing app, but they didn't launch our app! We still have the users, we were first to market, and we do have the best team that anybody could ask for!" More applause. Naomi left some room for it before continuing, "Ali has built a first-class architecture," she said as she gestured at their application architect. Claps arose as Ali discreetly waved his appreciation to the room. "Vera and her team have created a beautiful UI!" Vera rose and gave a graceful curtsy, then started directing claps to her design team surrounding her. "And Roy, well he does stuff with data that nobody really understands... but he brings the Artificial Intelligence that truly makes this app a Breeze!"

"It's not really Artificial Intelligence," piped up Roy with mock humility, "It's really Machine Learning..."

"Machine or human, it's learning that we need," Naomi quickly added, taking back control of the room. "And, of course, I couldn't get anything done without my right-hand gal, Evah." More claps erupted, especially from the testers in the back of the room.

"And last, but not least, we have united our Development and Operations teams using DevOps! Thanks to the extraordinary technical leadership of Jayson, the architecture of Ali, and the dedication and monumental follow-through of the testing team in automating our entire test suite, we can now say that 'We are Phoenix!'"

Somebody happened to have brought their copy of *The Phoenix Project*[1] with them, held it aloft, and echoed, "We are Phoenix!"

For a brief moment, Naomi wondered if they were mocking her. Then a couple of engineers in the back right started chanting, "We. Are. Phoenix. We. Are. Phoenix." Naomi let it go, and it started to build, and eventually the whole room was chanting. She didn't join in, but she had to admit that Gene Kim's book about DevOps had really shifted them into a new way of thinking.

She let the enthusiasm crest and continued, "So that's why we're here. We hear that you're wrapping up the last of the bugs this sprint, the smoke tests are running solid green, and automated test coverage is over 80%! That's fantastic!"

Naomi threw a side-glance at Roy. She knew she would have to deliver this next section without pausing, "So we want to stay ahead of Intuition and release the new version now, by the end of the next sprint or even this sprint." Roy leaned forward in his chair and started to speak, but Naomi was ready for this, "But we're a team, and we want you all to tell us what it would take to make that possible. So let's break into teams for the next thirty minutes and discuss."

Roy exploded out of his chair. "No! no. No. NO. NO! We agreed that this sprint would be mine!" Roy shouted over the rising din. "It's the sixth release and I finally get to add my data tracking!"

A third of the room glanced over at him, but Naomi had her answer ready to go, "I'm not saying that we can't do both, but we need to let the

---

1 "The Phoenix Project" by Gene Kim, *https://itrevolution.com/product/the-phoenix-project/*, 2013

teams figure out what they can and cannot do." She was pretty sure that they feared her more than they feared him.

"Bull!" erupted Roy again, now shouting directly at the VP. "Tim! This is crap!"

Tim waved Roy over to him, along with Naomi, "Not appropriate, Roy. Both of you come with me."

"Not appropriate?" Roy protested while walking over, "I'm not appropriate?! How about her blindsiding me with this bull—"

"Roy!" Tim snapped. "Keep it civil. We'll discuss this in my office," Tim said in a low voice.

Roy started muttering to himself and marched out of the room. Naomi gladly followed. She knew that the only person Roy would listen to was Tim, so she had already been strategically loading him up with the best arguments Naomi had in her arsenal.

Roy had already launched into his arguments before they crossed the threshold, "This is what you hired me to do, Tim. You wanted me to predict the future? I'll be your fuh—"

"Language," Tim asserted.

"I'll be your... your... your frackin' Nostradamus. Is that better?" Roy was already starting to dig himself a hole. Naomi chuckled to herself.

Tim just stared and nodded him on, so Roy continued, "Sorry. I can be your Nostradamus, but I can't be Nostradamus without data. It's not magic. It's science, Tim."

"We also decided," began Tim, "that we were going to decide these things as a team. That's why Naomi suggested we go with the Big Room Planning session."

"No," blurted out Roy, as his eyes rolled so far up into his head that the pupils disappeared, "Naomi suggested it because she knows that nobody in that room gives a rat's... gives a sh... cares at all about data."

"He's quick," thought Naomi, but this was chess and she'd already boxed him in.

"If we leave it up to a vote," Roy continued, "I'm never going to win. If you don't understand data, you don't understand why we need data, and therefore you should be disqualified from voting!"

Tim countered, "There are no literacy tests in a democracy." Naomi hated having fed that argument to Tim. It felt cheap, unworthy of its origins in the Civil Rights Movement, but it worked. Roy had no comeback.

Naomi moved into phase four of her plan, "Maybe the teams will still be able to add some... or even all of the data code. I mean, some of the teams finished early. I bet they've already started working on next-sprint's code. Let's see what they say. It's just that Intuition Bank's power play was completely unexpected, and we need to respond. If we don't respond fast, our investors will lose confidence."

Tim added, "How about this? When we walk back in there, you announce to the teams that they should also estimate how much of the data-tracking code they can fit in the next two days — safely, of course."

To Naomi, Roy sounded like her bulldog as he breathed out heavily through his flared nostrils. "Two days is not enough," he countered. "She's had four sprints, and I get two days. Seriously?"

"Well, that's what you've got," said Tim, ending the conversation.

Roy stood, stared at Naomi for a strong couple of seconds, and then marched back into the planning room. You could hear him already calling out to the teams for their attention.

Naomi looked to Tim in deference. "You were right about Roy," Tim said, "but I think you're also right that if we don't have an answer for executives now, they're going to be pissed. I'd rather have Roy pissed than our CEO pissed." Tim exited the office.

"You're right, Tim. I'm with you," Naomi said as she followed Tim back into the big room.

An additional fifteen minutes past the allotted time, and the numbers were in. Two of the teams had started working ahead into the next sprint, and fifty percent of those tasks were the data stories. They would test those, and add them to the release branch. The other three teams didn't want to risk breaking their builds by adding in new data code. They estimated that they could complete integration and regression testing in the remaining three days, and have a stable, full-system demo ready for the Sprint Demo. Roy was still impersonating a pot of water, silently simmering, but at least he was silent. Naomi breathed a sigh of relief. This was going to work.

TO GO, OR NOT TO GO

Three days later, Naomi entered the conference room with her morning latte in hand, "Did we do it?"

"We did it," replied Evah, already seated and ready to go, "Have a look." She slid a report across the table to Naomi with a yawn, "Not only did they finally get all of the unit tests to pass, and the smoke tests, but they also got to full 80% test coverage!" Then she glanced towards the door and back to Naomi and continued in a hushed tone, "Roy's not going to be happy, though. They only got half of the data stories done because of the extra time spent fixing the smoke tests."

"It was necessary," interjected a deep voice. They both looked up as Jayson entered the room, gently sliding the words into their conversation. Jayson was built like a mountain, six-foot seven-inches tall, with a massive frame that filled the doorway. But he was also as soft as can be — soft of voice, soft of personality, surprisingly graceful with that gigantic form of his, and with a soothing softness in his eyes. He added, "Since we were re-writing the security, every piece of the application had to be tested."

"That's alright, Jayson," smiled Naomi, warmly. "You'll get no complaints from me. Thank you for keeping us all safe."

But his softness was quickly shattered by Roy's voice outside the room. Naomi instinctually tensed.

"Surprise, surprise!" Roy was saying. "They didn't get all my stories done." The words were dripping with sarcasm. "What's the point, Tim? What's the point?! We won't know if it actually works or not."

Tim strode into the room, with Roy practically talking over his shoulder. Tim took his seat in the center of the table. Roy looked at Naomi, already sitting in the chair just left of center, curled his top lip slightly, walked the opposite direction, and flopped across the comfy armchair tucked into the corner like he was about to watch a game on TV. He even brought his own bag of chips. The crumple of the bag picked up where his words left off, wearing Naomi's nerves down to the bone.

Tim launched into it, "Go, or no go. That's what we're here to decide. Whether 'tis nobler in the mind to suffer the slings and arrows of Intuition Bank or push out a new release!" Naomi could tell that he was proud of himself for that one.

"We need to take back the media attention! We push now!" insisted Naomi.

"Stick to the plan!" called out Roy from his literal armchair-quarterback position. "You promised me one sprint of data collection. Once I have that, we'll know how to hit them back."

"That's one sprint of coding," fired back Naomi, "but then we still have to collect the data, which will take another sprint ...at least. It was fine when there wasn't any competition."

Tim held up his hand, "Let's hear from the others."

"I abstain," replied Jayson, "We'll build whatever you want us to build."

"I love a good fight," gleamed Don to Jayson's left. "Let's deploy!"

"I'm with Jayson," said Linda, noncommittally. "I checked with the Scrum Masters and they'll build whatever you want."

Evah was next, "The team worked really hard, and we're solid green right now. You know I always like more data, but adding more code also means more changes, and right now we're green."

"Hey y'all," asked Zach, appearing suddenly in the doorway. "Does anybody know why the CEO is walking around our floor? It sounded like he was looking for your office, Tim."

"They're in here, sir," came a voice from the hall.

"Please just call me Ahmed," they heard the CEO say.

"Ok, um, Ahmed. Well, he's right in here," said the intern as she ushered him into the doorway and quickly retreated back towards the safety of the front desk.

"Hello everyone!" he grinned enthusiastically. It was hard to tell if Ahmed really liked greeting people or if it was an act. He was fantastic at it, and Naomi admired him for it.

"Tim," he continued, "can I see you in your office? We have a problem."

"Oh, no!" Naomi thought, her heart dropping in her chest. "Is this about Breeze?" Her mind started racing through all of the worst possible outcomes that would bring the CEO down to their floor.

"Sure, Ahmed," responded Tim with poise. "Meeting adjourned until later," he said to the others as he got up and followed Ahmed out of the room.

Naomi followed the others out of the conference room. When she got to the doorway, she caught a glimpse of Tim disappearing into his office behind Ahmed, glancing back over his shoulder as he closed the door. She couldn't wait until Ahmed left, so she could ask Tim what Ahmed's problem was this time!

Chapter 2

Tim – Launch Missiles!

WHEN THE CEO VISITS...

"I always forget how nice your office is," commented Ahmed as he walked into Tim's office. "So many souvenirs!"

"Thanks," responded Tim. "Computer, set the shades to 75%."

"Ok. Setting the shades brightness to 75%," responded the automated speaker.

Ahmed ran his fingers across a drum head and gave it a light tap, "This drum is one of my favorites."

"Yes, the djembe," mused Tim, "I got that in Ghana about four years ago."

"And," asked Ahmed, "you really just go to the airport and buy a ticket to the country offering the biggest discount?"

"It's a little tip that my friend, Angela, introduced me to. Usually it's the country in need of the most tourism dollars," smiled Tim as he thought about the excitement of standing at an airport terminal surrounded by the possibilities. "I like to help out where I can. And I often end up in places I wouldn't expect. It's a lot of fun. You should try it."

Ahmed chuckled, "Oh, noooo. If my wife doesn't know exactly the hotel we're staying in, what the itinerary is, and where the hot tub is, she will not even pack a single bag."

Ahmed pointed to a painting behind the desk, "Is that the painting you were talking about?"

Taking a guess, Tim asked, "The one I bought with our Breeze app?"

"Yes," confirmed Ahmed.

"Yep," confirmed Tim, "I like to keep it in the middle of the action, to remind us of the goal. I geeked out a bit when the gallery owner tried to convince me to use Breeze for payment. I told her that I was in charge of the people who created it, and we geeked out about it together." The memory made Tim chuckle.

He continued, "She said it revolutionized her business. Since she is often selling paintings and sculptures well over ten thousand dollars, having an app that both handles the large transfers, and automatically produces the Currency Transaction Report was a game-changer for her. It enables her to handle impulse buys without having to worry about fraud."

Ahmed was also beaming, "Well, Tim, you were right! Launching this app was a good choice." Ahmed picked up another trinket from the desk and started turning it around, inspecting it casually, but Tim noticed a drop in Ahmed's face. His brow furrowed and Tim felt a clenching in his gut.

Ahmed sat down in the chair on the other side of Tim's mahogany desk. He gestured to Tim to sit. As Tim settled into his own chair, he was struck by how he felt like he was on the wrong side. Ahmed had this way of making whatever chair he sat in the head of the table.

Ahmed took a deep breath and explained, "We need to talk about Intuition Bank..."

Tim reluctantly but confidently cut Ahmed off, "We know," he said using a somber tone, "We thought they were on board, but it turned out to be good-old competitor research. But we won't let them get away with it, Ahmed. Trust me. My team is already on it." Tim wasn't sure if Ahmed looked convinced.

Ahmed began again, "I'm sure you are. The board has the utmost confidence in your team. The thing is, Tim... how do I put this..." Tim knew he had miscalculated. This was something different, so he quickly decided to be quiet and listen.

Ahmed stopped himself and restarted again, "You see, I was on the golf course this morning. I had bet Chester ten thousand dollars that he couldn't beat his score from last week. It was obvious that he was fooling himself, but he needed the external incentive. And, of course, he didn't." Ahmed paused, took another deep breath, and looked at Tim, but without the joy of someone winning a bet.

"Congratulations?" Tim slipped in with an easy questioning tone, and then went silent again.

Ahmed continued, "Thanks. But here's the thing. In the clubhouse he pulled out his phone... and showed me Intuition's app. Then he started selling me on their app, how easy it was to create an account, right there in the app, how it handled the reporting for transactions over ten thousand... He forgot that I owned Breeze... No, worse... He had forgotten that Breeze existed and was selling me on my competitor! That shouldn't be happening. I looked bad in front of the foursome. The other two even diverted their eyes."

That was why Tim could feel his gut ready to take a punch. He wanted to get up and hop on his exercise machine to make it go away. Trying to gain solid ground again, Tim seized Ahmed's next breath as his opportunity, "You're right, Ahmed. Of course you're right. It's not ideal, but I want to assure you that Naomi is already ahead of this. In fact, in that meeting you saw, we were actually talking about how we might be able to push the next release out early, thanks to our new DevOps practices."

"Good!" exclaimed Ahmed, slapping the desk with confidence, and sending an involuntary jolt through Tim. "I knew all I had to do was come down here and talk to you and you would fix it." Ahmed stood, and so did Tim. Ahmed took another deep breath and extended his hand, "We're counting on you, Tim. You know I don't like to make threats, so let's just say that if we can't turn this around... well, the Board is already on my back."

"You got it, Ahmed." They shook hands, and Ahmed turned for the door. He paused for a few more taps on the djembe, smiled, and exited, "Good luck, Tim!"

Tim followed him out of the room and gave Ahmed a curt wave, then shut the door. He moved the Japanese silk screen room divider blocking the exercising equipment, set the iPad on the bike's book stand, and started burning off some of his frustration as he verbally dashed off a message to the intern, "Schedule another meeting right away with the managers. Today if you can. Get them to clear their schedules if you have to."

He opened a new email and started voice typing again, "Hey, Roy. Just talked to the CEO. He needs the new release out ASAP. I hate to do this, but I'm going to have to ask you to hold your objections. I'll tell you more in-person." A couple clicks and it was on its way.

He paused, the djembe drum catching his eye. He dictated one more email, "Hi Angela! It's been a while. Hope you're doing well! Was just thinking about our trip to Africa. Would love to catch up. Also, I could use your insight. Do you have time today or tomorrow for a call? Cheers, Tim."

THE FIST OF FIVE

Reminiscing about their trip to Africa felt refreshing for Tim. "Remember when that lion leaned against our tour vehicle and wouldn't let us leave for two hours?" he asked, returning to an old memory that still stuck with him after all these years.

"Poor thing just wanted some shade from the hot sun," chuckled Angela's voice through Tim's earpiece. "If we had driven off and stolen his shade, he would have chased us down for sure!"

"It's a clumsy metaphor," Tim sighed, "but I've been thinking about that lion. I feel like we're stuck, and we're all arguing about what to do, and in the meantime that lion is still just lying there, both using us for his own benefit, and without a care as to its impact on us."

"I'm sorry, Tim," she said, matching his tone in empathy.

Tim felt bad for bringing the mood of the conversation down, but that's why they were talking. "Can I tell you what we're up to?" he asked, "and you tell me what we're doing wrong?"

"I'm happy to give you free coaching," cautioned Angela, "but if I do, you have to promise me that you won't share my ideas with the team. These are only guesses. I'm not there on the ground with you, so the best I can do is give you things to look for."

Tim relayed the highlights of the team's journey, while Angela mostly just listened. He told her all about the origins of the app, the initial customer research, the removal of account creation to get their first six-month "MVP" out the door, the steady quarterly releases since then, until the sudden interruption of Intuition Bank.

"That's a lot!" exclaimed Angela with a huge exhale. "Congratulations on just how far you've gotten! Running through the list quickly: the idea sounds smart. I love that you did months of customer research up front! The six-month MVP... well, let's come back to that. Anything that's more than about a month in size can't really be called a Minimum Viable Product, but that's a larger topic than we've got time for. I'll come back to the quarterly releases idea if and when we talk about real Minimum Viable Products. And now you're looking at accelerating your schedule, skipping the metrics, and deploying as soon as possible. Does that cover it all?"

"Sounds about right," confirmed Tim. "Gaah, why did this have to happen now? Intuition has really messed things up."

"This isn't about Intuition Bank, though," Angela said encouragingly. "That kind of competitive stuff always happens. The only thing you have control over is you. Focus on your game plan and collect that data."

"Ooh," exclaimed Tim. "It's almost time for the meeting with my team. If it's not a bother, I'd like to check back later and hear more about your surface insights."

"Sure. But before you go, are you still doing the morning gratitude journal?" asked Angela.

"Yep!" replied Tim. "At the top of the list today was appreciation that we're finally going to deploy the new version of Breeze. My second was a personal one, and my third was that you were available to take my call on less than a day's worth of notice!"

"Aww. Thank you!" Angela beamed. "Great. It's wonderful that you're still doing that for yourself, to ground yourself. Don't forget to do that for your team also. Acknowledge your team first, no matter what you do."

"Acknowledge first," Tim agreed emphatically.

"And," added Angela, "if I'm going to be able to offer any real advice I'll need a list of known problems... from all perspectives. Ooh! Remember how we used to do a 'Fist of Five'? That might fit the bill here. What if you have people rate the potential success of the new release, from one to five? Everybody should get a chance to speak, especially those with three fingers or less. Encourage everyone to speak honestly and gather as much information as you can. If you can get a recording, I'm happy to take a look at it, but more-importantly... remember... acknowledge first."

"Thanks, Angela," Tim replied. "You're always full of good advice. Have a great day!"

He hung up the call and started walking towards the conference room. He was amazed at how much lighter he felt. It had been all hands on deck the whole week, sprinkled with a lot of stress.

He met Zach at the door of the conference room. Vera, Evah, Linda, and Naomi were already seated looking over Evah's final report. He saw Ali's and Roy's names on the video screen. "Are Ali and Roy not here?" Tim asked.

"Ali is at his desk," Linda offered, "overseeing the final processes, but he's dialed in. Roy is working from home."

"Yeah," Naomi added, "He said he didn't need to be here in person." She paused, then asked, "Are we on mute?"

"Yep," confirmed Linda at the controls.

Naomi continued, "Frankly it will be easier for everyone with him not physically here."

Tim started addressing everyone, "I know it hasn't been an easy week," then he paused and pointed at Linda. She jumped to attention in her seat, and before he could ask, she said, "We are now off mute!"

"Thanks, Linda," confirmed Tim. "Can you also hit the record?" Linda started the recording.

"I know it hasn't been an easy week, everyone," continued Tim, "so I want to start with some acknowledgements. Ali, Jayson, Evah, and all the dev teams, thank you so much for all the extra hours. I never like to ask for this much time from you all, but this is a special case... all hands on deck... and you all really stepped up to the plate! Thank you."

Claps started spontaneously all around. Tim continued, "Roy, thank you for being willing to put aside the data features we promised you. Also something I did not like to ask, but I'm glad you understood that it was necessary, given the circumstances." Linda and Zach started clapping heartily. Ali and Jayson joined in, along with Evah. Tim threw a quick nudging side glance to Naomi who slowly started clapping.

"Lastly," Tim concluded, "but certainly not least, appreciation to Naomi for taking charge driving us to the finish line," followed by claps from everyone, except Roy, who sat there, his arms noticeably crossed on screen.

As Tim leaned back in his chair, Naomi saw this as her cue to speak, "We are now on the defensive. Intuition pulled a surprise punch on us, but we were actually prepared for this. We have to get back on the offensive and show who is the real heavy-weight in this industry. We have the money, the size, and the backing, plus our new release was already nearly ready to go. All we have to do is release! Are we ready to go?"

Roy piped up first, "I just want to go on the record that this may be the fast approach, but we don't have the data to know whether this will be successful. We have a hypothesis, but we have no confirmation from the customer that it is correct. The wealthy are typically different from your standard users who use consumer cash apps, and we need to understand their reaction to these changes."

Vera jumped in defensively, "We've already refined the user personas ten ways from Sunday." Tim found himself surprised. He had not seen his Design Manager come in. She was stealthy that way. She continued, "...and Naomi has followed those personas with the backlog refinement sessions and sprint commits. The teams have built the right software."

Naomi chimed in, "Vera is right. We have built the right software, and we are at WAR. Roy is also right, collecting data is important and we definitely want to do that, but we have been pressed to the defensive and have no time. We can collect that data after we have a successful release and celebration!"

"You don't know if it will be successful," Roy shot back. "You are simply guessing. The optimal approach is to measure and build the data based on a small user group to minimize the risk, and then, once validated, go all in."

Zach went next, carving a space for himself in the conversation, "Whether Roy is right or not, we have not gotten enough information on the latest changes and won't be fully ready to handle any incident and problem calls without heavily relying on the Development teams. We can do this, but it will slow down our response time and keep impacting the teams after release. Are you willing to make that happen?"

Naomi confidently responded, "Of course, Zach. We were expecting that, right, Tim?"

Tim nodded his head calmly, "Yes, and I agree that this is the best approach. Honestly, I haven't heard sufficient reason to stop or pick a different approach. Do we agree to release this sprint? Let's do a Fist of Five."

Naomi raised five fingers in the air. Don matched her, holding five fingers over his head as he walked into the room and took a seat. Tim, Vera, Zach, and Evah all showed four fingers. Linda held up three.

"Ali?" prompted Tim.

"Four," came Ali's voice as his picture popped on screen.

"Roy?" asked Tim.

"Two," shot back Roy as his picture popped on screen, two fingers being held much too close to the camera for proper etiquette.

Tim gave Roy a hard glare, "Roy, I believe we understand your reason for raising two fingers. Linda, would you please explain why you held up only three fingers? Be honest."

Linda looked around the room and at the screen, "I don't know. I'm hearing from many of the teams that there were a lot of last-minute changes. The interfaces changed. The flows changed. They're a little worried that they might have missed something."

Tim looked over at Naomi for an answer, who countered, "Evah said that her team has cleared all Severity 1 bugs. Only a few Severity 2 and Severity 3 bugs remain, easily fixed after releasing this sprint. We have the quality built-in and will support Zach and the Help Desk during this rapid transition."

Linda nodded her head and agreed, saying, "Yes, you are right. We run a tight ship..." Her pencil was tapping rapidly on the table.

Tim pushed her a little, "If you're worried about the hours, I've already cleared the overtime with Finance, but be honest."

Linda sheepishly added, "I have a feeling we should get more feedback from the users first and would like to have more concrete evidence."

Tim felt a wave of relief. He was sure she was going to say something technical, "Yes," he replied, "we would all like that! But what it really comes down to... well, you heard the CEO. We got beat, and we have to respond fast. Time is of the essence. We could be squeezed out of our competitive advantage if we don't release now. Also, if it turns out to be a dud, we can rollback any changes quickly to adjust to any negative feedback."

Linda shifted in her seat a little more, then planted her palms on the table, "Well I'm still pretty new to ABS and don't really know how many big releases we have done here, so I brought up only three fingers. However, let me call it four! I believe in us!"

That was good enough for Tim, "Okay, thank you, Linda."

He switched gears and turned to face Don, "Don, I know you've got five fingers, but I'd like to hear the sales perspective."

Don eagerly held up his hand and started ticking off items on his fingers, "First, we have full business agility and have strategized the best results possible. Second, we rock as a high-performance organization! Third, I have complete faith in Naomi and Vera. To me, they can do no wrong," he said with a twinkle in his eye. "Fourth, I have full faith in Zach's ability to turn any support call into a satisfied customer. Fifth... well, I forgot what number five was, but I am one hundred percent behind this and know that we will crush Intuition to dust! Sorry, Roy, looks like you've been outvoted."

"Yeah," agreed Tim, "Sorry, Roy. The room has spoken. Let's move forward with our release. Let's blow Intuition Bank and their 'Cynch' app out of the water!" Tim added with a wry smile. Everybody burst into nervous laughter.

"Right!" echoed the chorus.

Tim stood confidently and announced, "Meeting adjourned!"

CRASH AND BURN

Tim fired up his computer for the Monday morning video call. It had been a great weekend. He was even able to take the boat out and do some fishing with his son. He closed his Appreciation Journal, took a pleasant, calming, deep breath, and connected to his first video call. "Good morning, Angela! Thanks for fitting me in. I promise to keep it to five minutes."

"Good morning, Tim!" enthused Angela from Tim's screen. "No worries, and thank you for recording the status call."

"So, what's the verdict?" Tim responded, jumping the gun.

"Can I start with a piece of advice for next time?" she asked.

"Sure," Tim agreed.

"You... took some liberties with the Fist of Five there," she began.

"What do you mean?" challenged Tim. "I know I skipped the countdown before throwing up the fingers, but this team doesn't have any problem with being swayed by seeing the votes of others. Trust me."

Angela guffawed. "I can see! Ok, that's a minor thing. Does... what's his name?... Don? ...know how to do Fist of Five?"

Now it was Tim's turn to guffaw. "Ah! Don is a character, isn't he? He's been told, but he's also a bit of an iconoclast. He loves going against the grain. He always adheres to 'the spirit of the law', so I've decided to just go with his flow."

"Ok," conceded Angela. "Then I loved that you encouraged Linda to talk more! But I was concerned that Roy didn't get to talk at all."

"Roy," started Tim. "Roy's a handful. He's never shy about expressing his feelings, and I try to head off unnecessary fights when I can. Trust me, we already heard his opinion, and we didn't miss anything."

"Ok," said Angela cautiously. "So my main issue is that the Fist of Five is not supposed to be a vote. Nobody gets outvoted in a Fist of Five. You have to move into risk mitigation mode and create contingency plans to address the concerns of those voting two and below until you can get them to come up to at least a three. Fist of Five is a risk management technique, not a voting technique."

"Roy will not give up until he gets what he wants," answered Tim. "I've tried. He won't compromise."

"It makes me uneasy," Angela insisted. "I hear him using good words, like 'hypothesis,' and I'd like to hear more about the data he wants to collect. I don't want to say it, but without a risk plan to address Roy's valid points, I'm afraid that's going to blow up in your face."

"Wait," Tim interrupted. "I'm getting a third text from Evah. I better switch over to the team call. Can I get the rest of your thoughts later?"

"Ok," agreed Angela. "Good luck!"

"Thanks!" Tim ended the call with Angela, pulled up his calendar and connected to the Monday morning video call. The audio connected just in time for him to hear Naomi yelling, "Our requests are down 20% in just one weekend?! Someone is at fault here! Where was the mistake made?! I need answers now!"

Ali jumped in, "We're still researching."

Roy quickly added, "I told you to get the data first. See, Tim? This is what I was talking about."

"Hi, Tim," they all chimed in simultaneously.

"Welcome to the show," added Evah.

"What's the latest?" Tim queried.

Naomi obviously couldn't contain herself, "Roy, getting your stupid data doesn't matter here. Your insistence that your data is going to give us all the answers is... and I'm being charitable here... 'an exaggeration'. We'll get you your data, but first we need to get our user base back and growing."

Tim was a little stunned by the harshness of Naomi's words. She had always been tough, yes, but in a cool, calm, and collected way. Not like this.

Tim jumped in quickly, "Roy, I want you to know that we recognize your viewpoint, and that you have a valid perspective. We recognize the power of building smart analytics to understand and harness the needs of our special clientele. However, we have to get the basics down now, and then we can use data to refine our software."

Roy muttered, "It's the other way around," but kept silent after that.

Tim continued, "Let's figure out the root cause as to why the release backfired. Was any part of the release untested?"

Evah shook her head no as she took over the screen, "Nope. Every part of the code that was changed had active tests. None were disabled. And all of them are green."

Tim tried the next thing in his mental checklist, "Was there a missing library?"

"Nope," responded Ali, "we would have caught that in the build report, and with our robust continuous delivery pipeline, that would never make it to production. Also," continued Ali, tackling the next item on Tim's list, "we're following the 'Brent Protocols' we learned in *The Phoenix Project:* no production machine can be directly touched, so there isn't the risk of a production defect."

Tim prodded, "What else?"

Jayson added the tech perspective, "Let's see. We have universal error handlers, plus static and dynamic code scans, and they all have passed. As Evah will attest, all code goes through the same scripts when promoted from our QA to Staging to Production, and we have an extra smoke test in production."

"Yep," confirmed Evah, "our smoke testers have tried many different scenarios and found nothing technically wrong."

Jayson continued, "Okay, here's a compromise. Why don't we revert back to our previous version, add some basic metrics to help us discover the root causes, fix those causes, and re-deploy?"

Naomi began, quieter this time, but firmly, "No. We aren't going to back out of this release." Then she scrunched her face in a strange way and her eyes got wide, "I know! Let's have a full-fledged User Acceptance Testing and we will quickly get to the bottom of this issue! Evah, I'll need your help!"

Evah responded, slightly wide-eyed, "You got it, boss! I'll round up my best testers to start on this today!"

Tim chimed in, "Great idea, Naomi! Don, Linda, please bring in people to help out with this UAT. Hey, we're Agile. We know how to pivot, right? But," he added, pausing briefly, "while this seems reasonable, I can only give you two weeks. If we don't have the root cause, and the results aren't improved, we will revert back and follow Roy's plan. Two weeks. That's all I can give you."

As the team switched to planning out the UAT, their voices faded into white noise for Tim. His memory took him back to the day when he first had the idea. That was a great day. He was on the golf course, four under par, with two holes in one. The ideas were flowing. His golfing buddies were on board. They all agreed that it would be a 'breeze' to own the market space. That's even how the app got its original name, "Breeze Transfer". He longed for those days when it felt like it would be a breeze.

Chapter 3

Clyde – "Every Which Way You Can"

A HORRIBLE, NO GOOD, VERY BAD DAY

Clyde found himself thinking about the movie *Office Space* by Mike Judge. "Each day is worse than the day before, so every day you see me is the worst day of my life," or something like that. *"That is messed up,"* he thought. *"How did we get here? And how can I make sure we don't come back here again in the future?"*

Normally Clyde was a very positive person. He loved being a Customer Experience designer. He found great pride and joy in designing customer interactions, but these days he felt like he was drifting farther and farther away from the user. That was one of the problems with working at a huge multinational corporation. He had never planned to work at ABS. His first job out of college was working at a financial planning startup. That was where he met Vera. She was the most amazing Creative Director he'd ever worked with, so when they got acquired, he followed her to ABS to continue learning from her, but working for a big bank just never felt right. When they launched the internal incubator, he jumped at the chance of getting back into a startup environment.

"We're down to 1 minute and 5 seconds per transfer!" came Naomi's voice, shouting with agitated excitement as she burst into the Design space. "Considering that it used to take 1 minute and 37 seconds, I think that's a win! I told you that combining those two steps into one page would make the users' lives easier. Let's keep it up. This is war! We can't let Intuition beat us!"

Clyde knew that was supposed to be a rallying cry, but he did not like war. Wars were messy, people usually died, and it was seldom the people in charge. It was usually people like him, "red shirts" to use the term from Star Trek. People who worked in the background until something important happened. Then they'd get promoted just in time to promptly get killed on the battlefield.

The User Acceptance Testing was in full swing. Naomi had managed to invite nearly forty users to perform the tests in their pre-production environment. Most of those, though, were friends of Tim's. Clyde had learned from his favorite blog, "Angela's Angle," to never use friends and family members in tests to avoid generating "False Positives." He chuckled as he remembered the line, *"Moms of company employees don't count!"*

In reality, only a third of the forty test users had participated so far, but Tim and Naomi still received waves of feedback multiple times a day from the participants. After each wave, they would process the feedback and then Naomi would come blazing into the Design area with a new idea. The designers would then change the mockups and send them to the developers for implementation.

In parallel, Evah's testers would develop the matching automated testing scripts. If the changes passed the tests, they were deployed to the UAT server and the UAT testers were alerted to try out the new changes. The plan was that any idea blessed by the UAT would be included in the next release.

Except... that it didn't seem to be making a difference, so Naomi was back every day with new ideas. They all centered on one primary principle: a decrease in the number of clicks to complete a money transfer would make the steps so easy that "my half-blind grandmother could do it," as Naomi was fond of saying.

"What is that?!" Clyde heard Naomi exclaim. "I turn my back for a minute!" She was hovering over the laptop of the new designer, Sam, giving him step-by-step instructions on changes, and waiting impatiently as he executed them.

"I took what you suggested, and it gave me an idea that I wanted to try," Sam started explaining. "I did this before in my last job. We got great feedback from the users..."

"Are the users from your last job our users?" Naomi retorted. "I know our users. I'm talking to our users. Are you talking to our users?"

Clyde felt his heart gripping tightly in sympathy and found himself wishing they had cubes. Normally he wouldn't dream of it. He loved their open workspace. The 'Designer Den' they called it. He and Vera had designed it themselves. The programmers seemed just fine with their cubes, but the design team worked so much better without walls. Everything was shared.

He looked around at the open collaboration tables, the design library on one wall, and the art on the other walls. It gave him a sense of peace. All of the walls were painted in whiteboard paint and the creatives would draw on them from time to time, including Vera, who was an amazing artist. She could make whiteboard marker drawings look like paintings, and she would always add an inspiring quote of the day just outside her office. He spun around, both to read her quote of the day, and to put his back to the embarrassing scene happening behind him.

"A vision is like a dream -- it will disappear
unless we do something with it.
Do something big or do something small.
But stop wondering and go on an adventure."

– Simon Sinek

It was a beautiful quote under an even more beautiful sketch of a sunrise peeking out from behind a majestic mountain. Clyde peeked around the edge of the wall into Vera's office. Wow, she was organized. He knocked lightly on the door frame to catch Vera's attention and gave her a nod over his shoulder in Sam's direction. Vera perked her ears up, stood up, and marched quickly into the fray.

"Naomi, don't worry, I've got this," Vera said in a gentle but firm voice. "I know you're super busy. Let's have the team put together a couple of options for your review and then you pick the best one. And I'll even look them over first personally."

This seemed to satisfy Naomi. She thanked Vera with a confirming nod and headed for the exit. As she crossed the threshold the entire design staff let out a collective sigh of relief. Vera smiled through it all and turned to Sam, still smiling. "You have good ideas. Don't worry. Just don't make the changes in front of her, especially if the 'Naomi Meter' is on a ten. When she's blazing hot, handle with care." The whole room nodded in agreement. "Just tell her, 'We'll put together options for you to review,' like I did."

Clyde loved how the Designer Den was open to everyone in the company, but sometimes it had its disadvantages. It was their little oasis of sanity, and there were unspoken rules within its sacred walls. Under normal circumstances, everybody respected the rules, even Naomi. The designers loved having visitors and encouraged drop-ins with daily catered lunches. They even had a party area, with bean bag chairs, a pool table, and several chaise lounges. Having all the programmers and testers and analysts stop by on a daily basis to hang out was perfect for team building. Even Naomi was welcome... usually... when her stress level was an eight or below. They called that the "Naomi Meter".

But there was a cloud hanging over everything now, which even made the food feel emotionally soggy. It was now all about beating Intuition.

He felt trapped, like a worker on an old manufacturing line. He was waiting for the horn, but no horn was ever going to blow, because this work shift had no end.

They could get back to normal if they could just figure out what was causing the decline in customer adoption! "What are we missing?" he asked himself. *"What don't we know that we don't know?"* He had read about the "Unknown Unknowns" in an article the other day. He searched through his emails until he found it, from "Angela's Angle." This was definitely his new favorite blog. He found the part he was looking for, "Testing Automation is an essential tool for telling you what's wrong with what you already know. You need to add Usability Testing to figure out what you ***don't*** know."

A little bit further down was a two by two matrix with two lines intersecting in the middle. Both axes were labeled with "unknown" on one end and "known" on the other end. Angela explained, "There are the things that we know that we know, things that we know that we don't know, things that we already know but we don't realize it yet, and things we don't know that we don't know. These Unknown Unknowns are the most dangerous, and there's only one type of Usability Test that has any chance of uncovering them, the 'Open Test'."

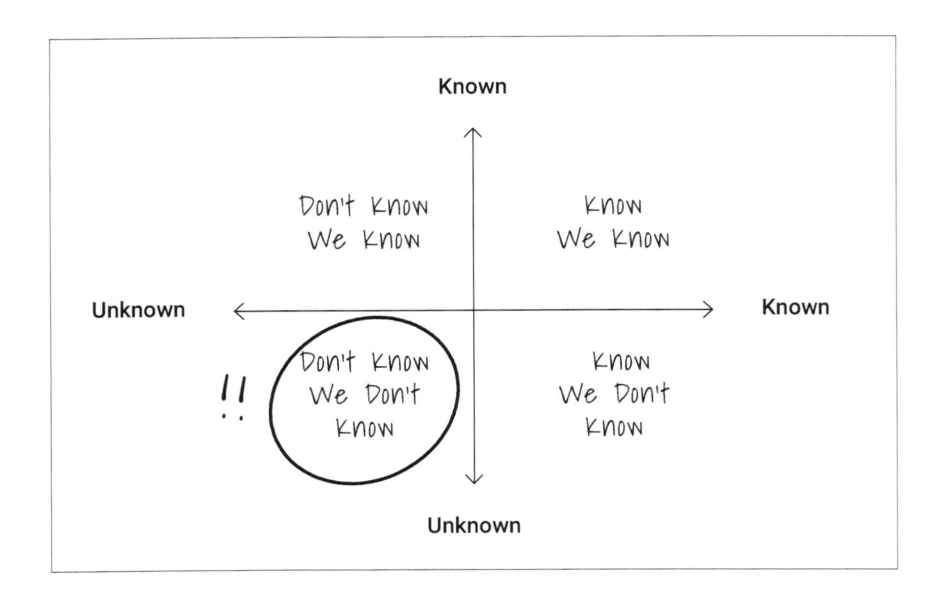

Clyde's brain shook back into focus. He scrolled until he found the descriptions of the three types of tests, "There are three types of usability tests: Open, Closed, and Guided[1]. The Guided Test is the one that's used most frequently. It walks through a known series of steps and is used to find bugs within a known scenario."

He scanned down to the start of the next description, "The Closed Test gives the tester a goal and the freedom to accomplish that goal in whatever method they wish. This type of test is commonly used in User Acceptance Testing or when you're trying to compare the behaviors of multiple testers with each other."

He moved on to the third description, "The Open Test makes no assumptions and is your best option for uncovering the Unknown Unknowns. The user is given no instructions. Just put them in front of the application and let them use it however they wish. Don't interrupt them. Just observe and take notes. If they ask questions, redirect it back to them with questions like, 'What do you think you should do there?'"

Clyde called out to Vera and spun his laptop around, "Vera, I've got an idea! I was reading this article the other day about Unknown Unknowns, which totally sounds like the situation we're in right now."

Vera sat on the end of the table and gave him a motherly look, "Go on, I'm listening."

Clyde pointed at the article on his laptop and explained the need for Open Tests instead of scripted User Acceptance Tests.

"Do you think Naomi will give you some users to do this?" Vera asked.

Clyde considered it for a moment then reasoned, "I had already brought this up to Naomi when I read it the first time and she said to me, 'stay in your lane.'"

Vera pushed him further, "Well, you're creative. Don't you have any ideas?"

Clyde smiled. He knew Vera's Socratic management style well. "Don might know some new customers who aren't on Tim's list already. Maybe they'd be interested in getting a sneak peek. I can also check with Zach and find out who contacts the help desk on a regular basis. According to 'Angela's

---

1 Also known as "Natural", "Scripted", and "Limited" testing: *"When to Use Which User-Experience Research Methods"* by The Nielsen Norman Group

Angle' you only need three to five people. After that, the amount of new information you get from additional test subjects drops off dramatically."

Vera responded excitedly, "Splendid idea! So what's the next problem?"

"Hmm..." Clyde thought it through. "Running the tests won't be hard. Sharing the results will be. It could literally become a 'he said, she said' kind of situation."

"What do we do in those situations when it's a choice between two designs?" Vera nudged.

Clyde gave a tentative smile, "We provide visuals and evidence and let the group mind hash it out... I know, I can record the tests! I've been creating these instructional videos for the help desk using screen recording software. It records the whole screen, including the computer sound and my microphone. If I run the tests over a video conference and have the user do a screen share, I can let people watch the tests themselves. Then no one has to take my word for it!"

Vera summed it up, "Great! I approve. You'll get a small group of users from Don or Zach, record the sessions, and bring them back here. It sounds like you've got a plan. In the meantime, I'll give Tim a heads up. Let me know if you need anything, and just don't let it slow down the new prototypes that Naomi wants for the new user login."

Clyde smiled again, this time more earnestly, "I can actually use those prototypes in the Usability Tests, so they will go hand in hand!"

THE USABILITY TESTS

On the day of the tests, Clyde got up early and readied the screen recording software. He also decided to include the design practice of A/B Testing. Test 'A' would include the previous, working release before the decline in user adoption as the control group. Test 'B' would use the newest release. Don was able to reach out to five potential customers to try out the new features live, and they all agreed to be recorded. Two of them had accounts already, but three of them did not.

Usability Test #1: New User, Old Version

First up for the day was one of the new users. Clyde had him test the old version of the software first. After reconfirming his consent, Clyde started the recording. The test subject had to get his personal assistant to come set up the screen sharing, but after that, he was ready to go. Clyde's only prompt was, "This is an app that allows you to transfer large sums of money to other people. For testing purposes, you can send a transfer to yourself and that will tell the system that this is a fake transfer."

The man expressed an immediate dislike of having to create his Breeze account via his existing bank account, "What do you mean I can't create an account for your app in *your* app?" Clyde just nodded and kept his mouth shut, taking notes. The test subject called his personal assistant again, this time to bring him the bank password. The assistant walked in and handed the man a sticky note. He typed the password into the computer.

As Clyde had seen many times before, he struggled with finding the link to create his Breeze account on the partner website, but unlike what Clyde had seen before, the guy actually just got up from the chair and stepped out of view. The assistant then sat down and proceeded to create the account for him, and then navigate back to the Breeze website. Clyde made several notes and took note of the time. The entire account creation process had taken 4 minutes and 26 seconds.

From that point on it really was a breeze. The first test user quickly found the button for creating a new transfer. When prompted to enter the email address of the user to transfer the money to, he entered his own email address, followed the legal prompts (scrolling through them quickly without reading), and finished the process. Clyde checked his watch again. The entire transfer was done in 1 minute and 30 seconds.

Usability Test #2: Existing User, Old Version

The second test was an existing user. Since she had already created an account, she had no problem logging in. Just like the first tester, though, she called her assistant to bring her the list of passwords for her accounts. Once logged in, though, she clicked the button to create a new transfer, entered her own email address as the destination, read the legal prompts quickly, and finished the process in just over 1 minute.

Usability Test #3: Existing User, New Version

Next up was the other existing user. Clyde sent him a link to the new version on their test server. Upon logging in he immediately said, "Oh, this is new. I don't need to log in through my bank anymore? Ok.

Whatever." He went through the steps to create his new account name and set his Breeze password. The total time was 1 minute and 39 seconds. After that, he sent the test transfer in 1 minute and 17 seconds.

Clyde's hopes were starting to drop. He was learning things about their users, many of whom were not that tech-savvy, but he hadn't seen anything that would be blocking adoption. These results all matched the UAT results.

Usability Test #4: New User, New Version

The first new user in Group B was running a little bit behind, and when she finally joined the video conference she was very obviously not in a good mood. "I'm sorry I'm late," she said. "I almost canceled, but let's go ahead and get this thing over with. What do you want me to do?" Clyde gave his usual speech describing the purpose of the test.

The woman loaded up the Breeze homepage and began the new user workflow. She easily entered her email address and chose a password and was taken to the security questions. "What's this?" she exclaimed, obviously irritated. "You want to know the bank where I have my car lease? How should I know? That's my accountant's job. What am I supposed to do with this? None of these options look familiar."

Clyde tried redirecting the question back at her the way the blog recommended, "Can you think out loud? What do you think the application wants you to do next?"

"Oh, geez," exclaimed the woman, exasperated, her eyes rolling back in her head. "Ok. Let me look... Here's an option that says 'none of the above'. Since I don't recognize any of these, I'll select that. There. It says I'm wrong. Ok, so it is one of the others." She tried two more answers before exclaiming, "You're going to lock me out for too many failed attempts? I don't have time for this. Tell Don that I'm sorry. I did what I could, but his application isn't working." And with that, she ended the call and was gone.

Clyde sat there for a minute dumbfounded. "Who doesn't know what bank their car lease is with?" he thought. "They have to pay the lease every month... Except they don't. They have people for that. Everybody so far has had an assistant."

Usability Test #5: New User, New Version

The next person did handle his own finances, so when he was asked to identify the bank that held his current mortgage, he got it right on the first try. He got blocked, though, when the security questions asked him to identify a street address from four years ago. He chose "None of the above" and was given an error. He countered, "I did? Did I own a house on one of those streets? Can you give me a city name? I can probably figure it out from the city name. It's hard for me to remember a house from four years ago. Do you realize how many houses I own? I flip houses. That's one of my major businesses."

Clyde said nothing and just replied with an, "Mm-hmm. Say more, please."

After searching his computer for about a minute, the test subject gave up looking. "Why do I have to do this anyway? Why can't you just use my phone to authenticate? It's got face recognition, fingerprints, passwords, lock codes. I mean, for Pete's sake, if it can't be trusted to authenticate that I am who I say I am, what's the point of all this crap?" It sounded like a great point, and Clyde added it to his notes.

The man switched to a browser and started searching for the address names in the multiple-choice answers. After searching all four address names he said, "Ok, this third one looks like it's in an area that I recognize." He selected it and clicked through successfully. "Finally!" Clyde checked his watch and notes that it had taken 5 minutes and about 20 seconds so far.

The next step for the new user was adding in a bank account. "Ok, next we add funds," he said. "That makes sense... looks like a wizard... selecting my bank... and it's asking for my account and routing number. Well, heck. I don't know what those are off the top of my head. I'm going to stop screen sharing while I do this step." The screen went back to showing their faces in full view. Clyde thought to himself that this was actually probably better to see the emotions on this guy's face during that whole thing.

The test subject continued narrating, "...Ok, I found one of my bank statements. Entering the account number. Where do I find the routing number? I don't have a checkbook with them... Let's see. That should be on their website. Hold on. Let's see. I remember that it wasn't on the homepage. Let me click into my Profile... Nope, not there. Account details? No, that's not the place. Let me try the help section. Oh, there it is! On the help page. What the heck is it doing there? That makes no sense. If you know that people need help finding it, why don't you just make it easier to find?" Clyde counted off another 2 minutes and 55 seconds before the guy shared his screen again.

The tester initiated the screen share again, "Sorry," the guy added apologetically, "that's not your fault. My stupid bank likes to hide the link for looking up the routing number. It always takes me a while to find it again, but I've entered the account and routing numbers now. It looks like the next step is sending a transfer. Let's see, I do owe Michelle thirty thousand. I can enter her email address in this box, but wait... I don't really want to make her go through this process just to get the money. What was that thing you said about making a test transfer?"

"You can make a test transfer by putting your own email address in the destination box," Clyde reiterated. He jotted down in his notes about the anti-viral nature of the process and how it discouraged this user from sharing the app.

"Perfect. I'll do that. Ok, let me read this legalese." The tester went silent for a good minute or so. "Ok," he said. "Sorry. I used to practice law. I don't click something I haven't read." He clicked the button and initiated the transfer. "What's next?" he asked. "Is that it? Ok. That part was a breeze. The other parts, not so much, but that part was good. A decent app you've got here. Do we need to do anything else?"

"Is there anything else you would want to do?" asked Clyde.

"Maybe add a couple more accounts," the guy said, "but not right now if that's ok with you. That's probably going to take a while. I'll do that later."

"Ok," responded Clyde. "Thank you so much for your time! You've been really helpful, and it's been super useful for me to see what you think about our app and how you navigate it."

"I hope I did alright," the man laughed. "Did I pass the test?"

"Definitely!" Clyde chuckled "I'm not sure we did, but you definitely did. Thanks again!"

"Ok," he said. "No problem. Happy to help Tim out. If I have time I can maybe do more later in the week. Have a great day."

"You too!" Clyde chimed in, and with that, the guy ended the video call. Clyde recorded the time. In total, they had been on the call for a little over 17 minutes. Clyde made a few more notes and then shut everything down.

It had been a brutal series of tests, but Clyde was elated. He had found it! He now had recorded evidence for Naomi and Tim to clearly see the reason behind the declining user base! He was excited and couldn't wait to share his discoveries with Vera.

NAOMI ACCEPTANCE TEST

Clyde turned off his camera in the video conference and got up to walk around in a circle. Clyde's stomach was feeling tied in knots as the leadership team watched the usability tests. He had spent all night into the early morning making a highlight reel. He had never been invited to the leadership conference call before, and didn't love the idea that his first invite would be pitting him against Naomi.

Well, it wasn't like Naomi was necessarily against the results. She had just refused to watch them, which had surprised Clyde. Naomi had changed tremendously compared to even just a couple months ago. She had always seemed so confident and self-composed, but now her responses seemed erratic and impatient. *"What happened to her?"* he thought. *"Has the threat of competition from Intuition impacted her that much?"* It had taken a direct appeal from Vera to Tim to put the results in front of the whole leadership team for a decision.

As the video finished, Tim offered Vera the opportunity to give her thoughts first. "As you can see," she said, "I think I made the right call. I wanted to let Clyde run with his passion, and it paid off. I'm sorry I didn't get pre-approval, but I also didn't want to interrupt everything else that was already in process."

Tim moved to the next two in his virtual round table, "Zach, Don, you two are closest to the customers. Do you agree? Are these users a good representation of how new customers are going to look at our new account creation process?"

Don nodded his head but kept uncharacteristically silent.

Zach was also nodding, but added, "I went back through the logs and what Clyde found is pretty consistent with the calls we have received. Most people don't see the problem as our problem, which is good news, but they're asking if there's a way to get around these beginning steps or choose different questions. They want to use the system, but they feel dumb that they don't know these answers."

Tim moved on to Roy next. Roy ruefully chuckled, "Okay, I'll say it straight. The results of our 'scripted' UAT were inconclusive and served no purpose. We were addressing the wrong bottleneck. We must examine this new bottleneck that Clyde discovered."

Finally Naomi boiled over and burst in, "This was not my fault! You were all in that UAT with me! You were there too, Roy! We followed our standard procedures and the only problems you all told me about were problems in the transfer process. Our test users failed us. Design failed us. QA failed us. Automated testing failed us. DevOps failed us."

"We did our best, Naomi," Evah squeezed in, almost in a whimper.

Roy tried to take back the conversation, "If you had let me..."

Naomi erupted. "If you say 'metrics', I swear to God, Roy!!! You wouldn't know what a user thinks if one came up and punched you in the face!"

Roy was opening his mouth, his eyes burning with rage, when Tim cut through the commotion, "Enough! Naomi, these are stressful times, but we will show respect to each other. You will apologize for attacking Roy!"

Naomi looked like she had been slapped in the face and took several moments to respond, "Yes... you are right, Tim... My apologies, Roy. That outburst was not needed."

Roy suddenly looked tired, "It really doesn't matter at this point. Regardless of the reasons, Clyde did something that the rest of us didn't do. It took guts and it worked. Focusing on his discoveries is what matters now."

Clyde sat down again in his chair and turned his camera back on.

There were a few moments of silence until Naomi added, quietly, "What I still can't believe is that you were all in on this secret test, and you didn't include me. I thought one of our guiding principles was Transparency. This is not transparency. This is betrayal."

Evah jumped in, "I didn't know about it either. Please don't throw me in that mix. I was just as much in the dark as you."

"I'm going to need a minute," was the last thing Naomi said before abruptly disconnecting from the call.

Tim took a deep breath, then smiled at Clyde. "It was an excellent find, Clyde. Thank you! You may have saved us. Okay, everyone, our current sprint is coming to an end. Will we be able to absorb this new information, design some quick changes, and get them ready for the start of our next sprint?"

Vera responded first, "I'm sure Clyde and I can hammer through our part today. Jayson and Ali, will you have time to review?"

Jayson looked calmly at the group and stated, "Yes, we'll make the time to review, but our teams are too busy to switch without weekend work, and they're beginning to suffer burnout, right Linda?"

Linda responded quickly, "Well yes, we are getting complaints about being overloaded."

Tim nodded, "I've said this before and will say it again. Heroics are not supposed to be the norm, so we have to get back to a reasonable workload."

"What about Naomi's latest improvements to the transfer flow?" Linda asked.

"Yep," agreed Tim. "That is a low priority now. Stop all work on that part of the application to free up capacity. Everybody's on this now."

Then, turning to Clyde he asked, "So, where did you get the idea of doing those usability videos?"

"I've been following this Agile coach," responded Clyde. "She writes a blog called 'Angela's Angle' and she suggested doing Usability Tests in one of her posts."

Tim jerked his head up in surprise, "This came from 'Angela's Angle'?"

"Yes," Clyde confirmed.

Tim pleasantly laughed, "She used to work for me! This is actually very serendipitous. I started chatting with her again recently and was considering if we needed to bring in an Agile coach. So far, we've been doing great without one, but well, things have certainly changed..."

His voice trailed off for a few seconds, but only a few seconds, before his booming voice filled the air again, "So how does that sound, team? Should we hire an Agile coach?"

Clyde and Vera responded, "Yes," in near unison. Jayson and Ali just shrugged their shoulders, and Linda quipped in, "Well, whatever you think is best."

"But," added Ali as his expression migrated to one of concern, "who is going to convince Naomi?"

Tim responded with renewed confidence, "I'll handle Naomi," and with that they ended the video call.

PART 2

AWAKENING THE ELEPHANT IN THE ROOM

Chapter 4

Angela – “Let Emotion Be Your Guide”

OPPORTUNITY KNOCKS

Angela was reading through a few emails when her phone unexpectedly rang. "Why hello, Tim!"

"Angela! How's your day going?" responded Tim's upbeat voice.

"Honestly, I've seen better ones," sighed Angela, "I mean, I love what I do, but some days are worse than others, you know? Today has been one of those days! My current client... their entire organizational structure is resisting the change, even six months in. I keep thinking of that quote from Peter Drucker, 'Culture eats Strategy for breakfast', and it feels like I'm breakfast! I think I'm just not what they want right now."

"I hear ya," Tim agreed with a knowing sigh. "If you were here I'd offer you something from the jar."

"Not the jar!" Angela guffawed. "Tim, you and that jar. I probably put on ten pounds from that thing."

"Ha! Sorry about that," Tim conceded. "You'll be happy to know that I've added healthy snacks now!" Angela couldn't help but laugh at the thought of a jar of healthy snacks.

Tim continued. "Those were good days, weren't they? Fantastic teams, fast learning, faster growth, and being able to really make a difference. Too bad upper management wouldn't let us expand. Say, were you upset about me leaving and going on to ABS? We've never really talked about it."

Angela paused briefly. "I was a little upset, but then again it did allow me to take your place as Manager! I understood, and forgave you a looooong time ago."

Tim laughed, "So, how would you like to recapture some of that energy, leave behind the old, broken companies just going through the motions, and come over here? We could really use you."

"I'm listening," Angela responded, "I feel like their 'corporate maid'. They want me to 'clean house', but they aren't willing to throw anything away."

"Well, this is not a clean house either," Tim assured her, "but I have to get this house looking beautiful again so that the CEO and the board aren't tempted to intervene. I have the CEO's full support, but he's a bit of an 'old school thinker'. I need my old star performer to help whip us into shape."

"Who you calling old?" Anglea quickly countered, on cue. They both chuckled, and she added, "But you have confidence that we can succeed?"

Tim clarified, "I do. You'll have my total support and I have full authority over Ares. We have a solid program and are following great processes. You won't have to teach anyone basic Agile. We read the "Phoenix Project" two years ago, have been practicing DevOps since, and everyone is absolutely motivated to overcome these setbacks. I wouldn't be here talking to you if I didn't fully believe we could overcome this! Give it six months and if it doesn't work out, I'll give you a shining recommendation if you want to move on."

"That's fair," she agreed.

"And no interviews," Tim added. "I already trust you, and we don't really have time for delays."

"Well," Angela quipped, "pushing a coach onto a team isn't exactly the best way to start, you know. Will the team resist?"

"Some may. Many won't. I just found out that one of them has been reading your blog, and is already using some of your techniques! I'm confident you'll fit right in in no time. I'll have Zach be your guide for your first two weeks. He's our Customer Support Manager and is really sharp. When can you start?"

Angela paused for a moment, "Hmm... Several folks will hate to see me go, but honestly, I'm ready to move on to where I can really provide value..."

"Okay, let's do this!" she said decisively. "I've been tapering down to only a couple days per week anyway. I can give you part-time now, and then transition to full-time after two weeks."

"That works for me!" Tim agreed.

AWAKENING THE ELEPHANT IN THE ROOM

Angela's first day at the Ares Innovation Center was shaping up to be a whirlwind. Tim started the day by spending over an hour in his office covering the current situation, describing the key players, and sharing Clyde's latest discovery.

After the intro, she and Tim moved to one of the conference rooms. "Sorry," Tim sighed. "You are coming into a burning house that is out of control, but hey, that's why I called you. Be on the lookout for interactions with Naomi and Roy. They are honestly going to be your toughest nuts to crack. Naomi in particular is really good and I trust her, but she's taking the downturn personally. She orchestrated a new release last week but our usage levels are still declining. Basically, Naomi is severely stressed, and when she gets stressed she gets easily angered, so she is going to need some gentle but firm guidance."

Angela decided to "mirror" Tim's statements back to him. "So, Naomi is upset because she crafted a new release last week, but usage levels are still going down?" It was very useful in new situations to help clarify people's thoughts. She found it endlessly fascinating that people will string words together in the moment, but then when you mirror those same words back to them, they will sometimes argue with their own statements!

Tim countered, "Well, no, I wouldn't say 'no increase'. Roy has discovered that the decrease is primarily with new users. Existing user growth is the same. Naomi thinks new users are deciding between Breeze and Cynch and we're losing. So we're doing an in-depth comparison of their account creation process and ours."

"Ah, so you are testing Intuition's app," Angela confirmed.

"Naturally," replied Tim, "I must admit that Cynch has a slick interface, and when talking to wealthy investors it's what they talk about the most, its speed and convenience. Now we can pivot fast but have a lack of clarity on where to pivot. That's where I need you to help."

"Let me make sure I'm with you here," interjected Angela. "You're testing the Cynch app with your wealthy investors and they're primarily talking about the interface? Speed and convenience? So you're pivoting – to what? – to match their interface?"

Tim reviewed the conversation in his head briefly before continuing, "I don't want to clone Cynch... unless that's what we need to do... It's just that all our customers talk about is moving money quickly, easily, and securely."

There was a knock on the open door and Angela looked up to see a young man standing in the doorway. "Are you Angela?" he asked.

Tim glanced up, "Yes. Okay, Angela, let me introduce Zach, our Customer Service Manager. Zach is my 'secret weapon'. He's very well connected to all of the team because of his job. Please join forces with him to make changes stick around here!"

Zach gave a "pffft" sound, rolled his eyeballs, and smiled, "Okay, Tim. You know that praise will get you everywhere."

Tim laughed and started walking away, "Angela, I'll leave you in his capable hands!"

Zach smiled broadly and said, "So you're here to save us from the clutches of Intuition's stranglehold, right?"

Angela countered, "Well, I'm no superhero, but I can help teams do things they've never done before!"

Zach laughed, "The truth is, you couldn't have come at a better time. We need someone from the outside to help us. Someone with full autonomy who isn't afraid to say what they see without fearing the fate of their job. Do you know that story of the chicken and the pig[1]?"

Angela nodded, "A chicken approached a pig and said, 'We should start a restaurant together.'".

Zach finished the punchline, "To which the pig said, 'No thanks! You'd only be involved, but I would be committed.'"

They both chuckled and Zach added, "And here at Ares, we are definitely the pigs. You would be the chicken. You have a lot less to lose, so please show no fear in giving advice, but also don't be surprised if it gets scrambled!"

Angela smiled. She loved a good pun.

Zach kicked them off, "Okay, what would you like to tackle first?"

Angela looked at Zach, "My initial approach is always about people and building healthy relationships with the teams. That way, I can help enable you all to solve your own problems through any new tools and techniques. I find an environment of psychological safety vital to producing high-performing teams."

Angela continued, "For me, that process starts with alignment: alignment of me with your teams, and alignment of the teams with Agile principles. The best way I've found to foster alignment is through conversations. Do you think you could help me set up interviews? I'd like to meet each team and see how they interact with each other."

"We can do that," Zach confirmed. "They're going to be resistant to adding more meetings, especially while we're under pressure. Everyone is already concerned that this will eat up a whole sprint. But if Tim tells them to, they'll show up."

---

1 See *"The Fable of the Chicken and the Pig"*, credited to Ken Schwaber

Angela interceded, “I’d like to minimize my disruptive effect and be as non-invasive as possible. I know from my days as a developer that you need big blocks of time to solve big challenges. Maybe I can just take over a retrospective, or add some extra time before or after an existing meeting?”

“Sure. Great idea,” Zach agreed. “I like how you think,” he smiled.

“When all is said and done,” Angela explained, “I only need two hours from each person. One hour together with their team and one hour with others in their same role.”

“Ok, that’s not too bad,” Zach remarked. “It seemed like a lot more.”

“It will be a lot of time for you and me, maybe,” Angela responded, “but not that much for the teams.” She continued, reviewing her interview checklist, “Ok, adding onto the team events will help me to get to know the team perspectives, but I would also like to talk to them outside of their teams. Sometimes people are too polite to tell the truth in front of the people who stress them out. Do you have any Community of Practice meetings, all the Scrum Masters at once, all the developers, all the product people, and so on? That might be a great chance for me to talk with people grouped by their roles.”

“We do have a bi-weekly Scrum Master lunch-and-learn,” Zach shared, “plus QA gets together as a group every week. Let’s see... The Designers are almost always together, so that will be easy, but we haven’t started one for the Product Owners or developers yet. But Tim said that I can schedule them from his account and make the meetings mandatory.”

“Uh,” uttered Angela cautiously, “I’m less okay with the idea of mandatory meetings. Please use them sparingly.” Zach nodded. “Are you going to be with me for all of the interviews, Zach? Tim said you had cleared your whole schedule this week.”

“Yep!” Zach confirmed. “I can already tell that this is where I want to be.”

That left a warm feeling in Angela’s heart, “That’s so nice of you!”

Zach added, “I’ll have to check in with the Help Desk from time to time, but they can also operate just fine without me. Which reminds me, I better check my messages real quick.” Zach took a moment to glance at his phone alerts and scroll through the notifications.

Angela jotted down a note about Zach’s team being able to operate autonomously. A manager that relaxed about their team was often a sign of having good systems in place, but it would be good to verify that.

Zach finished scrolling, "All good! Nothing they aren't already handling on their own. What else can I do?"

"Well," Angela began, "did Tim say that you've seen my blog?"

"Only recently," Zach answered. "Clyde turned me on to it. He's been following you for months, and used your blog about Usability Testing as his template for our sessions."

"Oh, good!" exclaimed Angela with a smile. It was always fun to meet real people that actually found her content useful. She continued, "If you saw the one about Usability Testing, ideally I'd like to follow full Usability Testing protocols here. By that I mean that for each interview, one of us takes the lead and the other takes on the role of observer and scribe."

"Ooh," said Zach, "yeah, I remember that part. Clyde and I tried it during our tests and traded off roles to see what each side was like. One person asked the questions and interacted with the test subject. The other person didn't speak, just wrote down the responses and any other observations. It was hard sometimes to keep quiet, but also quite fun!"

"I find the observer role the most important," Angela replied. "When you're required to follow along without having any control over the situation, you have a much more powerful learning experience. So I'd like to go through the schedule and see where it makes sense for you to be the lead, and where I should be the lead."

"Ok," said Zach, reticently. "If you think I'll be able to do it well enough."

"I get the feeling you'll do just fine," Angela assured him. "Do you also remember the emotional scale from that article?"

"I do," said Zach cautiously, "but I'm not sure I totally understood it, so we didn't actually use it. I might need you to go over it again."

"Sure," Angela agreed. "When I'm an observer I like to focus on emotions. One recent discovery of neurobiology is that the decision center of the brain is closely tied to the emotional memory areas of the brain. Jonathan Haidt[2] calls it 'the Rider and the Elephant'. You first have an emotional reaction to a situation – that's the elephant part – and then the rational part of our brain – the rider – reacts to the movement of the

---

2 For more on Jonathan Haidt's work see his books, including "The Happiness Hypothesis".

elephant. So, if you want to truly understand what someone is saying, you have to understand the emotional context driving it."

"Huh," responded Zach. "Well, we follow the Spock approach around here. No emotions. Rational thought only." He paused.

"Here's the thing," Angela inserted. "From recent research, it looks like that may be biologically impossible. I know we're talking about Star Trek and fiction here, but there is actually a biological component to what Gene Roddenberry was writing about in Spock's dilemma of being half-human. As Spock realized over time, the idea of avoiding all emotions in pursuit of pure logic is a fool's errand. Everything we do has an emotional component, and if we choose to not consider that part of the conversation, we're ignoring incredible amounts of valuable information. Emotional Intelligence is just as important as Cognitive Intelligence."

Zach's eyes narrowed, betraying a look of skepticism. "You don't look convinced," Angela said. "Don't worry, I'll show you what I mean as we go along. It can be hard to explain sometimes until you see it, and then you can't unsee it." Zach shrugged his shoulders, nodded his head in agreement, and started typing some thoughts into his laptop.

Angela grabbed a marker and started writing on the whiteboard in the room. "You don't need to understand the whole theory to apply it, though. I use a scale that allows anyone to capture the core elements of emotional reactions, and then go back and make sense of it later when you have more time." She wrote the numbers zero through three on the whiteboard, "Level 0 is whether or not people are just paying attention. If they're on their phones or checked out, that tells me that the topic doesn't affect them, and I make a note. If most of the room is at this level, I move on to a different topic."

0 – Not paying attention / not emotionally or intellectually invested
1
2
3

She continued, "Level 1 starts when people seem to be actually listening. The key here is to see if you can get them to talk about the topic, instead of you talking. That opens the door to the emotions."

"Ok," Zach replied. "Level 0 is no engagement. Level 1 is talking."

Angela clarified further, "Once they start talking, then the real information starts appearing. If the person is adding to the conversation but without emotion, we label that Level 1." She wrote a few more details next to the number 1.

0 – Not paying attention / not emotionally or intellectually invested
1 – Paying attention / intellectually-engaged / not emotionally invested
2
3

She continued, "You have to be careful sometimes with Level 1 reactions. They're engaged, but it's more of an intellectual exercise, and they're not fully invested. People can talk for a long time about a topic they're not really invested in, simply because it's easier than talking about emotional topics."

"I've seen that happen," Zach blurted out. "We have meetings that go on for hours but go nowhere."

"Right?" Angela agreed. "So emotion becomes the key to keeping the conversation on track. Level 2 is when people start to get emotional in response to something they hear. Usually, you see emotion first in the face or the hands." She added some more details to the whiteboard.

0 – Not paying attention / not emotionally or intellectually invested
1 – Paying attention / intellectually-engaged / not emotionally invested
2 – Emotionally invested / face and hands ONLY
3

"Lastly," Angela added, "Level 3 is what we call the 'full-bodied emotional response'. Their whole body gets engaged, leaning in or turning away, sitting up straight in their chair or even standing up. This marks a super-important topic!"

0 – Not paying attention / not emotionally or intellectually invested

1 – Paying attention / intellectually-engaged / not emotionally invested

2 – Emotionally invested / face and hands ONLY

3 – Emotionally invested / full-body response

Angela concluded, “Here’s how it all works during the interviews. While the lead person is asking the questions, the observer is looking around the room and watching for emotional reactions. We especially want to watch for Level 2 or 3 emotional reactions from somebody who doesn’t speak. Does that make sense?”

“Gotcha,” confirmed Zach. “Level 0 is no emotion or attention.” He paused. Angela nodded.

Zach continued, “Level 1 is engagement and attention, but no emotion?”

“Yep,” confirmed Angela.

“Level 2 is emotion in the face or hands?” asked Zach.

“Yep,” replied Angela, “whether they’re talking or not.”

Zach continued, “Level 3 is full-bodied emotion, whether they’re talking or not.”

“Check,” confirmed Angela with a nod.

“Ok,” added Zach, “if I see someone with a Level 2 or Level 3 reaction, how do I let you know? Do I jump in? Do I tap you on the arm or something?”

“Good question,” Angela added. “Usually when I have a partner we have a text chat going.”

“Ooh!” exclaimed Zach. “I set up a shared online doc space for us yesterday. It has simultaneous editing, so if we’re both editing that doc, I can leave notes for you there and vice versa.”

“I like it,” said Angela. “That way whoever is leading can decide to either tackle it on the spot or mark it for follow-up later.”

“Why would you wait?” Zach asked.

“If I think it could put someone in an awkward position,” Angela shared, “I’ll ask for a follow-up conversation rather than bring it up right away.”

“Now that sounds like Emotional Intelligence to me,” Zach said. “And

I can also tell you in the notes if I think that person would prefer a quiet follow-up, or would not mind being called on in the session."

"Excellent!" Angela responded. "Make sure to add the person's first name, just in case."

"Ooh," Zach added, "should I write down which emotion I'm seeing? Like, 'She's really angry,' or 'He seems concerned.'"

"I used to do that," Angela replied, "but then I discovered two problems. First, taking the time to identify the right emotion can easily distract you, and second, it's too easy to be wrong. What you could do if you want to, though, is identify positive versus negative emotions. So, you could write minus two, minus three, or plus two, plus three."

"Ok. Roger that." Zach agreed. "It still feels weird, though, talking about emotions at work."

Angela laughed, "Emotion is allowed in the workplace. The key is to be aware of it so that we can adapt to it like Jonathan Haidt's 'Rider and the Elephant'. Ok, I'll take the lead on the first few meetings so you can practice watching emotions in the room, and watch me tailor the conversation to the emotions. Then we'll divvy up the remaining sessions. How does that sound?"

Zach nodded as Angela continued on, "The most important thing to me is how we do the interviews. The topics will be hard to predict, but we can control how we run the sessions."

She took a deep breath and exhaled. Zach did the same. She moved down her checklist and then looked him in the eyes and continued, "That's the interviews and the qualitative data collection. Next comes the quantitative part. Are you ready?"

Zach nodded, "I think so."

"I understand your hesitation," Angela said reassuringly. "Just let me know if I'm going too fast."

"We're good," Zach reassured her.

"Good," Angela mirrored. "This next part is really more about logistics and not as intense. I'd like to visit as many team sessions as I can and just watch. Product sessions, design sessions, DevOps discussions, you name it, I'd like to be a fly on the wall. We need to see what's happening with our own eyes. Interviews only tell part of the story. One of my favorite quotes from the Usability testing world is, 'People are notoriously bad at predicting their own behavior.' It's never an intentional deception.

It's just human nature that everybody has unconscious biases. Through observation, I can see your behaviors and you can see mine. My other favorite quote is, 'If we knew the answers to our own problems, they wouldn't be problems.' Observations help us to see the patterns in reality, and then the interviews tell us why those patterns are happening."

"Ok," Zach confirmed, jotting down a note for himself. "I'll get you a list of all the stand-up meetings. Some of them happen at the same time, but looking across several days, you can probably attend them all. A few of the teams switched to one-week sprints during the crisis, so there will be several Sprint Planning and Sprint Review sessions this week. You're also welcome to attend all of our Help Desk summary meetings where we recap the most common or most intense calls of the day."

"Thanks! Sounds interesting. I will. Are there any Story Refinement sessions?" asked Angela. "I like to attend as many of those as I can."

"Yes," confirmed Zach, "but only three of the teams have Refinement sessions this week." That was a bit disappointing to Angela. There should have been a lot of them given the current crisis.

Zach continued, "But I did get you into one of our Graphic Design brainstorming sessions with Vera's group. They're super excited to walk you through all of the works in progress."

"I don't want to interrupt what they're doing," said Angela apologetically.

"No," said Zach reassuringly. "They recap all the time with each other. It's an integral part of their process. Nothing out of the ordinary."

Angela nodded cautiously in agreement. "Now this last part may be the hardest from a scheduling perspective. I'd like to hold a two-hour kickoff meeting to introduce myself to the leadership. We can do it in person or virtually. I want to hear their perspectives, ask them about their goals, give them a chance to ask questions, share the alignment plan, and also reassure them that my goal is not to cause trouble... Well, unless it's good trouble," she said with a grin and wink worthy of the Cheshire Cat from Alice in Wonderland.

Zach smiled back enthusiastically, "Tim already asked me to set one up! So you'll meet everyone at the end of today. Sound good?"

"Looking forward to it!" Angela beamed. She thanked her lucky stars that she had Zach.

Zach added, "Starting tomorrow, we'll also meet with the leadership team going forward every day at eight thirty for the Assessment

Stand-Up. They want to hear what you learn each day, and they want to have a chance to add their own insights."

"'Alignment', please," interjected Angela, "instead of the word 'Assessment'. I'm also okay with 'Discovery' and 'Gap Analysis', but I like 'Alignment' the best. 'Assessment' sounds too much like I'm here to judge you all. It's really important to me that we don't use words that establish an adversarial relationship."

"Sure," responded Zach, "but can you say more?"

Angela clarified, "Certainly! Thanks for asking! 'Assessment' puts me on the outside and in a place of false authority," Angela said while tenting her fingers in a mock imitation of an evil villain, "'holding your fates in my hands'. In truth, I only have the authority that people let me borrow. I also have no desire to wield authority. If people only do things because I say so, as soon as I'm gone, they'll just go back to what they were doing before. I find it better to talk about 'alignment'. First, my alignment with what you all are doing, and then later, I may ask you all to align what you're doing with Agile learnings. Do you think that would work here?"

"You're the expert," Zach responded.

"Actually I would consider you the expert on Ares Financial. That's why I'm so happy that you volunteered to be my partner in this. I'm just here to provide new ways for you and Ares to channel your existing expertise."

That made Zach smile.

"Thank you, Zach!" she smiled back. "I'm so happy to have you by my side! I've also really enjoyed getting to talk about these things. I hope you have too!"

"Definitely!" he exclaimed. "Anything else?"

"I think that's enough for now," Angela said with a chuckle.

"Agreed," Zach chuckled back. "Then... would you like a tour of the place?"

DAMAGE CONTROL

"This definitely does not fit the definition of 'good trouble'," Angela said, mostly to herself. She started retracing her steps in the leadership kickoff meeting. It started smooth enough. Tim gave an inspiring speech regarding Angela and her abilities that left her feeling a-buzz, but also a little uncomfortable with the praise. Next, they introduced themselves, Naomi the Product Manager, Vera the Creative Director, and Linda the Scrum Master Manager. Ali was there as the Chief Architect, along with Jayson who seemed to be the Development Manager. There was also Evah, who ran Quality Assurance, and the guy who was talking now. His name was... Roy. Right! Chief Data Scientist. When it was her turn, Angela began with an overview of the upcoming alignment interviews.

After the overview, she showed a famous video called, "The Backwards Bicycle" by Destin Sandlin[3]. They easily picked up on Destin's main point, that "knowledge does not equal understanding". Knowing what needs to change doesn't always mean we know how to make that change happen. Many in the group, especially Roy, were fascinated by the video, giving it nods of approval.

The transition point must have come after that. Angela started answering questions about the alignment interviews, and that's when Tim excused himself for an important meeting. Once he was out of the room, the conversation migrated away from the agenda and to the current state of the Breeze Transfer app.

That's when Naomi started to drive the conversation, "None of these ideas are new," she stated. "We're just re-discussing the same ideas over and over again. Everybody needs to stop pretending that they have the answer."

Angela tried to regain control of the proceedings, "So I'm hearing that these are hypotheses which have been presented already?"

Naomi held up her index finger towards Angela, "Sorry, Angela. If you could hold on for just a moment."

Angela could feel no animosity directed specifically at her, so she decided to sit back and observe. That had definitely been at least a Level 2 emotional reaction – hands and face. Angela wondered which emotion was driving it. She left herself a note to talk to Naomi about it later.

---

3 Destin Sandlin, host of "Smarter Every Day," is an engineer who explores interesting problems. In "The Backwards Brain Bicycle" he discusses the difference between knowledge and understanding: *https://youtu.be/MFzDaBzBlLo*

Naomi stood and continued. She appeared calm and collected but that move definitely turned it into a Level 3 emotional response. "I've already agreed to roll back to the previous version. Why are we still discussing additional changes?"

"My data says that rolling back at this stage won't help," Roy interjected, leaning forward firmly onto his feet while still remaining seated on the couch.

Angela noted the full-body engagement. Roy was trying very hard to employ a Spock-level denial of emotion, but his feet gave him away. *"Is Roy's response passion for his idea, or a reaction to Naomi?"* She wrote in her notes.

"Your data?" Naomi said, dismissively. "Don't you mean Clyde's test?" That was definitely anger there.

"Yes," Roy conceded through clenched teeth. "Clyde's test put a name to what I was already seeing in the data." He was trying valiantly to cover up his anger, but that suppression was actually just increasing the pressure, making him sit stiffly at an angle that looked very uncomfortable and even threatening.

Ali tried to break the tension, "I wish it was that simple, Naomi. However, there are several security concerns and each participant bank still has its own APIs and interfaces to connect." They had obviously moved on to a new tangent, but Angela was more concerned with the nervousness in Ali's voice. Angela jotted down a note to speak with Ali separately.

Suddenly Roy exploded onto his feet, shouting, "When are you going to get it, Naomi?! This is going in the can and you don't know why! People are getting burned out with all these changes and the micromanaging." He gestured at Linda, who immediately shrank even further into her chair like a turtle in its shell.

Roy looked at Jayson and Evah, "They are beginning to look like rats in a maze." Jayson and Evah both put their heads down and pretended to look busy, but Jayson's reaction seemed more like avoidance, while Evah seemed to be holding back something.

Roy redirected to Vera, "You know Clyde has evidence showing what's really happening and we should leverage that! This isn't the fault of the designers, nor QA, and definitely not DevOps," Roy said as he pointed to Vera, Evah, and Jayson, in turn. Roy finished his outburst pointing at Naomi, "It's your fault for not listening to me!"

That had brought them into a full whirlwind. Vera had tried to raise her hand and interject, but Naomi cut in instead. Most likely Naomi had not even seen Vera. She was completely fixed on Roy as she spoke sternly, "Oh there you go blaming others. At least the teams are making changes quickly. We don't need data right now, we need a new release before Intuition takes us down!"

Roy snorted, "There you go with your doom and gloom message again of the death of Ares! You might as well put a gravestone on our name. That will really increase morale!" he said, his words dripping with sarcasm.

Naomi's face went red and she looked like she was about to jump across the table, when Jayson just stood and said, "ENOUGH!!" with the full weight of his giant, 6-foot-7-inch frame, immediately grabbing everyone's attention. He didn't do anything else. He didn't even speak, but everyone got the message.

"I apologize, Angela," Naomi said. "I look forward to you helping to fix our 'virtual graveyard'" she said with air quotes, "but I've had enough." And with that, Naomi abruptly walked out of the meeting.

Everyone just stared at each other wide-eyed, then at Angela, sheepishly embarrassed. Then they quietly started collecting their belongings and headed for the door.

Zach leaned into Angela and whispered, "So that's a Level 3 emotional reaction, right?"

Key Points of Learning

- Mirroring
- Committed versus Invested
- Emotional Intelligence
- Measuring Emotional Reactions to Find Root Causes
- "Knowledge does not equal understanding"

Chapter 5

Zach – Seek First to Understand

ACTIVE LISTENING

Zach ran up the stairs of the parking garage. He knew he shouldn't have answered "one more email" but he was in charge of customer support, and his team had some angry customers this week. Normally it didn't matter where he answered emails, but today was different. Today someone was waiting on him. He checked his smartwatch. "Only 14 minutes late. Not too bad," he said to himself, trying to steady his breath. He opened the door to the lobby and saw Angela sitting on the benches by the security desk.

"Hi, Angela!" he called out.

"Good to see you again!" Angela waved back, smiling her welcoming grin.

"I'm so sorry I'm running behind," he apologized. "My team hit me with an emergency this morning. Never a dull moment, huh?"

"Quite alright," Angela said reassuringly.

Zach gestured to the man behind the desk, "Let me introduce you to Carl." Carl touched his hand to the brim of his hat and gave a gentle nod and a smile. Zach continued, "Carl is great. He's usually here in the mornings to greet us all. He's been a fixture of the mornings for about – what is it? – three years now?"

"Yep, three years is what I heard," added Angela, smiling warmly at Carl. Carl smiled back. "Carl was telling me all about his first day," Angela continued. "Did you know that he has two talented daughters who are both interested in tech?"

"I did." Zach smiled as he glanced down at the picture on the desk of Carl with his daughters.

"Oh, yes, ma'am," Carl chimed in. "Zach here has offered to help my oldest get an internship when the summer rolls around." Zach felt a warm wave spread out from his heart. It was a good sign that Angela cared enough to treat Carl as a real person. Most people didn't bother to get to know the people at security, the cleaning staff, the cafeteria workers.

"Are you ready to go?" he asked Angela.

"You bet," Angela replied.

As they walked to the elevators, they heard a familiar voice, "That was some meeting, huh, Angela?" Naomi was standing at the elevators with coffee in hand. Zach took a deep breath and held it as Naomi elaborated, "I bet you're starting to see what I'm up against. My apologies for abruptly leaving during your kickoff presentation. It had nothing to do with you."

Naomi extended her hand eagerly as she continued talking, "Welcome back. We didn't really get to talk in private yet, but Tim has been raving about you. We're super excited to have you here!" Ding! The elevator opened and they all got inside.

Naomi kept up the conversation, "Well, Zach here will tell you that we've got a top-notch team. The developers are smart and the testers are very diligent. They'll eventually hunt down the remaining bugs standing in our way. But that's what you're here to help with, right? Agile has always been great for the developers. I heard you were an amazing Scrum Master. I bet you will whip them into shape."

"Product too," Angela slipped into Naomi's monologue. That brought Naomi to a quick stop. "Agile isn't just for software development anymore," she added with a smile. "I've worked with dev teams, product teams, factories, HR teams, and even an ad agency. Agile is just a set of tested techniques for how to break down work and tackle it efficiently and effectively in small pieces to decrease risk. It works everywhere." Angela smiled again in a way that seemed non-threatening, to Zach at least. He hoped it was having the same effect on Naomi. "I even used it with a tenth-grade class last year. I have a niece the same age as one of Carl's daughters, and we used it to organize her class project. They had so much fun!"

"Carl?" asked Naomi.

"Downstairs at security," explained Zach.

"Oh, right. That Carl," Naomi quickly countered. "I didn't know he had daughters."

"Yes," effused Angela, "they're adorable, and very much into tech. I'm so happy to see girls taking an interest."

"That's fantastic," agreed Naomi. Ding! The elevator doors opened and Angela and Naomi stepped off into a conversation about girls who code.

Zach noticed he was holding his breath again and exhaled. That went better than he had expected. Angela corrected Naomi, redefined the conversation, and turned Naomi into an ally in less than a minute. Did she do that consciously? If so, he needed to learn how. The doors started to close. Startled to attention, he stuck out his hand to stop the doors and extracted himself from the elevator to join Angela by the front desk. Naomi was headed off to her office and Angela was reaching over the desk to shake the hand of the intern.

Over his left shoulder, he heard Roy's voice, "That's her, right?" Roy kept going, not waiting for Zach's reply, "Did Naomi say anything that I need to know? I saw them walking off the elevator together."

Zach responded quietly, "We were just talking about Agile and its many uses. Let's let her get settled before we just launch into things, okay?" Roy grunted and it sounded like consent.

Angela turned around and with a big smile jumped right in, "Roy! I'm looking forward to our chance to chat one-on-one! Tim was gushing about your ability to mine critical information out of the data. I'm a big fan of good metrics. There's nothing like a clear set of success and failure criteria to bring clarity to a problem, right?"

"Right..." started Roy cautiously. "I like that you just said success AND failure. You have to measure both since failure is also a learning opportunity. I don't know how much you've heard already," he continued, giving a glance towards Naomi's office. "This place does not openly tolerate failure... so, of course, they fail all the time."

Zach glanced at this watch, not sure if they had time for this rant. He heard Angela chime in, "We're definitely going to sit down and have a one-on-one, and I want to hear all about your experience and what got you started with Data Science." Switching to Zach, she said, "My apologies, Zach. Are we running behind?"

Zach glanced up, "Oh, uh, yeah. We should probably keep moving. Yeah. Let me show you where you can put your stuff." He gestured towards the conference room.

"Nice to see you again, Roy." Angela shook Roy's hand and followed Zach's gesture towards the conference room.

"That was impressive," Zach whispered to Angela when they were out of Roy's earshot. "The way you handled both Naomi and Roy was impressive. How can I learn how to do that?"

Angela smiled, "Tim mentioned that you were a good observer of people. You saw what I was doing? I call it 'validating'. It also helps to build rapport. Let's see... Steven Covey included it in his book 'The 7 Habits of Highly Effective People'. He used the phrase, 'Seek first to understand, then to be understood.' 'The 7 Habits' is one of those classics that has really withstood the test of time,"

Zach pulled out his phone, "I've heard of the '7 Habits'. It's on my list to read. I'll bump it to the top."

Angela continued, "And Covey is not the only person to talk about it. It's a core tenet of diplomacy. Acting teacher, Sanford Meisner, had another way to teach the same concept that he called 'The Repetition Exercise'. And another favorite format of mine is 'Green Light Statements' from Natasha Todorovic-Cowan at Spiral Dynamics. All different approaches to the same realization: We constantly make assumptions about each other and it gets us in trouble. When we switch to listening and honest curiosity, that's when we begin to truly understand each other."

"The... Repetition... Exercise," muttered Zach, as he tried quite unsuccessfully to keep up. "How do you spell Meisner?"

"M-e-i-s-n-e-r...," Angela started spelling it out, then stopped. "Tell you what. Let me send you some links. I'm so glad you're interested!" she exclaimed with delight.

She added, "I love it when I uncover a technique that multiple people have also discovered independently throughout the years. It tells me that I'm onto something good when multiple minds reach the same conclusions from multiple different starting places."

"Let's see," she said, putting together a list of techniques for him, "I'll send you Covey[1], and Meisner[2], and Natasha[3], and David Rock's[4] book, 'Quiet Leadership'. Let's see... Marshall Rosenberg's[5] 'Nonviolent Communication'..."

"So many..." Zach marveled.

"Sorry," Angela said apologetically. "I'm not saying that you should read them all. I just thought that you could pick one that resonates with you the best."

"Oh, I probably will read them all," Zach admitted, "...eventually."

She stopped short and exclaimed, "Ooh! I definitely want to throw in 'Never Split the Difference' by Chris Voss[6]. He used to be the lead hostage negotiator for the FBI. Have you ever heard the phrase, 'We do not negotiate with terrorists'?"

"Of course," Zach said confidently.

"Well, he's the reason why that is *no longer* the policy of the United States," Angela countered.

That stopped Zach in his tracks, "I wasn't expecting that... Not negotiating with terrorists is not the policy of the US?" He paused again, trying to sort through the double negatives.

Angela clarified, "He found that *not* negotiating always resulted in the worst possible outcomes. Terrorists are terrorists because they want to change the world around them. You have to listen. More importantly than that, though, you have to find a way to let the other person know that you hear them and that you understand them."

"But", she added with strong emphasis, "and this is the critical link – there's a big difference between listening to terrorists, and giving them everything they ask for. What he put together with his team was a fantastic outline of how to both listen and understand without giving in to their demands."

Zach's mind was already swimming, and they hadn't even been there for 30 minutes yet. "Is this the same thing as 'mirroring'?" He asked. "But I didn't see you repeating the same words back to them."

"Yes, but you don't have to repeat the same words," Angela clarified. "Don't get me wrong. Mirroring is a great place to start, and I still use that form from time to time, but the most important thing is to keep the focus entirely on the other person and not yourself. I actually messed up. In the elevator with Naomi. Did you notice?"

Zach's eyes drifted up and to the left looking for the answer in his memory, but couldn't find it. "How did you mess up? I thought what you did with Naomi was amazing."

Angela explained, "I jumped to Agile's defense about not being just

---

1 "The 7 Habits of Highly Effective People" by Stephen R. Covey: *https://en.wikipedia.org/wiki/The_7_Habits_of_Highly_Effective_People*

2 "The Repetition Exercise" by Sanford Meisner: *https://en.wikipedia.org/wiki/Meisner_technique*

3 Natasha Todorovic, "Green Light Statements": *https://spiraldynamics.org/*

4 "Quiet Leadership" by David Rock: h*ttps://davidrock.net/books/*

5 "Nonviolent Communication" by Marshall Rosenberg: *https://en.wikipedia.org/wiki/Nonviolent_Communication*

6 "Never Split the Difference" by Chris Voss: *https://en.wikipedia.org/wiki/Christopher_Voss*

for developers. Did you see how it made Naomi stiffen? After I realized that I was standing on my soapbox I had to pivot. Tim had mentioned that Naomi volunteers at one of the coding charities for young women, so I thought that I might be able to reconnect with her as a woman in tech."

"That's amazing!" Zach exclaimed. "Oh, I see! That's why you made the comment about your niece's class project, right? What a very clever way to get Naomi under control."

"Nope!" interjected Angela quickly. "It's not about control. I don't want that to be your take-away."

Zach was obviously puzzled so Angela continued, "I had made that conversation about my needs to not be put in a box as a dev-only coach. So it was also my responsibility to bring the conversation back around to her."

"But there was nothing wrong with what you said," objected Zach. "Agile is not just for development. It is for products, Human Resources, schools, and anywhere teamwork is needed. You shouldn't feel like you don't have a right to speak or stand up for yourself, or Agile. We need that here! We desperately need some outside opinions!"

Zach refocused his eyes on Angela.

She just smiled, took a deep breath, and looked at him with gentle eyes. Zach noticed and did the same. After a few seconds, Angela began again, "The way I would express what you just said is that it's good to have boundaries. You can't be a pushover. Sometimes you have to take a stand. And it sounds like you've found an area where you need to set some boundaries."

She paused again and held up one finger. Then she pointed it at herself, "But I'm in a different place than you. I can't be the coach for Ares Innovation if I make it about me. I have to meet you all where you currently are. That's another version of using Covey's 'Seek First to Understand' and it's critical at the start of any coaching engagement. First listen, see, and learn. If people don't feel understood, then they will shut you out. It is better to show them I am here to solve their problems and not my own problems."

Zach started, "That makes sense..." then paused. "But I'm also going to have to ruminate on that for a bit."

Angela started unpacking her things. "Sounds good to me," she said. "And let me know if you want to talk more later."

Zach nodded – about ten times too many – a huge grin spreading across his face.

DOUBLE ACES

Later that week, Zach found himself in the Leadership Alignment meeting, trying to keep up but really only catching every other word. It didn't help that he hadn't gotten enough sleep. He took another sip of his cappuccino to try to shake off the grogginess.

Angela was providing a recap of the team interviews that the two of them had conducted over the previous couple of days. The interviews had been fascinating, but not because of what the teams had said. He already knew that information. Watching how Angela interviewed people was what had fascinated him, so when he got home last night, he downloaded a copy of the Chris Voss book "Never Split the Difference" and only forced himself to stop reading when he realized that he couldn't both finish the book and sleep.

He was still replaying the interviews in his brain, noting where Angela had borrowed from Voss' book. Voss had three phrases to help mirror someone else's comments without using the words "I" or "me" and making it about you. *"It looks like... It sounds like... It feels like..."* He ran through the list a couple more times in his head to further cement it in his memory. *"It looks like... It sounds like... It feels like..."*

As he started listening to the conversation again, he began to piece together what was happening. It was all the "usual suspects" including Tim, Ali, Roy, Evah, Jayson, Linda, Naomi, and Angela. Angela and Linda were sharing the results of their review of the Features and User Stories. Something about how the documentation was not centralized. Vera's group had the design information in their design tool, the business requirements were managed by Naomi, and the user stories were tracked in a virtual Kanban board. No one knew where the architectural diagrams were, so Ali promised to send links when he got back to the desk. Evah had gotten a little defensive, saying that the test scripts had to be maintained in the automated Test Suite software, which Angela assured her made complete sense.

After laying out the problem that they had discovered, Zach could see Angela switch into listening mode. He started mentally tracking which responses from her were repeats of other people's words, and which responses were new information.

"If this were just me," Angela clarified, "it would not be a big deal. On-boarding someone is always a hefty task. What I noticed, though, is that some of the team members also didn't know where to go to find details about the user stories. They only had what was attached to the card in the Kanban board. When I asked where the documentation for the features was kept, they just said, 'We ask Linda'. Not an uncommon dilemma, by the way. According to research by McKinsey[7], teams can spend on average 20% to 30% of their time just searching for documentation." Zach tallied three statements echoing the words of the teams and one addition from Angela about the statistics.

Linda added, "I had the same problem when I joined earlier this year. It took me months to learn where all of the pieces were, but you get the hang of it. So now I make sure that everyone can get what they need. All they have to do is ask."

"Yes, it definitely looks like you've mastered the system, Linda!" Angela said in a congratulatory tone, deftly incorporating Voss' recommended phrase of *'it looks like'*. Then she clarified further, "Anyone who needs something reaches out to Linda, and I admire how she was able to put her finger on it and get each team member what they needed. Great facilitation, Linda!" Zach noted that the point about admiration used the word *"I"* but the whole statement was still squarely focused on Linda.

Angela continued, "And I wonder if we could make Linda's job a little easier. For example, it looks like the teams all start work at the online Kanban board, which is great. From there it also looks like all of the relevant, modified code is attached to that card. Also great!" This was a new thought by Angela, going in a new direction.

Jayson smiled, nodded his head, and said, "We make sure every file is there during code review. No one gets to mark a card as finished if the code is missing."

"Bravo!" Angela cheered. "In addition, all of Evah's test cases are linked to each card from her testing suite, so you can see a list of all of the test scripts associated with each User Story and bug. Great job, Evah!" That was all about Evah, Zach noted.

Angela clarified, "That's all I was thinking of, leaving the information

---

7 *https://www.mckinsey.com/industries/technology-media-and-telecommunications/our-insights/the-social-economy*

where it is and linking to it from the User Story." Evah lifted her head up a little higher and smiled broadly.

Angela kept going, "Is there a way that we could link all of the other content to the cards? Since people start there anyway? The designs, the architecture, the business research?" That statement was definitely from Angela's point of view.

"The metrics?" Roy interjected. "None of that matters if we're still building the wrong thing, I mean, sure. They follow the standard format, 'as a user I want to do something so that I can accomplish something,' but that's only half the picture. We need to collect data to truly understand the customers."

"Yes, that is one of the ultimate goals," Angela added to validate Roy, "to truly understand our customers. Thanks, Roy. And it sounds like you disagree, Roy, that the User Stories are well written." All of those statements reflected Roy's expressed point of view.

"Yeah," said Roy, but that was all he said.

Zach tried a validating statement out loud, "Roy, it feels like you would like to add to our standard story format."

"What is all this touchy-feely nonsense coming out of your mouth today, Zach? Why do you keep starting every sentence with, 'It feels like'? It doesn't feel like anything. It is. These User Stories suck. If they were good stories, every single one of them would have a metric. They'd have instructions on how to capture metric data at each step of the process so that we can verify if Naomi's grand designs are actually having the impact they should, or if they're *crap*. My money's on the latter."

"Crap?!" blurted out Naomi. "Do you see how he talks to me, Tim?!"

"Roy, we've talked about this," Tim quickly interjected. "You can't use that kind of language."

"It's not the language, Tim," Naomi cut him off. "I can take the language. What? Do you all think I'm some kind of delicate flower? Don't let my appearance fool you. This woman is not a flower..."

As Tim worked to soothe the tempers of Naomi and Roy, Zach noticed a new line of text that Angela was still typing in their shared notes doc, "Some people don't like talking about feelings. As you can see, they have feelings. They definitely have feelings. But they don't like talking about them. That's why no single system of active listening can ever be the *only* system. Keep trying. It's hard but it's worth it. Don't worry about Roy. He's just one opinion. Continue using 'It feels like…' if you want to. He's pushing back, but it's also working. He started off like a broken record, but did you notice that he's left those statements behind? Now that he knows that we've heard him, he's moving on to new insights that he wants everyone to know. Sometimes people fight because they don't feel like they've been heard."

Double Aces Origin Story

As Zach finished reading he suddenly became aware that the room had gotten a lot quieter. He also noticed that Angela was standing. She wasn't doing anything. She was just standing there. What did he miss? He quickly looked around. Nobody else was standing. The room had fallen into a momentary hush.

"I'd like to try something that I think will help," Angela finally said, breaking the silence. "It's a form of structured discussion that came out of the educational world. It's called the 'Double Aces'."

Angela walked over to the whiteboard as she talked. "When working with young kids, teachers found that to get the best out of their students, the first thing they had to do was praise whatever their student was doing, right or wrong." She wrote the word "Praise" on the board and continued, "Then they would ask the students questions about the choices that they had made." She wrote the word "Question" on the board. "Only after those two steps would they suggest any points of 'Polish' for the student to do differently." She wrote the word "Polish" on the board and underlined the first letter of each word. "P-Q-P was what they called it. Praise. Question. Polish."

Zach noticed Linda writing in her notebook, which prompted him to write it down as well. Angela continued, "Well, an interesting thing happened. Because they were doing this all day with their students, they just naturally started doing this with each other, even when there were only adults in the room, and they discovered that this had nothing to do with age. It was just a fantastic way to give feedback!"

Brain Biology

"Now," she continued, "thanks to the research of Nobel-prize-winning economist Daniel Kahnemann and his colleague Amos Tversky, we also know why it works — biologically. It turns out that our brains have two modes of operation that he labeled the 'Pattern Matching' mode and the 'Logic Processor' Mode."

"I'll describe the 'Logic Processor' first," she explained, "because this is the mode with which we are all the most familiar. You might call this the 'Spock' mode. Can I assume that you're all familiar with the famous Star Trek character?"

"Of course," Roy confirmed. All of the other heads nodded around the table as well. "I try to live by the Spock code," Roy added with a smile, holding up his hand with split fingers forming the Vulcan hand gesture for "Live Long and Prosper".

"Live Long and Prosper to you too!" Angela returned, returning the gesture with a wide grin. "So the 'Logic Processor' mode is capable of great things. It can ponder new situations, perform complex calculations, and build new associations and pathways in the brain."

She paused and got serious for effect, "But this ability comes at a cost. It is a slow process and uses a lot of energy. If you spend 30 minutes in deep 'Logic Processor' thought, you can burn as much energy as 30 minutes on the treadmill!" That statement was an obvious surprise to most people in the room, as betrayed by their expressions.

"Now imagine," she continued, "running on a treadmill all day without stopping. You'd be exhausted! So we actually don't use our 'Logic Processor' very often. Anyone want to take a guess of how often we typically use this part of our brain?"

"25%?" Evah tossed out.

"Maybe 20% or less," Linda suggested.

Angela pointed her thumb downwards.

Roy tossed out, "15% seems like a fair guess."

Angela pointed her thumb downwards again.

Linda's eyes grew wide with surprise. "10%?!" she said incredulously.

Angela started rotating her thumb upwards, and then quickly turned it back downwards to emphasize the point, adding the final answer, "5% to 10%." Most of the room had a look of surprise across their faces, except Tim and Jayson who seemed to be unphased.

"Now, technically," Angela explained, "our Logic Processor brain developed later in terms of evolution because we already had another brain system that was extraordinarily effective, 'Pattern Matching'. So effective, in fact, that even in modern times we still use this part of our brain ninety to ninety-five percent of the time! It's so pervasive, in fact, that one component of this process is referred to as 'The Default Mode Network' because if you ask someone to sit and do absolutely nothing, this part of our brain turns on by default."

"The best way I can describe it," added Angela, "is as a 'difference engine' by which I mean that the first thing that we see in any situation is what is different — what is wrong. When I look around this room, if I had to pay attention to everything in it, that would be a lot of data to process. So our brains figured out that we can efficiently ignore anything that we see that already meets our expectations. That leads us to only focus on the differences." Linda started scribbling furiously in her notebook again, prompting Zach to also take more notes.

"This is what I've been trying to tell you all," Roy jumped in. "This is what I'm trying to do with the data. Just as Angela is describing, you have to identify a baseline of the expected behavior so that we can set up algorithms to find the anomalies — the unexpected."

"Thanks, Roy," Angela smiled. "That really helps to highlight this as a universal truth, proven in research many times over."

"If I may, though," she continued, "I'd also like to talk about the hidden downside." Roy nodded his head and waved her on. Zach noted for himself that Angela didn't contradict Roy, or attempt to exert control of the room. She just acknowledged his contribution and then redirected it back to what she was doing.

"For illustration," Angela elaborated, "let's walk through what happens in our brains by default. When you start a conversation with someone, your brain immediately, by default, starts trying to predict what the other person is saying. Then, by default, you respond to what you *predict* the person is saying in your head, not what they are actually saying. Ninety to ninety-five percent of the time that prediction is close enough to what the other person actually says that neither of you notice. It's only when that prediction is so noticeably wrong that one or both of you notice. Someone says, 'That's not what I said,' or 'That's not what I meant.' Hopefully, you stop and rewind the conversation, ask questions to clarify what was actually said, and hopefully develop a curiosity for understanding the real point of view of the other person."

"Oh, god, I've been in that conversation," Linda scoffed.

"Me too," added Jayson.

"And now you know why," Angela offered. "It's biological. Now I'm going to connect it to the words on the whiteboard to show the genius of what those teachers discovered." She pointed to the last word first. "Polish: By default we trade statements back and forth, offering points of polish on each other's ideas until we hit a point of conflict." She pointed to the middle word, "Question: If we're being gracious, we might ask each other questions to see where we differ." She moved to the first word, "Praise: If we can reach an agreement – and that's a big if – we might offer praise for the other person's ideas."

"Are you seeing it?" she asked. "Our Default Mode is the exact opposite of Praise, Question, Polish. If you reverse the order, you turn off the Default Mode and turn on your 'Logic Processor'. It's amazing how it works!"

"I want to say that again," she continued, "to turn on our 'Logic Processor' we have to consciously reverse the order of our conversations." She paused to check in on how it all was landing with the group.

Linda ventured the first question, "So, wait, by default our brains work in the exact wrong order? If that were the case, how are we all still alive?"

"A question I often ask myself," Roy retorted.

"Fair question," Angela responded. "When the situation is a known challenge and calls for us to do something we already know how to do, then 'Pattern Matching' is far more efficient. This is where the power of 'gut instinct' comes from. Ninety to ninety-five percent of the time we can and should trust our gut, but when the situation calls for new thinking, that's when following our gut can get us in trouble."

"Yep, that sounds like us," Evah quipped, with good humor and an edge of snarkiness. Linda looked up from her notebook and burst out into a laugh of recognition. Others joined in on the joke, but it just as quickly settled into an uneasy, self-conscious chuckle all the way around the table. All except Naomi, who looked even more stern.

Angela summed it up, "When our gut instincts collide with each other and we find ourselves in conflict, that's when we need to slow down, reverse the order of the conversation, and consciously engage our 'Logic Processor' brain."

Harmony versus Disharmony

"Can we give it a try?" she asked. Everybody just quietly looked around at each other, including Zach. The idea sounded great, and Zach was eager to try it, but he wanted to watch someone else go through it first.

"Roy," he heard Angela say, "as the consummate experimenter, can you assist me in a demonstration?" Zach's eyes went wide with surprise at her bold move.

"Sure," agreed Roy, hesitantly. "I'm willing to try anything, once."

"No you're not," Naomi muttered, and then quickly shifted in her chair and went silent. Zach was sure that she hadn't meant to say that out loud.

Roy bristled and was about to respond when Angela jumped in, "Thanks, Naomi. A perfect starting place!" she said, winking at Naomi, who actually looked a little embarrassed. Angela turned to Roy, "What about Naomi's comment would you like to praise?"

"Absolutely nothing," said Roy, pursing his lips in frustration.

"I thought not," Angela replied, "which is why I want to give you two other words. When P-Q-P was brought over to the business world, it was discovered that people found it really hard to praise something when they disagreed. So we found two other words: Appreciate and Acknowledge." She wrote "Appreciate" and "Acknowledge" in line with the word "Praise" on the whiteboard, and Zach did the same on his laptop. Then she wrote the word "Harmony" above "Appreciate", and the word "Disharmony" above "Acknowledge".

"When we agree with the other person," she added, "we say that we are in 'harmony' with their statement and can 'appreciate' it. When we disagree with the person we say that we are in 'disharmony'. When you are in disharmony we ask you to acknowledge something about the statement instead."

"I don't appreciate Naomi's comment, and I also don't want to acknowledge it," Roy said emphatically.

"Right," agreed Angela, "it wasn't a nice statement and it sounds like you don't condone it. But let's set aside how it was said for a minute and just focus on the content."

Appreciate or Acknowledge

"A statement can be both wrong and right. What aspect of what Naomi said has some truth in it? This is the experiment part... Naomi's words were, 'No, you're not.' What is the continuation of that sentence?"

Roy filled in the blank, "No, I'm not willing to try anything." He looked at Angela, "But that's wrong."

"Yes," Angela agreed, "AND... what's also right about that statement?"

Roy's face scrunched in puzzlement. "...That I'm not willing to try everything she proposes?"

"Yes!" Angela emphasized.

"What?" Roy asked.

"That you're not willing to try everything that Naomi proposes," repeated Angela.

"Well, that's obvious," Roy snarked.

"Yep," confirmed Angela. "That's your 'difference engine' at work. It's an obvious statement, so your brain logged it away and moved on, just as it was designed to do."

She paused but Roy didn't take the bait, just stared back at her looking confused. Angela clarified, "In many cases, it really is just as simple as saying the obvious. That's all I'm asking you to do. Can you summarize that obvious statement?"

Roy paused, looked around the room to see if anyone else was going to intervene, but they all seemed to be waiting for him, so he went for it. "No, I'm not willing to try anything." He paused.

Angela smiled, so Roy continued his thought, "Because..."

“Wait,” inserted Angela, “We’ll get to that ‘because’ part later. For now, it’s just the acknowledgment part. Can you say that again?” She looked at him again, expectantly.

“No,” began Roy a third time, “I’m not willing to try just anything,” and then stopped, albeit with a mild look of annoyance on his face.

Clarify or Confirm

“Excellent!” exclaimed Angela. “Step two in P-Q-P is the questions part. Another thing that we discovered when bringing this to the business world is that it’s a very specific type of question that we’re after. It’s called a ‘Clarifying Question’.” Angela wrote the word “Clarify” on the white-board along with a question mark, this time in the right-hand column under the word “Acknowledge” and in line with the word “Question” in P-Q-P.

She clarified, “When we don’t understand something that the other person said, we count that as being in ‘disharmony’ and we ask questions to understand it better.” She turned back to Roy. “Roy, is there anything that you would like to clarify about what Naomi said?”

Roy jumped right in, “No, I’m pretty clear on what Naomi thinks.”

Angela turned to the others, “This is another thing that was discovered. Sometimes there is nothing to clarify, but it’s really important not to skip over the Question step if we really want to engage our ‘Logic Processor’ and disrupt our ‘Pattern Matching’. Here we say that we are in ‘harmony’ with the statement, but we are going to ask a question anyway.” Angela scribbled the word “Confirm” on the board, under the word “Appreciate” and in line with the word “Clarify”, following it with a question mark as well. Zach followed her lead in his own notes.

	(HARMONY)	(DIS-HARMONY)
Praise	Appreciate	Acknowledge
Question	¿Confirm?	¿Clarify?
Polish		

Angela turned back to Roy, "So if you don't have a clarifying question, ask a 'Confirming Question'. Can you give that a try?"

Roy thought for a while. Zach felt uncomfortable for him and guessed that he was trying out several versions in his head, based on how his eyes were darting back and forth. He tried to get Angela's attention to offer a suggestion to Roy, but Angela wouldn't look his way. Linda also tried to pipe up with a suggestion, but Angela held up her hand to stop her. Finally, Roy looked up and reengaged with the group, "I guess the thing I want to know is does Naomi think that I disagree with everything she does? She certainly treats me that way."

Angela looked in Naomi's direction, who was surprised by the sudden attention. "Uh... well... it certainly does seem that way. I can't remember the last time I heard you agree with something I said."

"What about last week?" Roy asked. "Those UI changes you presented for the payment cancellation. They matched the data about where the users were getting stuck."

"You agreed with those?" Naomi asked.

"Yeah," confirmed Roy.

"And you told me so?" asked Naomi.

"No. Why should I? There are a lot of things that I agree with. When I agree I don't get in the way. It's implicit. When I disagree, then I speak up."

Angela turned to Roy and asked, "So you only speak up when you disagree?" Roy nodded. Angela continued, "And you never speak up when you agree?"

Roy paused, then nodded, "Mostly..."

Angela summed it up, "Perhaps you can see how if Naomi only hears what's wrong — and again, I want to emphasize that this is normal and biological. It's baked into our DNA. But, if all she ever hears is when you disagree with her, that she might be led to believe you always disagree with her?" Roy seemed to be lost in thought. Zach glanced at Naomi. She also seemed lost in thought.

"Wooooaaah," exclaimed Linda, "that's trippy." It was so unexpected that Zach accidentally chuckled under his breath, which made Angela chuckle a little, and started a wave of chuckles around the table that broke the tension. "Sorry," said Linda, "I shouldn't have said that out loud."

Enhance or Evolve

Linda raised her hand and asked, "What's on the last line next to Polish?"

"Polish is not always needed," explained Angela, "but if you want to offer words of Polish, it is absolutely vital to connect the point of polish to the other person's original statement. Ask yourself, how can you enhance or evolve what the other person has already contributed?" She wrote the words "Enhance" and "Evolve" on the board, under "Clarify?" and "Confirm?", and on the same line as "Polish". "If you are in harmony with the statement, how can you 'Enhance' it? If you are in disharmony with it, how can you 'Evolve' the idea into a better form?"

Stepping back she pointed at the two columns of words, "As you can see both columns on the right start with the letters A-C-E — Ace — hence 'Double Aces'."

Angela wrote "Double Aces" at the top, to give the exercise a title.

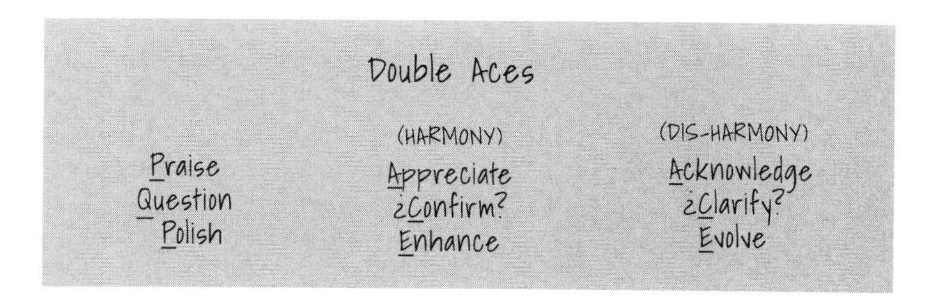

As Linda and Zach added to their notes, Angela wrapped up the meeting, "This is probably a good place to stop. We'll have plenty of more chances to practice this. Roy, thank you for leading our experiment! It's not easy!"

"It's literally against our nature," she emphasized, "but it's also so very important to consciously break our normal patterns. Can we have some applause for Roy?" Angela started clapping. Linda and Zach joined in. Then everybody else joined. Even Naomi was clapping politely and, it appeared, sincerely. Roy actually looked a little shy but nodded in acknowledgment.

Everybody finished collecting their things and headed towards the door. Zach could see subtle smiles on quite a few faces. Angela dropped back down into the chair next to him with a short exhale. She turned and smiled at Zach, "Do you think there is any coffee in the break room? I'm exhausted. That required a lot of my 'Logic Processor'!"

MINDSET MAPPING

At the start of the next week, the leadership team got together again to review the complete feedback from all of the interviews. "Good morning, everyone!" began Angela, maybe a little too cheerfully for eight-thirty in the morning. "I created copies of my notes in case anyone wants to follow along. I like to use the Agile Mindset Mapping Index[8] to organize my thoughts. The acronym is A-M-M-I, and it's pronounced like the name 'Amy'.

"Agile... Maturity... Mapping... Index?" confirmed Linda.

"Ah no," corrected Angela. "It's an Agile Mindset Mapping Index. Think of it as a library catalog system, but for Agile specifically." Linda fixed her notes as Angela continued, "The team behind AMMI compiled and cross-referenced several decades of shared experience within the Agile community. They looked at both what worked and what didn't work and compared the results, especially when something worked in one organization but not another, or it worked in one team but not in another team. They discovered over sixty independent variables that together determine the difference between success and failure for any organization. They've dubbed it 'The Science of Failure'."

8 Find more information about the Agile Mindset Mapping Index (AMMI) at *AskAMMI.org*.

Agile Levels

Team Level

"To understand the layout of the catalog," Angela clarified, "let's first talk about the many levels of Agile." She wrote the word "Team" on the whiteboard, "The team level refers to a group of people that collaborate together on a shared collection of work on a regular basis, usually daily. It has nothing to do with where you work in the organization, though. For example, you all are a Team of leaders because you interact and collaborate with each other daily. There can be an executive team, a leadership team, a product team, or a development team. Think about who collaborates with you on a daily basis."

"Wait," Evah clarified, "my testers are on teams but they also interact with each other on a daily basis. So are they a team, or are they on separate teams?"

"Great clarifying question, Evah," Angela answered. "Let me ask you a clarifying question in return. When your testers get together on a daily basis, are they getting advice from each other, or are they actually testing the same things together?"

"Well," Evah said, thinking it through, "daily conversations are more about advice, and they all have their primary teams, but when it's crunch time, like at the end of a sprint, they all jump in to help each other out."

"Good to know," Angela said. "In that case, I would say no to them being a testing team together. They each belong to a team, and I would say that when they hop over, they temporarily join the team with the backlog that needs help."

"How about my designers?" Vera asked. "They collaborate together on the same designs, and then deliver those designs to the development teams."

"From what I have seen," Angela responded, "the designers do operate as their own team separate from the development teams, and pass work back and forth with the development teams. Any other questions?"

"I do," Jayson said, raising his hand. "We have some teams where they work on the same things, and other teams where half of the developers work together, but they don't ever work with the other half of the developers."

"Ah, great example," Angela agreed. "I saw that too. I'll talk more about it with you after I present my findings, but you're right. In some of the cases that I saw, we may want to split them into separate teams, and in other cases, we might want to leave them in the same team but encourage more points of collaboration."

"What about Roy and I?" asked Ali. "We're all over the place."

"I would say," Angela answered, "that for your main backlogs of work, you each act as a Team of one, plus you belong to this leadership team here. So some of the Team level techniques will apply to your work, but since your work affects multiple teams, your Range of Control covers multiple areas in the next level of Agile practices, the Product level."

Product Level

Nobody asked any more questions, so Angela moved on, "Ok, if you have multiple teams whose work comes together to form a complete deliverable, we call the next level the 'Product' range of influence. You might hear this referred to as a Release Train, a team-of-teams, or a 'program'. The name doesn't really matter. What matters is that both information and work travel between multiple teams on a regular basis. Another way to think of it is from the point of view of the customer. If a customer sees you all as one entity, then you are probably a team-of-teams working on the same Product level."

"What if," Evah challenged her, an air of joking in her voice, "you have a team-of-team-of-teams?"

"Yes," answered Angela jovially, "that is the same thing. It actually doesn't matter how many levels you have. For example, Microsoft might have multiple teams working together on the Templates feature for Powerpoint. They might work together with all the other teams to form Powerpoint itself. Those Powerpoint teams also work together with the Microsoft Word and Excel teams to form Microsoft Office, and Microsoft Office is also part of a suite of online Office tools. This is more about the regular, periodic interactions and integration that has to happen between teams."

Organization Level

"Which brings us to the next grouping, Organizations," Angela said, changing focus again. "Now, let's start with a simple case. Sometimes you might only have one product in an organization."

"Like when you operate like a startup as we do, right?" Zach confirmed.

"Exactly," Angela agreed. "More often, though, multiple products exist together as part of the same organization, and the interactions between these product lines are the focus of the Organizational level. The dividing line largely comes down to a shared budget. Let's take Zach's example of Ares Innovation acting as a startup. You have your own budget, but does ABS Bank add to or take away from your budget?"

"Yes they do," Tim confirmed. "While we do generate revenue, we are not entirely self-sustaining yet. Sometimes we receive less investment, or they have to reclaim some of our budget for other projects in ABS. It doesn't happen often, but it does happen."

"Then," Angela added, "that creates a great contrast. With a true startup, they live or die by the amount of money in their bank account. They can go seek investors, but the money is not shared with anyone else. So in the extreme case, a very small startup might be made up of a single Team, working on a single Product, forming a very small Organization."

"Ares Innovation by contrast," she continued, "can seek more budget from ABS Bank, and ABS Bank can take money out of the Ares budget, so you operate together as part of the ABS Organization."

"Now just like Microsoft," she clarified further, "you can have multiple Organizations nested with each other, just like you can have multiple products nested inside each other. At Microsoft, there is a shared budget between all of the Office teams and the Office Online team, and at an even higher level there is a shared budget between them, and all of the other products that Microsoft makes. It's about the nature of the interactions. Interactions driven by products and features are classified at the Product level, and interactions driven by budgets and portfolio strategy practices are classified at the Organization level."

Points of Collaboration

"Now, within each of these three levels," added Angela, "we subdivide our activities into six groups – People, Design, Planning, Implementation, Verification, and Operations." She wrote each of the 6 areas on the board as she said them.

People	Design	Planning	Implemen-tation	Verifi-cation	Opera-tions

"I notice they're all nouns," began Vera. "Does that correspond with the roles?" she asked. "Managers deal with people, Designers design... Product Owners maybe do the planning... If Verification is Testers, then Implementation is probably developers, and Operations make sense. But why not just say that, and where are the Scrum Masters?" Vera seemed a little frustrated, trying to recategorize everything in her head.

Angela clarified, "It's more about collaboration than roles. There are many flavors of Agile, and all of them are valid, but each framework defines the roles differently. So the roles are not consistent, but there is consistency in the points of collaboration between all of them. Managers and employees get together and collaborate with each other so 'People' is the first Point of Collaboration. People also collaborate around Design and around Planning. We use the word 'Implementation' instead of 'Development' because Agile also works outside of software and hardware, including with HR teams, non-profits, legal teams, and even in the Performing Arts. Agile can basically work anywhere in a business where you have teams working towards a common goal. Likewise, 'Testing' is more of a software or hardware term, so we use the generic term 'Verification', and the last point of collaboration is fairly universal, 'Operations'."

"Match these six points of collaboration with each scope," continued Angela, "and you can differentiate between Design practices done at the Team level, Design practices shared between Agile teams at the Product level, and Design practices at the Organizational level. Likewise, you can talk about Planning practices at the Team level that an Agile team does for itself, Planning events that teams do together at the Product level, and Strategic Planning that you do at the Organizational level."

"Mostly, though," she continued, "it gives me a way to catalog my notes and keep track of everything we talk about, when, and with whom. Any area on this list, if missing, could be a potential point of failure, so all levels need attention as part of understanding our complex ecosystem."

Angela passed out copies of her notes from the interviews. Zach noticed that she had reorganized them according to the different Agile levels and the six areas of collaboration. There were six sections of notes about the Teams, six sections about the Product level, and six sections of notes about the Organization as a whole.

Table of Contents:

Teams

- Team People
- Team Design
- Team Planning
- Team Implementation
- Team Verification
- Team Operations

Products (Team of Teams)

- Product People
- Product Design
- Product Planning
- Product Implementation
- Product Verification
- Product Operations

Organization

- Org People
- Org Design
- Org Planning
- Org Implementation
- Org Verification
- Org Operation

Range of Influence

"Makes sense," added Ali, "I like how that works out into a set of levels. Focus on the Team level, when that's mastered move up to the Program level, then to the Organizational level."

Angela was obviously running a few things over in her brain before responding. "You don't really grow out of the Team level and leave it behind. AMMI is sometimes misused that way. Easy to do, since 'leveling up' is so common in video games. Hmm... Let me bring in one more concept to tie it all together. It's called the 'Range of Influence'."

She drew a curve on the board. The curve was highest in the center and then sloped down to nothing on both sides. She then divided the curve into sections using vertical lines. There was a single tall slice in the center with two medium-sized slices on either side, leaving two small slices on the outsides.

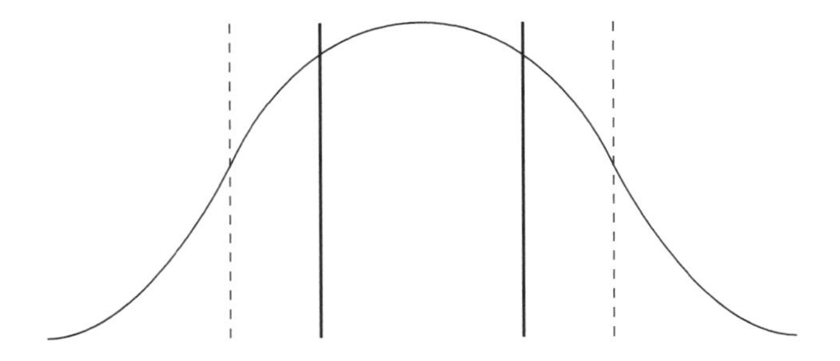

"This graph," she explained, "represents all the things in your life that affect you. The section in the middle represents the things that are within your 'Range of Control'. Some of these decisions may be your direct choice, or maybe you are part of a team deciding together." She wrote the words "Range of Control" between the middle lines.

"Just outside your Range of Control," she continued, "is what we call the 'Range of Influence'. In these areas, you know the people making the decisions and could have input into their decisions, but the decisions are not yours." She labeled the areas to either side of the Range of Control with the words "Range of Influence".

"The areas all the way on the outside," she added, "represent the decisions that affect you but which are outside of your influence." She wrote the words "Outside my Influence" next to the outer tails on the graph.

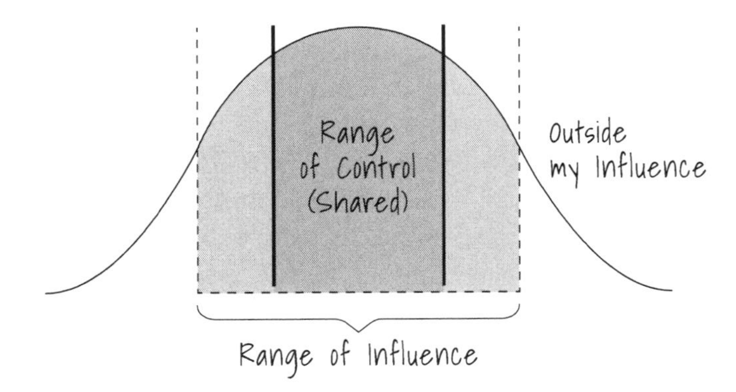

"The goal of this graph," she concluded, "is to help everybody identify which Agile practices are within your power to change, which you have influence over, and which you have no power to change. This also helps us to be realistic with our expectations."

"Let's look at the notes together as an example," she offered, holding up her copy.

"The first several pages contain all of the practices at the Team level," she pointed out. "Since we all belong to a team, all of these practices are either within our Range of Control, or within our Range of Influence, but only when it comes to our immediate team."

"For example," she said, pointing at the first page, "this section labeled 'Team People' is about Retrospectives, learning new skills, and listening to each other. Everybody can do these things."

She flipped to the next page, "The section labeled 'Team Design' is all about the design work done by individual teams. We say that stuff is within the Range of Control of the designers and the Product Owners."

"Likewise," she continued, moving to the next page, "we would say that Team Implementation and Team Operations are within the Range of Control of the developers. And so on."

"But," Angela clarified, "the developers don't work on the designs, and the designers don't work on the code. It would be unfair to hold the designers responsible for the code and the coders responsible for the design. Those are outside the 'Range of Control' of each respective role. But the designers and coders do talk to and consult with each other, so we can say that those areas are within their Range of Influence..." She paused for a few seconds, and Zach let it all sink in.

"So, putting it all together," she summarized, "we say that everything at the Team level is either within the Range of Control or the Range of Influence of the team members. Make sense?"

Zach nodded his head along with several of the others. He figured that made sense. The teams did collaborate with each other about each of the areas listed, and even though no one person did everything at that level, they did have influence over their teammates.

"Now let's go to the Product notes for contrast," Angela said, flipping forward a bunch of pages. "This is the area where you all operate as leaders. Naomi is in charge of Product Design, Evah is in charge of Product Verification, and Jayson and Ali oversee Product Implementation. Those are squarely within each of your Range of Control as leaders, but you don't write the actual code or the test cases. You have influence over Team Design, Team Implementation, and Team Verification, but you don't do that work yourselves. Team level practices count as your Range of Influence."

Intrinsic Motivation

People glanced through the notes quietly for a little while, then Ali piped up, "I notice that each area, like Team Design, has three practices inside, and next to each practice there's a scale? 'Never', 'Some', 'Half', 'Most', and 'Always', with one of the words circled for each. How often is 'sometimes'? Is it 20% of the time? 40% of the time?"

Angela confirmed. "Yes, those words just represent how often the teams talked about each area during the interviews. If nobody had heard about the concept, I marked it as 'Never'. If everybody was already doing it, I used the word 'Always'. Sometimes half of the teams were doing it, and in other teams it was either less than half the time or more than half the time. In my experience, greater precision is a waste of time. That's why I don't use percentages, but if you do, stick to something like twenty 5%, 50%, 75%. Just summarize the major patterns: some of the time, half of the time, or most of the time."

Evah picked up where Ali left off, blurting out, "But there's like twenty practices at the team level, twenty more at the product level, and another twenty for organizations? Do you really expect us to track all sixty things at once?!"

Angela replied with softness in her voice. "You, as managers? No. The goal is to get the teams to track all of the practices at the Team level themselves. We just have to do it gradually. It's important to not overwhelm them and only add new practices when they are truly helpful. The Product level practices are to be tracked by the Product Manager, Product Owners, Scrum Masters, and functional managers, and the organizational leaders track the Organizational practices."

"I just don't see that happening," Evah retorted. "If we don't watch them like a hawk, they always try to cut corners."

"A common problem," Angela agreed, "but it can be done. I'm not saying that it's easy, but the key is connecting each practice to something that the teams already care about. The popular Agile term for it is 'Intrinsic Motivation'. The teams are already frustrated by a bunch of problems which came up in our interviews. One by one we will connect each problem with one or more of the techniques. When they experience how the technique makes the problem go away, they will intrinsically want to do the practices so that they can avoid their problems."

Evah scrunched up her face in disbelief. "I don't know about that," she said. "It sounds too good to be true."

"Well," countered Angela, "let me give you an example from the first category of practices, People practices at the Team level. Most of your teams hold retrospectives every single sprint, and they seem to really enjoy the process."

Linda chimed in, "It gives them a time and a place to talk about any difficult issues."

"Yeah, but," countered Evah, "some of the teams don't do them."

Zach knew the answer to this one so he spoke up, "I saw the reason why after going through the interviews with Angela. Angela had a checklist about what makes a great retrospective that she downloaded from the AMMI website. She asked each of the teams if they met regularly, and about the format and stuff. Then she asked some questions that I hadn't thought about yet. She asked if they took their improvement items and added them to their backlog, and did they assign anyone to shepherd the improvement to completion. Of the teams who consistently did retrospectives, someone always volunteered to lead each improvement, and some teams even added them to the backlog. But on the teams that didn't do retros, none of them did either of those things."

Angela clarified further, "It's one of the first things that I check when I start to hear people make comments like, 'We bring up ideas for improvements but nothing ever gets done about them.' Often everybody assumes that someone else is going to do it. Just assigning them can make all the difference in the world."

"That's a great point!" Linda commented, enthusiastically writing it in her notebook.

"In the Design area at the Team level," Angela continued, switching topics, "I noticed that you consistently make great use of Research Spikes."

"Oh, yeah," Jayson confirmed. "Teams sometimes design themselves into a corner. They have a great idea, so they start building it only to find out halfway through that it's not going to work. Then they have to scrap days or weeks worth of work and start over! So I introduced 'Spikes'. They have to plan out a proof of concept first, and review it with me before they begin working on a new idea."

"See," Evah interjected, "he has to review it with them."

"But I see Angela's point, Evah," Jayson countered. "Yes, I ask them to review their spikes with me, but they create the spikes on their own. I don't have to remind them to create spikes. They want to avoid the pain of throwing out weeks worth of work more than I do. People only have to make that mistake once and they're converts."

"Exactly, Jayson. Yes, thank you!" Angela said in appreciation. "And another great example from the Team Planning category is Definitions of Ready and Definitions of Done. Your teams are doing a great job with those!"

Linda beamed, "That's one of the first things I like to look at when I join a team. Consistent Definitions of Ready and Done. If teams don't have them, I hold sessions with each of the teams to write them down and update as needed on a periodic basis."

This time Evah asked a question, "Do you have to follow up with them to make sure that they do it?"

Linda replied, "I've only had to really do it once per team to start. When I got here, there were several of the teams that didn't have one. They kept getting into the middle of the sprint and getting stuck because they didn't have something, so I showed them how to use the Definition of Ready to make sure they had everything before they got started. They latched onto it pretty quickly. It gave them a reason and a reminder to ask for things that they needed. Then after they gave their Product Owners a Definition of Ready, the Product Owners in return gave them a checklist of things they wanted to see at the end. That became their Definition of Done."

"Perfect example, Linda," Angela said enthusiastically. "You paired a technique with a problem they were already feeling."

"Wait, but that's the same problem," Ali interjected. "In both cases, the teams were getting stuck, but one solution is listed in the Design category, and the other technique is listed as a Planning technique. Why aren't they in the same category?"

"Good question," Angela answered. "The frustrating thing about problems is that there can be multiple causes. You can solve for one cause, and then the problem comes back again, but from a different angle. That is actually why we keep them separate, so that it is clear that getting stuck in the middle of a sprint might have two causes, a lack of sufficient design, or a gap in planning. You need to check both."

"Can I ask a different question?" Linda asked.

"Sure," Angela replied.

"I see that Daily Standups are in the next section," Linda began, "under Team Implementation. First, why is that not a planning technique? And also, that is one thing I do have to reinforce regularly. With certain teams, it's like pulling teeth to get them to show up for the Daily Standup."

"Ah," answered Angela, "the answer to both those questions is actually the same. Are you thinking about your team that is working on the new user workflow?"

"Yes!" confirmed Linda, nodding her head.

Angela explained, "I saw that too. It's actually a common anti-pattern in Agile. Your Product Owner on that team runs that Daily Standup, and he runs it like a project status meeting."

"What do you mean?" asked Linda. "He uses the three questions: What did you do yesterday, what are you doing today, and are there any obstacles? I figured that it didn't matter if the Scrum Master or the Product Owner led it, as long as he was following the right format."

"It's not about who runs the meeting," explained Angela. "It's about the intention behind the three questions. He's checking in on the teams to make sure that they got their work done. He's making it about his needs and about accountability. That's not what the Daily Standup is for. The Daily Standup, from the team's point of view, is a fast collaboration technique. It's not about is it done, but rather is it ready for the next person in line to get started. For example, if a developer says that they finished a story and it passed all the automated tests, then the Product Owner knows that it's ready for review. Or if someone has been working on a task longer than expected, then the Scrum Master knows to get them help, or if their other tasks need to be reassigned."

"You have to be very careful," Angela spelled out with greater clarity, "not to make team members feel bad if things don't go as planned. Skip the blame, address their problems as they arise, and focus on helping each other. Using accountability as a weapon kills a Daily Standup. If team members feel dread going into a Daily Standup, that is what demotivates them from wanting to be there."

Zach could tell that those insights were a jaw-dropping kind of moment for many as he looked around the room. They were for him too. He couldn't wait to get started on Angela's ideas.

"So how can I get the Product Owners to want to write test scripts?" Evah burst out. "We need to start doing BDD if we're ever going to reach the highest levels of performance in the 'Phoenix Project' book."

"And Planning Poker," added Jayson. "I do have to force some of the teams to do Planning Poker. I'd like for them to want to do that, not just because I said so."

Naomi jumped into the fray, "Getting my Product Owners to do regular Story Refinement sessions can often be like herding cats."

"How about 'Technical Debt'," offered Ali.

"And data," Roy added. "Nobody wants to collect data. Let me see if you can solve that problem!"

Angela laughed and responded, "Not everything all at once! Yes, we will get there. However, balance is the key at this stage!"

Managers in Agile

"Wait! If this does work," Evah quipped, "we'll be out of a job." A light, uneasy chuckle went up from around the table.

"Oh, there's plenty for you to do!" said Angela, reassuringly. "And let me address that head-on. There is a huge fallacy in some Agile communities that managers are somehow unnecessary in Agile because teams become 'self-managing'. While we do strive for them to be self-managing for the practices at the Team level, the practices at the Product and Organization levels are usually outside of the teams' Range of Control."

"That's where you as managers come in," she continued. "When you no longer have to spend time managing team practices, that frees you up to work on the practices at the Product and Organizational levels. A lot of the work in these areas never gets done, but is sorely needed. Things that only you can do by the nature of your positions."

"Well then, it sounds like we need to run some training sessions!" Zach said enthusiastically, in an obvious attempt to push the group towards action. "Shall we make a list of topics? Then you can design a class for us, and Linda will get everybody registered to take it."

"Ooh, are we voting?" asked Linda. "I'd like to hear more about these Working Sessions."

"And I'd like to challenge these scores on MVPs," insisted Naomi. "We have MVPs. We are definitely building MVPs."

"And I don't buy this 'Intrinsic Motivation' line," added Roy, "Let's take data, for example. These teams don't know how to use data. If we left it to 'Intrinsic Motivation', nobody would collect data."

"These are all very good suggestions," confirmed Angela, "but effective transformations have to start by establishing trust with the teams through fixing problems that they care about. After we make their lives easier, then they'll be more likely to make changes for us. It's a give-and-take. We make changes first that positively impact them, and then we ask them to make changes that affect our work."

Roy jumped in, "No, we have to focus more on Data-Driven Marketing and Sales."

Naomi's voice changed to a more commanding tone, "Oh there you go again, Roy! Not everything with the word 'data' is a priority and for good reason!"

Roy smiles, "Without data, you are simply guessing! You're relying on your intuition, something that has been shown lately to often be ***flat-out wrong!***"

Naomi's voice increased, "At least I make decisions and don't spend all my time collecting data and then sitting on it like a dragon with a hoard of gold!"

Roy was just about to respond when Angela quickly interjected, "Tell you what! We're going to end the day here. I have an exercise that we can do tomorrow that will help us collectively pick the next best thing to tackle, and I'll tell you all about it then."

Naomi and Roy continued giving fiery stares to each other until Roy broke it off, "Fine. I need a break from all of this arguing anyway!"

He got up and added with a tone of sarcasm, "Enjoy your time here, Angela!"

Zach could tell from the look on Angela's face that she was worried.

Yes, something was going to break, and soon...

Key Points of Learning

- Active Listening
- 'Double Aces'
- Agile Mindset Mapping Index (AMMI)
- Range of Influence
- Intrinsic Motivation
- Managers in Agile

Chapter 6

Naomi – “The Pursuit of Happiness?”

SELF AWARENESS

"Dear Lord, Clyde! Why is this so hard?!!" Naomi vented at her monitor. On her right screen, she had a video conference with Clyde. On her left screen, she had a new customer video that Clyde had recorded. The customers were still struggling with the new workflow and were just abandoning the tests. "They don't seem to want to put any thought into opening a new account at all!"

"I was thinking the same..." Clyde started to confirm, but he was cut off.

"Why didn't you test the new workflow?" Naomi said, blazing ahead. "I sent you the new designs two days ago." She knew in her gut that she was grasping at straws, but didn't want to admit it.

"This test was assigned to the previous workflow," he tried to insert. "For integrity..."

"Integrity," she scoffed. "Integrity is doing the job I was hired to do! Integrity is delivering on promises! What's going on with this screen?!" The screen was starting to get a fuzzy white haze over it. She banged the side of the monitor, like that was going to help. Technology. Nothing worked right. The screen got whiter. No, it wasn't just the screen. The white haze was getting stronger! She looked around the room and it was everywhere and getting stronger! "What's going on?!!" she blurted out.

"Naomi?" she heard from Clyde's voice, but she couldn't see his face anymore. She couldn't see anything anymore! White dots dominated all of her eye-sight like she was staring at a very bright light.

"Naomi, are you okay?" Clyde asked again.

"No, I am not! I can't see!"

Clyde responded, "See what? Do you mean my screen? Did the screen share stop working again?"

Naomi responded with exasperation, "No, you fool! I have no eyesight! All I see is white haze!!!"

"What?!?" Clyde exclaimed. "Oh no, are you serious? Is there anything I can do? Want me to call an ambulance?" Panic started to creep into his voice. It only made Naomi's panic even worse. He gasped in amazement which just underscored for Naomi the absurdity of the situation.

"No!" Naomi growled, "Give me a moment!"

She closed her eyes and tried to relax. She reached out for the desklamp, fumbling with it. Her hand hit the shade of the lamp and it started teetering. She quickly reached out to grab the base so that it wouldn't fall and accidentally knocked into something solid. What was it? She didn't know! She couldn't see! But at least she had the lamp in hand, steadied it, and felt her way up the base to the light switch, turning it off.

She sat there for a few seconds with the lights off, her hands still holding on to the lamp as if it was going to fall again if she let go.

Clyde hesitatingly asked, "Any better?"

Naomi was startled a little. She forgot that he was there. Responding in the most normal voice she could muster, but with her eyes still closed, she said "Yes, I am doing better." It was a lie, but it was the only control over this situation that she had. "Clyde," she continued, eyes still closed, "I am going to need a break. Please excuse me. We are done for the day." She reached out to where the laptop was supposed to be with her other hand and closed it, severing the connection, and turning all the screens black with it.

She sat there in what should have been darkness until the white "snow" slowly, ever so slowly, started to fade, but she still could not see! Was it seconds? Was it minutes? She didn't know. She couldn't see the clock either! "Just relax," she told herself. She had heard that advice somewhere. Just relax. And breathe.

"Why was no one coming to help her?" she thought. She had to have made a great deal of noise. *"No, just relax."*

If she admitted it to herself, she knew why. Working from home for these past couple of weeks was supposed to be her best idea lately. More time with the family. She was not going to lose them too, at all costs. More time to work, without cutting out the family. More time to create new ideas for the design team, review mockups, draft workflows, and test new deliveries from the team, all without the constant interruptions of people stopping by her desk. She was going to be in control of life, and not let life control her.

But all this stress had driven her from cool and confident to angry and hot-tempered. She had become a live wire and even the kids no longer came seeking her. It was just too much to bear. Even Sam was spending more time upstairs, giving her "space". Naomi was hit with a sudden and all-consuming wave of sadness.

"Relax. Breathe," she urged herself in earnest, and the wave gave way to tears that trickled down her cheeks. She just let them flow for a while and tried to stay sitting upright for as long as she could. When she was just too exhausted to maintain her composure, she crumpled over in her chair and just let the tears come.

When the tears stopped, she opened her eyes and tested her vision. All of the items in the dark room started to come back into focus with the light from the streetlamp shining apologetically through the window.

Okay. That had gone too far. That was one of the most terrifying moments she had had in her life! She needed time to pause, reflect and think. She opened the laptop again, but for only one reason. She drafted an email to Tim, explained her situation, and asked for the rest of the week off. She clicked send and closed the laptop again.

"How did I let this happen?" she asked the darkness around her. "It was too much", Naomi thought, *"Her life had become hellacious. What changed?"*

Everything had been going wonderfully for her at Ares. Even before joining the Innovation Center, she had been a superstar. She was promoted from analyst to Product Owner within months, then to Product Manager, and finally to Director of Product Services when she made the change with Tim.

It had been, what? Six years since graduating from Havard? Her first choice after the MBA was joining the fast-paced hustle and bustle of the brokerage side of American Banking Services, but it became evident that the better choice would be financial wealth management. As one of the youngest members of that business unit, Naomi proved herself more than capable of handling the work as a junior analyst, quickly moving up the ranks. She had always been known for fast learning, quick decision-making, and uncanny problem-solving through new ideas and better techniques. It was one of her professional superpowers.

She remembered two years ago when she heard that American Banking Services was creating a new business unit that was supposed to "pioneer the future of our company" and aggressively sought out joining the group. Tim was so impressed by Naomi's confidence and motivation that he offered her the position as a Product Manager with only one interview.

Naomi knew she had clinched it on Tim's final question, "Why should I choose you over more experienced Product Managers?"

"I take ownership over my teams," Naomi explained. "Their problems are my problems and I'll solve them. The buck stops here." Of course, there was more to it, but Tim had said that he was most impressed with her confidence, creativity, and tenaciousness.

Naomi no longer felt confident, creative, or tenacious. All of that had evaporated in the wake of the Cynch app, and the 'buck' was speeding past her, all the way into Intuition's pocket! She had become a hot mess and that scared her!

God, had it already been three months since her world had been turned upside down by Intuition's launch?! How quickly she had gone from 'hero' to 'zero' in a mere three months! First, the team thought they could conquer it with evening work and full confidence that they would overcome. Then their confidence was replaced with uncertainty as it spilled over into weekend work. She was now at eighty plus hours every week and desperately trying to cling on to anything at all.

On top of that, Angela had already usurped Tim's trust, his new golden child. It had almost made Naomi abandon her plan of working from home. Angela had introduced some new prioritization scheme, "Weighted Shortest Job First". It was etched in her brain now because everybody kept repeating it, especially that darn acronym. "'W-S-J-F' says we should work on this first," or "I didn't get that done yet because it's not at the top of the W-S-J-F priority list." What happened to the Product Manager setting the priorities? Wasn't that written in the Agile Manifesto somewhere? Doesn't the Product Manager set the order of priorities? Last she checked, she was the Product Manager!

She felt her blood pressure rising again. "Relax," she told herself again. "Okay, just breathe." She used her smartwatch to track a few breathing cycles for her. It didn't help that it was late Wednesday evening and Naomi had already drunk three cups of coffee, taken three aspirin, and even taken antidepressants. In the early days of work-from-home, she'd still get out and go to the coffee shop for lattes, cappuccinos, and expressos. Those were nice little breaks, but no more. Now it was about getting the nearest caffeine shot with the least amount of time and effort. The tyranny of the urgent and always feeling like she was square in the center of the headlights of a big eighteen-wheeler truck with the name "Cynch" speeding up behind her. As frustrating as Angela's presence was, the real problem started with "Cynch". God, it was such a rip-off of her product! Not even as much fun to say.

Holy crap! What was the name of their product? Naomi had forgotten. Cynch was dominating her consciousness. "Breeze!" There it was! She breathed a sigh of relief and began chanting the name to herself like a mantra, "Breeeeze. Breeeeeze." It made a great replacement for the word, "Breathe". After a couple more minutes of thinking about breezes blowing through palm trees on a beach, she finally started feeling normal again.

When was the last time that she went to a beach? When was the last time that she was able to focus on herself? How do you focus on yourself? She wondered what the Internet would say. She opened the laptop and quickly closed all the applications. Save? Yes. Doesn't matter what it is. Save it and close it. Close everything. Quit everything. She opened a browser window and searched for "finding yourself".

Meditation was a common theme. Naomi decided to try a meditation app. She did a search for "top meditation apps" and spent the next two hours going through the introductory lessons, breathing, how to sit, what to wear, and body awareness. She even tried a yoga breathing technique called, "Bhastrika pranayama" for some further energy. That led to multiple sessions on focus and purpose, and although she felt better, they did not help quell that uneasy feeling within herself. It seemed to be really helpful to a lot of people, but not really being the patient type, she opted to keep looking.

She started reading and watching an endless string of self-help videos and blogs. It was a bit overwhelming how saturated the Internet was with self-help content. Julia Cameron and Katie Byron looked interesting. By the time she made it to Brené Brown, it was well into the early morning.

Brené was talking about being vulnerable and truly listening to others. She particularly resonated with the part about listening and empathizing with people. Brené compared it to going into a deep hole with that person and saying, "I'm here." As she described it, it became more and more clear to Naomi how this was a very different approach from attempting to solve their problem, different than introducing your own perspective, and different from trying to "look on the bright side".

Naomi started watching and reading everything published by Brené, including her movie, "The Call to Courage". She was a complete sponge. She soaked in the content and really identified with the need to show vulnerability. *"It's okay to admit that you don't have all the answers,"* She realized. *"Being right has been more important than being kind, especially since Intuition screwed us over."*

That was when her "Aha!" moment arrived!

"You're not really listening," was the phrase that kept repeating in her head. It was almost as if she was not saying it, someone else was saying it to her, but she was also saying it at the same time. It was worth a try. After all, what she had been doing was definitely NOT working. It also occurred to her that what she was facing was too hard for her to solve alone. She really didn't know what to do and needed to try a different approach.

Clyde's face popped back into her mind. Clyde had ideas. Some good ideas. She hadn't listened to his ideas originally, but several of them turned out to be truly fruitful, once she was forced to try them. That was the problem — her problem — she had to be forced to incorporate them. Clyde's ideas were worth considering. Angela's too. She already respected Tim's ideas, and Angela often represented Tim's ideas when she thought about it. She respected Vera's ideas and Evah's ideas... but whose ideas had she not been respecting? Zach... it's not that she hadn't been respecting Zach's ideas, but she also hadn't really been paying attention. She couldn't remember any of Zach's ideas, or if he had offered anything. The same was true of Clyde and Linda. She wrote a note to herself to listen to Zach, Clyde, and Linda. Who else? Jayson... he always had solid ideas. Ali, yes. Roy... She shuddered, physically. She didn't want to, but she had to admit to herself that she definitely didn't listen to Roy. She took a deep breath and made a commitment to listen to Roy.

She looked up and looked around the room for the first time in hours. The clock on the wall read 4:25, as in 4:25 am. She blinked in astonishment. No one had stopped by to say good night or encourage her to come to bed. She knew why. Because she didn't listen when they did. Tomorrow she will start listening. She wrote "LISTEN" in bold letters at the bottom of her page of notes, closed the laptop, and stood up. She grabbed a sticky note, and her pen again. She wrote "LISTEN" on the note, and stuck it to the top of her closed laptop. She made a vow to herself to spend the entire next day listening to her family... not responding, not sharing her own opinions, not solving their problems, just listening. These next few days and the whole weekend would be about listening to her family.

Naomi breathed a big, long sigh of relief. She had a clear direction to take and started immediately feeling better. It was time to make a change for the better!

OFFICE SPACE

Naomi collected her things from her car, closed the door, and double-checked her appearance in the reflection of the car window. She was looking good, she was feeling good, and most importantly she was feeling confident, or at least more confident. It had been a great weekend, a family weekend. They played games together. They ate together at the dining room table. They watched a couple of movies. They got outside and went for a hike in the woods. God, that was refreshing and rejuvenating! She even got some time to reconnect with Sam after the kids went to bed. It had been a normal weekend. She missed those. She smiled at herself in the reflection, a genuine smile. She was so happy to see a genuine smile looking back at herself in the reflection. She almost teared up again, tears of joy, but this was not the time.

"This week is about listening," she said to herself as she grabbed her coffee and walked to the elevator. She was early — she was always early — so she had the elevator all to herself. She liked it that way. Start the day with calmness and then let the day build. She found herself looking forward to seeing any new recordings from Clyde. She had on her checklist to stop by and check in with Zach, ask for his thoughts, and take Linda for a cup of coffee to ask her how she was integrating into Ares. She wasn't sure how to approach Roy yet, but she had the bright idea to talk to Jayson about how to bridge the gap with Roy. Jayson would probably have some good insights.

Ding! The elevator opened and she walked through the open doors. Her confidence and composure, though, didn't get off with her. She was hit simultaneously with both the emotional memory of what she had left behind and a jarring new sight to behold. The arrangement of the whole work area had changed. It reminded her of the layout that the graphic designers used in their area. Instead of "cube land", the teams each had their own open area in a big square with modular workstations populating the edges of the square. The dividers were gone, now replaced

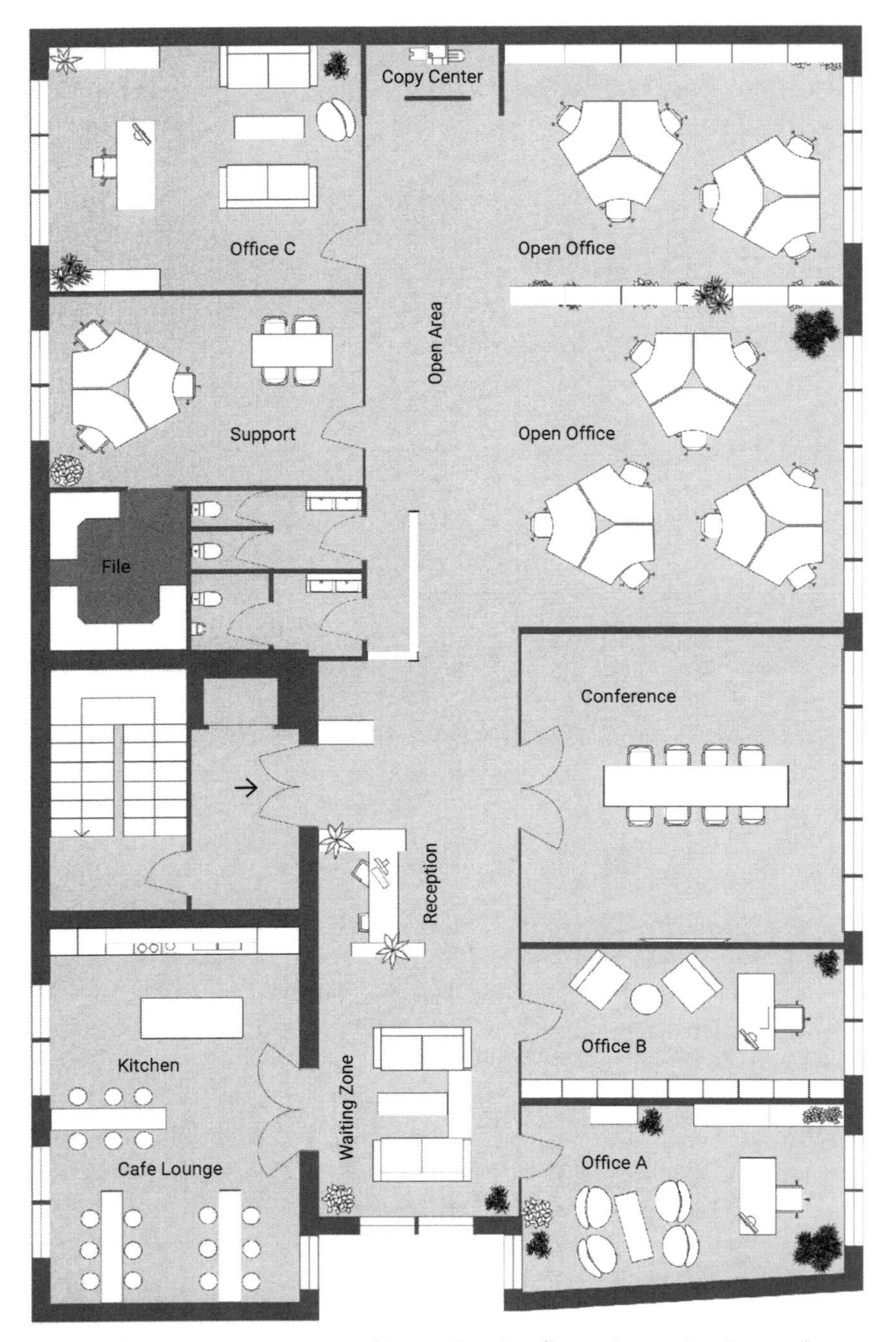

Example layout. Image courtesy of RoomSketcher (*https://roomsketcher.com*)

with new modern chairs and free-standing desks, some of them at sitting height and some of them raised to standing heights.

There were walls in each space, but now they were rolling whiteboards that were covered with sticky notes and papers with blue tape. Were the teams using physical Kanban boards now? What about the online Kanbans? She felt an instant sense of dread that nothing would ever be up-to-date in the tracking software ever again. The center of each open area was littered with couches, coffee tables, and bean bag chairs. I mean sure, the designers got a kick out of these things, but programmers were a different type of person. She started to feel the mama bear awake within her. Did the developers really want these changes, or were they forced on them?

She was snapped out by surprise when one of the Scrum Masters walked by and waved, "Hello, Naomi! Welcome back!"

Naomi was still too shocked to really speak. She replied with a simple "Good morning, Geena," and gave a polite wave back. She took a deep breath, and physically, but subtly, shook off the surprise from her whole body.

First things first, reestablish a home base. She started walking towards her office on the far wall. Good, it was still there, but something else was odd. Several of the other offices around hers had been emptied. Had people been fired and nobody told her?! One of the offices was Evah's! No, if Evah had been fired, she would have told her. Also Linda's. Maybe Linda was let go? Last hired is often the first fired in a crisis, but Linda had been in several of the video meetings last week, and nobody had said a thing.

It was odd. In place of the usual desks and bookshelves, the offices now held conference tables, chairs, and even more rolling whiteboards filled with sketches in marker. She couldn't wait for Evah to arrive. Why had nobody told her about all these changes? More importantly, why had nobody *asked her* before making all these changes? Naomi felt that wave of anger flow over her again.

"Naomi! Welcome back!" She heard Tim's voice calling out. She looked around and saw Tim emerging from his office and walking towards her. She started walking towards him. "Are you doing better?" he asked. "How is your eyesight?"

"Thanks for asking, Tim. My eyesight is clear. That was definitely due to stress and the time off certainly helped. Thank you. I filled the time with family, meditation, and also some self-help videos too."

"Ooh. That's awesome. What did you learn?" asked Tim, a little too enthusiastically for Naomi's tastes.

"I've learned that when I leave the office for a while, chaos takes over!" She said, gesturing around at all of the changes stretching out around her.

Tim sounded a little surprised, "Oh you mean the change of layout and the new furniture? Naomi, don't you remember we all agreed to move to a more open layout, like the Design team space, for improved intra- and cross-team collaboration? It was before the Intuition launch, of course, but the furniture just happened to arrive while you were out, so we just pulled the trigger on the new design."

"Did we actually order all of that furniture?" Naomi conceded. "It's been so long, I had honestly forgotten, but this is not what we designed."

"True, we didn't stop there. Angela had helped design open spaces at several companies in the past and brought us pictures and examples. We looked through them all, debated the benefits of each layout, and weighed them against our personal needs. This is the result. Specially designed by the team for the team!"

Naomi began fuming that she wasn't involved. "But I also didn't anticipate you would go and do it without first letting me know! Was this really the best use of teams' time?"

"That's exactly the right question!" Tim agreed. "Here let me show you how we decided. It's pretty ingenious." Tim gestured for Naomi to head to one of the emptied offices.

"Where did everybody's offices go?" she asked.

"Oh, right. You missed that too," Tim realized. Naomi's eyes narrowed a little bit, with more dread creeping in. Tim continued, "It's a concept called 'Campfires and Caves'[1], which is part of the reason it caught my attention. You know I love spelunking! Campfire is the term used to represent collaborative spaces, like these new spaces here, or the space that the Designers built. It's all about open spaces, where people are intermingling and talking, with projectors, rolling whiteboards, or big tables to review works in progress."

---

1 "Campfires, Caves, and Watering Holes" are terms coined by Professor David Thornburg

"Good God," Naomi blurted out with exasperation. "How is anyone supposed to get any real work done?" It was worse than she thought. Now Naomi imagined they were all sitting around campfires, eating 's'mores, and singing "Kumbaya"!

"Exactly!" said Tim, jumping at the opportunity. Naomi was a little taken aback and puzzled by his enthusiasm. Tim closed the gap, "That's why it's vital to have Campfires AND Caves!"

He smiled. Naomi didn't.

He continued, "Time to focus and work by yourself is also just as important. That's where the 'Caves' come in. As Angela pointed out, you have two options. You can either set up your main work environment as caves and then create collaborative campfire spaces to get together, or you can set up your main work area as a campfire and then have private spaces where you go for peace and quiet and shut out the world. We gave each of the teams an option and they each voted as a team. The Riverlands and The North teams both voted for campfire spaces. The others voted to remain as caves. It makes for a wonderful little natural experiment."

"So now I'm confused," Naomi asked. "Are these offices shared 'caves' now? Am I sharing my office now with developers? I'm... listening. I'm trying to, but... I'm also a bit frustrated. I had to scrape and claw my way up to an office. This seems... unfair... to say it lightly."

"Angela actually said the same thing," Tim assured her. "I really think you're going to like her as you two talk more." Naomi needed more convincing, and Tim was clearly happy to provide. "Angela said that it was very important that everyone with an office door must make the decision for themselves whether they wish to have a campfire or cave as their home base. The leadership team even talked for a while about who liked which environment, why, and what made sense for whom. For example, I'm very often closing my door to hold private meetings or phone calls. I would have to constantly be finding a cave throughout my day, so living in a campfire just didn't make sense for me. Ali and Roy opted for the same."

"Linda, on the other hand," Tim offered as a contrast, "said that she really didn't want an office. She liked campfires and offered up her office for a cave. So we put some desks in there as a quiet room. One of the developers offered the analogy of the quiet car on a train, so that became the agreed-upon rule. Anyone can go in there and use a vacant desk, but you can't talk."

Naomi had to admit that that was a fair solution. She also appreciated that it was voluntary. She couldn't believe, though, that Linda would give up her office so fast. Well, actually, that was Linda. She was never in her office. She was always at someone's desk, or in the break room, or in the lunchroom, or running a meeting. Then she paused. "So, I'm guessing that Evah made the same choice since we're standing in her office now?"

"Yep," confirmed Tim.

"So," Naomi continued, piecing the clues together, "If this is a quiet room, why is there a big TV in here and a conference table?"

"Ah," said Tim. "Great point. Since most of the teams opted to stay with cubicles – in cave configuration – we also needed campfires for them. Since her office was on the larger size, Evah offered it up as a smaller campfire for The Stormlands team, because they have fewer members. The existing conference rooms are going to act as the other campfires. Plus! Every campfire space can also become a cave space if you reserve it on the company calendar."

"So," Naomi recapped, "whether you start with an office – which we're now calling 'caves' – or you start in one of the open spaces, whenever you need a quiet space or a collaborative space, you can reserve one."

"Right!" said Tim. "In theory." Naomi's left eyebrow raised involuntarily. Tim explained, "We're already starting to see a scramble for the campfire spaces."

"The campfires?" Naomi asked quizzically. She was expecting the opposite.

"Yeah," Tim confirmed. "They get booked fast since we're using a first-come, first-serve basis. At first, we gave each team dedicated rolling whiteboards so that they didn't have to keep erasing the boards between meetings. They could just take the whole whiteboard with them, but they were a bit unwieldy, and at the same time not big enough to hold all of the Kanban boards and diagrams."

"Angela said the same thing happened in her old company," he added. "She said things got a lot easier when each team was granted a dedicated team space, a room all to their own, where they can leave things up on the walls, and that's always free for team meetings. So, eventually, we want to have a dedicated campfire room for each team, which led to Ali's suggestion of covering the walls with whiteboard paint! Have you seen whiteboard paint?! You can write on the whole wall, and then just wipe it clean! It's pretty awesome. I'm trying to coordinate some more office space with the Facilities department."

"But I'm going on too long about the campfires and caves," Tim realized in an apologetic tone. "I really want to get back to your question about 'How do we know it's the best use of the teams' time?' We came in here to talk about the Transformation backlog."

ECONOMIC PRIORITIZATION

Tim started tapping on his phone. "Check out this feature we got with the new campfire screens. You can share the screens from any device on the WiFi." Tim's phone appeared on the screen. He rotated the phone to landscape and opened a spreadsheet. "We have this saved on our private cloud. I'll send you the link."

In bold letters at the top of the spreadsheet, it said, "Weighted Shortest Job First (WSJF)". This is what Naomi had been wanting to talk about. It was a lot of numbers but in no particular order. She was wrestling with the anger that 'User Account Creation' was nowhere near the top of the list. Her number one priority was actually not on this list at all!

Tim was being quiet, probably letting her read the screen, so she took a couple of deep breaths subtly. She was determined to try her best at being vulnerable and have the courage to sit with her discomfort, listen, and learn.

WEIGHTED SHORTEST JOB FIRST (WSJF) – TRANSFORMATION

Job	Business Value	Enabler Value	Time Criticality	Job Size	Score
1. Open Space	5	13	13	1	31
2. Hackathon	1	8	5	1	14
3. Agile mindset improvements (AMMI)					
MVP 1: AMMI + 2 improvements	8	13	13	2	17
MVP 2: Big Room Planning	5	3	1	2	4.5
4. Customer Usability Testing	21	8	21	5	10
5. Pirate Metrics (AARRR)	3	1	3	2	3.5

"Ok. Great. I wanted to talk to you about this W-S-J-F stuff." Naomi said exasperatingly.

"Oh, a bunch of us have started pronouncing it Wiz-Jiff," Tim shared with a smile. "It's kind of fun to say. Jayson said he heard it pronounced that way before, and it's starting to stick."

"Ok. WizJif." She fought the smile that came with saying it, though, because it really was annoying her. "I thought I was supposed to set the priorities as Product Manager. Now everyone's pushing back on my requests and throwing this in my face."

"Wait, did you not get the WSJF introduction?!" Tim exclaimed abashedly. "Oh, I'm so sorry, Naomi. I didn't realize. Yeah, this must seem very confusing for you. Let me see if I can do it justice and walk you through it."

"Angela introduced this in that first week after you walked out of her kickoff meeting. Not very professional, by the way," Tim said with a stern look. Naomi diverted her eyes.

Tim continued, "Angela expressed that she really wanted you to be part of this, but it was really hard to get a hold of you, so I told her to go ahead and we would fill you in. Dang, it! That's my fault for not filling you in. I'm sorry."

It was Tim's turn to divert his eyes. He shifted them back to his screen and continued, "She said that it is typically used to prioritize product features or Epics, but also works great with planning transformations. She wanted to use it to make sure that we only worked on what was absolutely necessary, right now. As she expressed it, 'We don't want to get trapped in transformation for transformation's sake.'"

"Agreed," was all that Naomi said. She was trying not to be confrontational. After all, this week was supposed to be about listening, right?

Tim continued, "Ok. Here's the quick background. W-S-J-F has two parts, "weighted" and "shortest". Imagine that you only have two things to work on."

"As if," quipped Naomi.

"Right?" returned Tim with a chuckle. "But putting it in really simplistic terms, imagine that you have two things that you could be working on, and they both will take the same amount of time to complete. Let's say three days."

He drew a graph on the whiteboard, ticked off multiple days on the horizontal axis, and wrote the word "Value" at the top of the vertical axis.

"At the end of three days you deliver one of them, we release it, and it generates ten thousand dollars in revenue."

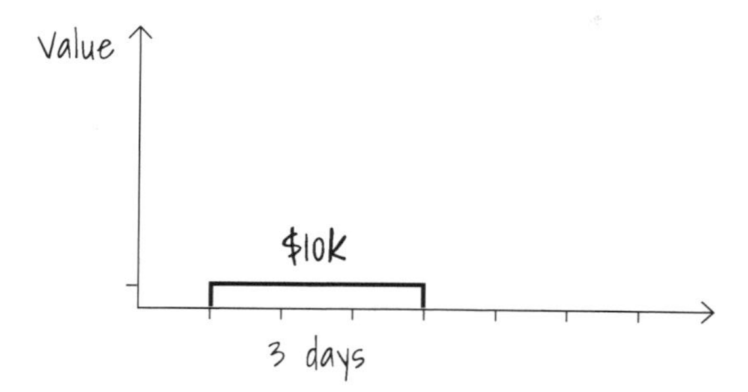

He drew a mark for ten thousand dollars on the vertical axis, drew a small box, and wrote "3 days" under it on the horizontal axis.

"The other job also takes three days, we release it, and it generates a hundred thousand dollars in revenue."

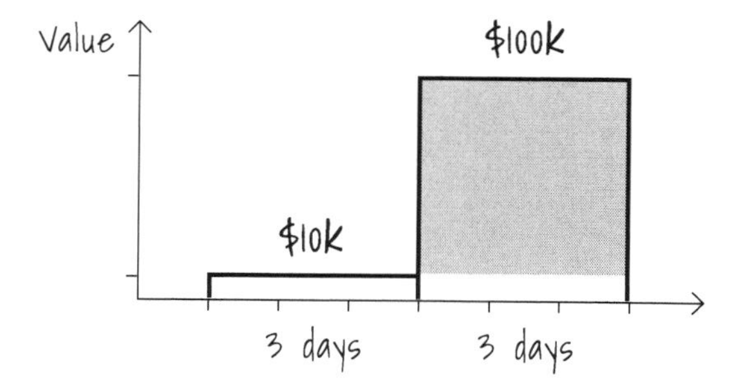

He drew a mark for one hundred thousand dollars at the top of the vertical axis, drew a much larger box next to the original box, and also marked it on the horizontal axis as three days.

"Which do you work on?" he asked Naomi.

"This seems like a trick question," Naomi said cautiously. "The obvious answer that you're showing on the board is that the hundred-thousand-dollar job is more important, but what if we can't sell it right away? Or what if it takes a while to realize that revenue?"

"Yeah... Great questions," Tim added. "We did get to that part eventually. It fell under a concept called... what was it... uh... 'Time' something... I remember that Evah asked something like that."

Naomi smiled with some internal pride for Evah, until Tim burst out, "'Criticality'! 'Time Criticality' was what it was called. It's built on top of the concepts of 'Cost of Delay' and 'Economic Prioritization' developed by Don Reinertsen[2]. I ordered a copy of his book and started reading it last week."

"But I'm getting sidetracked," Tim said, a little flustered. "We will get back to that. We start with the simple, and then we get more complex. That's also part of the genius of this. Break it down into simple terms first for clarity, and then it makes it easier to find clarity in more complex situations. There are so many things that we can't predict — like timelines — but right now, at this moment, we know that the potential of one item is ten thousand dollars, and the potential of the other item is ten times the value of the other."

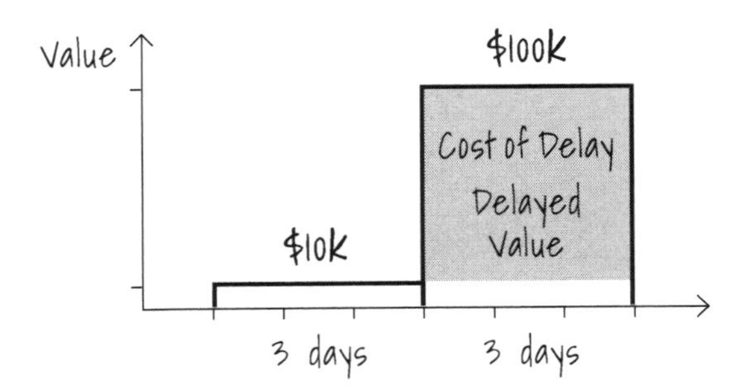

He wrote the words "Cost of Delay" and "Delayed Value" on the board, pointing to the hundred-thousand dollars that were delayed by the ten thousand dollar task.

Tim smiled and moved on, "Ok. Great. Now imagine that you have two things that you could work on that are both valued equally, at a hundred thousand dollars each. The first involves one day of work before you can send it out the door, and the other involves ten days of work before you can send it out the door. Which do you work on?" He paused for Naomi's reply.

Naomi wanted to play along but just couldn't, "I know you want me to say the one-day job, but it's never that simple."

---

2 For more information about Don Reinersten, see his book "The Principles of Product Development Flow".

"No, it's not," Tim agreed, "but the simple tells us information about the complex."

"Well, sure," Naomi agreed back, "but, for example, how long have we been working on the ten-day job? What if we're at the end of a six-month-long stretch and we only have ten days left? Then ten days is nothing!"

"Exactly!" Tim burst out, excitedly, "and that's how we've been thinking about it all wrong. We make decisions about the future based on our past, not the present! Let me explain. It doesn't matter how we got here. Right now, looking at the work to get done, one of these jobs we could get out the door tomorrow and start generating revenue ...tomorrow. The other would keep us busy for the next two weeks. As Reinersten explains, it's all about sequencing!"

Tim was obviously super-excited about this idea. The joy on his face was slightly infectious. He kept going, "Let's look at our two possibilities."

On the whiteboard, he drew two axes again. He marked one as days and the other as value. "If we work on the six-month job, spend two weeks on it, and get it out the door, we get it into the marketplace after ten days."

He ticked off ten marks on the axis of days and then drew a box which he labeled as '$100k'.

"There's no value for ten days, but then it gets deployed and we start earning our one hundred thousand dollars. Hooray, our six-month project is done! Then we come back and work on the one-day job and get it out the door on the eleventh day, and start earning two hundred thousand dollars." He drew a second box at eleven days, and labeled it as '$200k'.

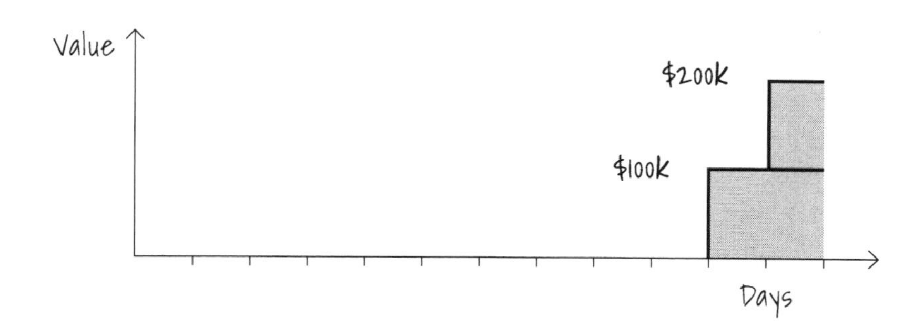

"Buuuut... if we reverse the order and complete the one-day job first..." He drew a new chart next to the other one and added a box stretching from day two to the end. He labeled it '$100k'. "Then we work for ten days and finish the six-month project on day eleven for the second hundred-thousand." He drew a second box above the first, from day eleven to the end. "The six-month project is still done, one day later, and we still earn the second hundred-thousand dollars, but look at the difference! Look at when we get the first hundred-thousand!"

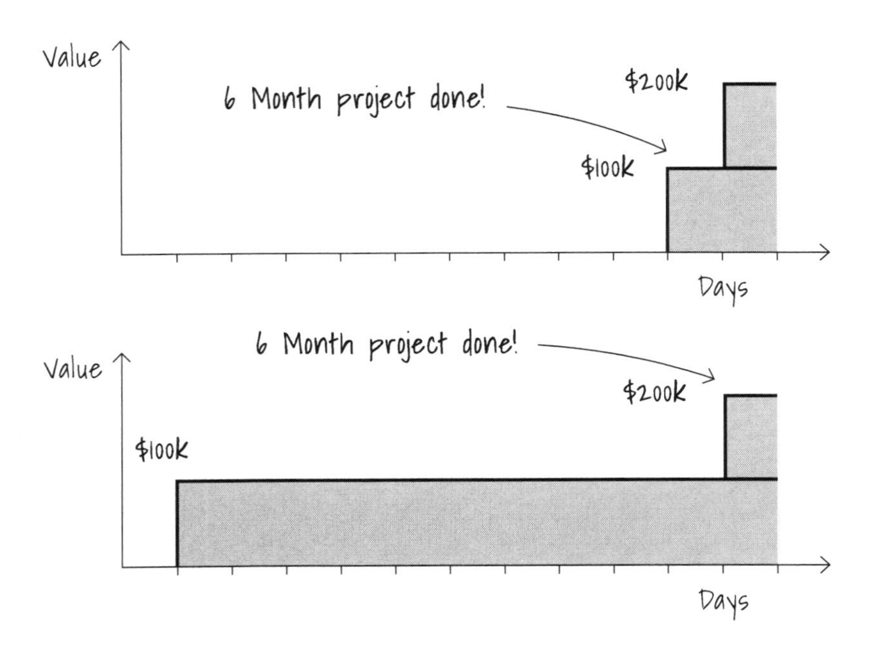

He drew arrows on both graphs to mark the point at which the six-month project would be done. Naomi got the point. The point was earning revenue earlier, *"but if it was that easy, wouldn't they be doing it already?"* she thought.

Tim paused and looked at her expectantly. He was going to make her say it out loud. Naomi obliged, "If we do the ten-day job first, we get the two hundred thousand on days ten and eleven. If we do the one-day job first, we get the first hundred-thousand on day two."

"Yes," Tim enthused, cutting her off, "in either case, we get the second hundred-thousand in eleven days, but if we do the shorter job first, we get the first hundred-thousand dollars *nine days earlier*! This is why Reinertsen calls it the 'Cost of Delay'. We are *costing* ourselves money by *delaying* the wrong things. With every choice, something is always going to be delayed. The question is, 'Which delay is the best delay?' This could be the difference between having a good executive report or a bad executive report or having to report good quarterly earnings or bad quarterly earnings. With no change in people, by only changing the order of the work, we earn revenue two weeks earlier. That's why I'm so excited! I thought you would be too."

"Don't get me wrong, Tim," Naomi countered, "this sounds great. Getting revenue nine days earlier would be fantastic. It's just never that simple." She was feeling exhausted that she was having to constantly battle all of this new-found enthusiasm from everybody. Everybody was floating off into the clouds, and she kept having to grab them by the ankles and drag them back down to earth.

That's why the next thing Tim said stuck with her, "But Naomi, haven't you seen how everybody's spirits have been lifted over the past couple of weeks? It does work. We've been making small decisions based on job size for the past several weeks, and people feel better about the outcomes. They're getting things done, and they are beginning to feel a whole lot less overwhelmed while doing it. The clarity is amazing!"

Naomi had a momentary thought of dread, a quick clench in her stomach. Maybe she was the problem, bringing everybody down. Were they really this much happier without her here?

"Hi, Naomi! It's so great to see you!", Evah said joyfully, poking her head into what used to be her office. She noticed what was on the screen. "Are you walking her through WSJF, Tim?"

Tim enthusiastically nodded his head.

"Oh," exclaimed Evah, "this is powerful stuff, Naomi. I can't wait to have your voice in our WSJF prioritization sessions!"

"Yeah," Tim confirmed. "We've gotten as far as the Cost of Delay."

"Oh! That's the biggest part for me," Evah added. "When I learned that changing the order of things made such a huge difference, I started applying it to all our work. I went looking for what was waiting and found several small, but really important testing tasks and asked for volunteers. Since these were testing tasks, when they were done, everything was done. We started closing out user stories, the Burndown Charts started looking better, and people started feeling less stressed. It sounds too good to be true, but it really isn't!"

Naomi couldn't deny Evah's joy and enthusiasm. Evah had always been her right-hand gal. They were always in sync with every decision — eventually.

"I was just about to walk through how the scoring works," Tim said, gesturing Evah to a chair beside Naomi. "Would you like to join us?"

Evah accepted, "Sure."

"So," continued Tim, "Job Duration defines the word 'Shortest' in Weighted Shortest Job First. The 'Weighted' word is defined in three parts."

He pointed to the columns on the screen.

"Business Value, Enabler Value, and Time Criticality. Business Value represents the value of the job to the Product side of the house."

Evah jumped in, "We tried to represent your priorities as best as we could here, Naomi. I hope these values are what you would have done."

"Yes," Tim added, "Evah, Vera, and I offered the values under the first column. Jayson, Ali, Roy, and Linda provided values for the Enabler column. Then we all voted on Time Criticality."

"So," Naomi clarified, "Business Value represents the needs of Product, and Enabler Value represents the needs of Technology?"

"Yes, and to be clear," Evah interjected, "Angela was insistent that we understand that there are many ways to do the scoring in WSJF. Dividing up Product needs and Technology needs is just one way to do the voting."

"What do you mean by voting?" Naomi asked.

"Oh, it was just like Planning Poker," Evah shared. "We even used Planning Poker cards. We walked down each column, then chose values from our hands, turning them over at the same time, and then if we had different numbers, we discussed it until we agreed."

"Yeah," added Tim, "I'd never played Planning Poker before. It was actually quite fun, and the conversations were really useful. We had this debate about whether Open Space was really necessary, which led to Linda sharing some research she collected about how much time we spent every day waiting for meeting rooms."

"It really was insightful," Evah agreed. "I learned a lot."

"We also learned," said Tim, "that you have to go column by column from left to right. Angela was very explicit that you can't go row by row.

You have to go column by column because it's about relative value. We started by picking the least important item on the list and giving it a one. That for us was the Hackathon since we already had a queue of new ideas coming from you and the Design team. Then we picked the most important item, Usability Testing, getting those items tested with the users, and gave that a twenty one. Then we went down the column playing Planning Poker for the rest, voting and discussing until we had the numbers. Everybody got to talk, by the way, even though only three of us voted."

Evah picked up the narrative, "Then we went down the Enabler column the same way. The tech folks picked their most important and least important, and then we went item by item watching them vote, and discussing things as we went."

"The last column we all voted on," Tim concluded, "Time Criticality. Figuring out the urgency level. We had quite a bit of debate, but we eventually settled on the Usability Testing and the Agile Mindset changes as the most urgently needed. Then we followed the same process to fill in the rest of the values."

"But," interjected Naomi, "Big Room Planning is important. It's not a one. We all agreed that getting the team together was important for empowerment."

Evah jumped in to clarify, "Oh, it's not that Big Room Planning is unimportant. It is very important. This isn't about absolute value. It's entirely about relative value. It's not urgent *right now*. More accurately, It's the least urgent thing right now compared to the other topics, hence the value of one. In a couple of weeks, it might jump up in urgency and rise to the top."

"Yeah," Tim emphasized, "getting back to sequencing, these numbers are supposed to change. Could be monthly, or bi-weekly, or even weekly."

"Would you agree, Naomi?" Evah asked. "Big Room Planning is not that important right now?"

Naomi paused, looked through all the items, and considered it for a moment before responding, "If this is just about relative value, then yes, Big Room Planning is not what we need right now. But I probably would also have given Pirate Metrics a one."

"Cool," Evah breathed a sigh of relief. "I got that right. I thought that was going to be the same answer that you would give."

Naomi gave her a little smile. It was nice to have someone watching your back. She could always count on Evah.

Tim redirected them back to the spreadsheet, "Great! So that brings us to the last column on the right, assessing Job Size. We decided to use Fibonacci[3] weeks for that. Angela said that our predictions about the sizes of things get less accurate as the jobs get larger, so it started with 1 week, 3 weeks, 5 weeks, 8 weeks. After that, it jumped up to 13 weeks (about a quarter) and we stopped at 21 weeks (about half a year)."

"The teams have always told me," Naomi interjected with some suspicion, "that they're not allowed to give me estimates with actual days. Is that not true?"

"No, that's still true," answered Evah. "It's not about actual weeks but about the relative size. That's why we had to use Fibonacci, since these are only guesses and we'll be less accurate as the size gets bigger."

"Putting it all together forms an equation," Evah said as she stood and walked to the whiteboard. She started writing an equation on the board. "We add up the first three numbers and divide that total by the estimated Fibonacci weeks. Value divided by Job Duration."

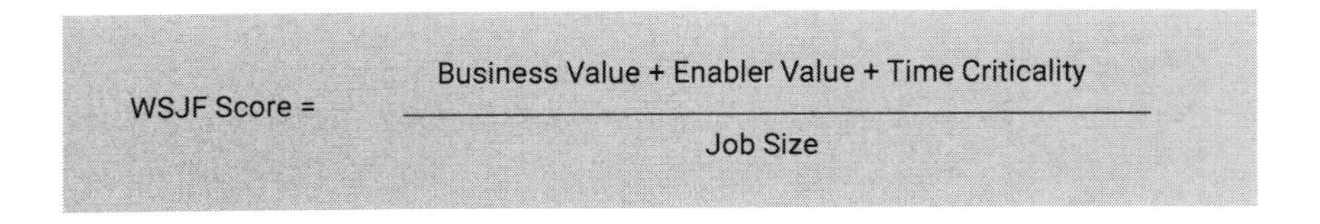

"If the job size goes up," she continued, "the value of the job goes down because it delays getting other things out the door. If we can get it done faster, the value goes up. That's where Minimum Viable Products come into play. We asked ourselves if we could get any of these items done faster? If we couldn't, we looked for a subset of activities that could be done faster, but that still had value by itself. That's how we got to the AMMI self-diagnostic with two changes per team."

---

3 The Fibonacci Sequence is made up of numbers where the next number in the sequence is the sum of the previous two numbers, e.g. 1+2 = 3, 2+3 = 5, 3+5 = 8, or 1, 2, 3, 5, 8, 13, 21, etc.

"Hi, Naomi!" Zach waved as he walked by the door smiling.

Naomi could see a lot more bodies walking around behind Zach. The workday was beginning. "What time is it?" she asked.

"Oh! eight fifty-five," Evah answered, looking down at her watch.

"I haven't even settled in yet," Naomi said as she looked around at her bag and laptop scattered on the chairs and the table around her.

Tim looked chagrined, "Oh my god, I'm sorry. I never let you settle in. I was so happy to see you, and then we got to talking about the Campfires, the Caves, and WSJF."

"Oh!" exclaimed Evah, "That's right! We're in my old office. I call this room 'Yosemite' now. Remember that trip I took with my family last year? Say, do you want me to give you a tour of the new layout? I can show you where my desk is now," she said with a smile.

Tim interjected, "Let's let her get settled in. That's my fault. Sorry about that, Naomi."

"It's okay," Naomi acquiesced. It did make her feel good that everybody was so happy to see her. Well, at least Tim and Evah were still happy to see her, and Zach.

"Thanks, Evah," said Tim as he got to his feet. "And welcome back Naomi," he said warmly and genuinely.

Naomi smiled back appreciatively, "Thank you!"

They all headed back to their starting places for the day.

THE MOB RULES

As Naomi and Evah walked through the new open space for the Riverlands team in the afternoon, she noticed that the whole team was clustered around the main conference table. "Why is everyone still huddled together around that table? They've been like that all day."

"Oh, they're mobbing," Evah told her.

Naomi didn't find much comfort in anything with the word "mob" included. Was Marlon Brando now the "Godfather of Coding"? She started thinking of all those Mafia films and couldn't help but wonder if they were up to something illegal.

She took a deep breath, thought about Brené Brown, and turned on listening mode, "Can you tell me more about this 'mobbing'?"

"Oh, yeah. Sure," Evah clarified. "The full name is 'Mob Programming'.

Jayson said it originated from Extreme Programming and was popularized by Woody Zuill. I watched a video about it online. You can search 'mob programming', or I can send a link to you later. It's this time-lapse video of a team working in the mob programming style. They all get together and work on one user story at a time."

"One story?!" Naomi burst out.

"Hold on," Evah said cautiously. "I was wondering the same thing, but it gets better. I had to see it myself, which is why I watched that video."

Naomi took another breath and switched back to listening.

Evah continued, "They start by reviewing the story together, so they're all on the same page. They ask questions. If there isn't an answer in the group, someone volunteers to go off and get the answer. They might go talk to someone or do some research online, but every question has someone responsible for getting the answers. Then they all break off and research their questions. In the video, you'll see some people leave the room and come back. Others will go to their desks and return. Others will pull out their laptops and work independently right there at the table. No one is sitting idle, and they're actually not all working on the same thing."

"What about that guy?" Naomi asked, pointing to one of the testers standing behind a programmer. "He's just standing there watching *her* work. It's...weird."

"Oh, Troy?" Evah asked. "He's actually reviewing the test cases while Veni is typing. That's the next phase after the questions are answered. Then they break into pairs and start building the solutions. You might have a pair of coders working together on the database, or a coder paired with a tester working on test cases, or a coder paired with a business analyst working on the UI. Do you see how he's holding some sheets in his hand that he keeps checking? Keep watching. Every few minutes he'll lean over and say something to her."

"Also," Linda's voice added, "he's learning how to code."

Both Naomi and Evah were a little startled. They hadn't realized that they had stopped right next to Linda's desk!

"Oh, I'm sorry," Linda added. "I didn't mean to interrupt your conversation. I just find this all so fascinating to watch too!"

Naomi figured she might as well bring Linda into the conversation. "What do you mean he's learning to code?" Naomi asked. They were in

Linda's space, after all, and it's also not really possible to not bring Linda into a conversation.

"Well," Linda began, "We've been focused on fostering cross-functional people — people who can do multiple tasks in a story. The goal is to have everyone become engineers, not testers and developers. Everybody codes and everybody tests."

Naomi shot a glance over at Evah, with her being the head of the testing department.

Evah got the glance and picked up the cue, "Yeah, this is really good for my people. I mean, not everyone wants to become a programmer, but some of them do. The others want to learn more about product design. The newer automated testing tools also require programming, so my people have been learning to code for a while now. For example, Troy there has been learning to code, but it's been all class assignments so far. By watching Veni work, he learns how she writes code as an experienced programmer. Plus, every thirty minutes or so they switch places. Then he sits at the keyboard and types, and she helps to make sure that he does it right, coaching him as he types."

"And he likes that? Someone looking over his shoulder?" asked Naomi. Nobody seemed to like it when she looked over their shoulder as they coded. It stung a little, but she kept it to herself. She wasn't a programmer, after all.

"Yeah," Linda replied, "the ones who are learning have been saying that they love getting the feedback right at the time that they make the mistake. It creates good coding habits, and prevents bad ones."

"And here's the thing," added Evah, "they're producing fewer bugs. I thought for sure this process was wasting time."

"Right?" Naomi agreed. "They could both be working on two items during this hour, instead of only getting one thing done between the two of them."

"Right?!" Linda added, "but Angela clued me in on a little secret! DevOps researchers measure productivity across the entire lifecycle of the user story, from research all the way to delivery to production. The data shows that teams using mob programming are taking twice as much time to do the research and the coding..."

Naomi started shaking her head in agreement. She knew it.

Linda kept going, though, "...but when they get done, the testing and the code review are also done. I've been observing that here too. They're doing testing and code review in parallel. So the time we normally would spend afterward, waiting for code reviews, or testing, then sending it back for refactoring and retesting is actually more than cut in half. We still do testing, but they're finding almost zero bugs. Our DevOps metrics of 'Percent Complete and Accurate' have shot up a lot! Since we're finding fewer bugs, we aren't sending stories back to the coders at the end of the sprint, so we're getting stories done in fewer days, earlier in the sprint, and there is almost no rework!"

Linda had been on a roll, so she took a moment to breathe.

Evah confirmed, "Yeah, Angela used the phrase 'shift testing left'. We've been working on following Acceptance Test-Driven Development (ATDD) principles, and this is allowing us to get to over eighty-five percent ATDD compliance! My teams that are doing the most automated testing are creating the tests first, before the code is even written."

"What about that group over there?", Naomi asked, shifting everyone's focus. "There's four of them, and they seem to be in a fight. Shouldn't we break it up? Wait, is that Jayson over there? Why isn't he stopping it?"

"Oh," said Linda, "that's a Coding Ku... a Kumba... wait... I'll remember it... Nope. No, I won't. Hey Jayson!" She called out. "Do you have a minute?"

"Sure thing, Linda," Jayson said as he walked over to join the trio. "What can I help you with?"

Linda clarified, "What's that thing called that those four are doing? It's a Kumba-something, right?"

"Ah," Jayson said knowingly. "It's pronounced Koo-mi-tay, A Coding Kumite." Naomi's eyes rolled internally again. So many new practices were being thrown out seemingly without much thought! She hoped she had only rolled her eyes internally. First 'Mob Programming', now 'Coding Kumites'. What were they? Some sort of crime-ridden Agile Kung-fu organization?

"Kumite," Jayson started explaining, "is a Japanese word for martial arts sparring sessions. Whenever there's a disagreement..."

As Jayson continued Naomi could feel her blood pressure rise again. *"Making people feel good is not our job. Our job is to solve the challenges with Intuition!"* she thought. *"Angela is organizing the chairs on the Titanic, allowing teams to play around instead of performing real work!"*

Naomi decided that listening time was over. "Where's Angela?" she said, abruptly and angrily. "I'd like to talk to her about her prioritization approach."

"It's on," she heard Linda say. She was not doing a great job of masking the excitement in her voice and it just fueled Naomi's frustration.

What bugged Naomi the most was that she knew that it was *she* who had brought the Breeze application to where it had become, and it was the creativity of her ideas that had brought them success so far. Angela's ideas went nowhere and disrespected the knowledge and experience of leaders like herself. She was tired of fighting them.

She looked around the office for any sign of her, but she was not to be found in any of the open spaces. Naomi took off for the cubes, with Evah in tow. She crisscrossed up and down the rows. Several folks had seen her but that was all more than an hour ago. Wow, Angela moved fast!

When they had circled all the way back to Linda's desk, Evah suggested, "Linda, can you see if you can find Angela? I'll take Naomi to the main conference room and you can meet us there. The leadership review will be starting soon anyway."

Naomi was conflicted. Evah was the only one that seemed to care, and yet she had also bought into Angela's hype. She'd have to figure that part out later.

THE END OF THE LINE

"I found her!" Linda said as she walked into the room, interrupting the end-of-the-day leadership review, already in progress. "Angela and Zach will be here shortly. They were hiding in one of the user testing rooms. Well, not really hiding," she said with a clever smile. "Not that kind of hiding. It was a user test, so they were hiding from the user, or at least they couldn't be interrupted, but when the test was done I went in and told them what was going on. They said that they'd be right over."

"Why were they having a user test without her?" Naomi thought to herself. *"Angela has her fingers in everything! No, that's a battle for another time. Stay focused,"* she told herself.

"Thank you, Linda," Tim said. Linda took a seat with the rest of them, all except Roy for some reason, and nobody knew why. It didn't really matter. Naomi was just glad that she didn't have to deal with him today on top of everything else.

Tim continued where he had left off when Linda entered the room, "Naomi, you have a lot of talent, but the point here is to consider solutions from the entire team."

"I do, Tim," Naomi countered. "I admitted my mistake with Clyde, and I spend most of my time now exploring multiple ideas with the design team."

"You're right," Tim agreed. "That's too harsh. You do consider other ideas, but other parts of the team don't feel as heard as the design team. The changes on this list aren't Angela's ideas like you keep alluding to. They come from all over the division, and we need to respect everyone's contributions."

"What was that Disney movie?" Ali offered up. "The one with the rat?"

"Ratatouille," said Jayson. "Angela told us about the Ratatouille Principle[4], based on that food critic character's quote at the end. 'Not every idea can be a great idea, but a great idea can come from anywhere.'"

"Right, I forgot about that," remembered Tim. "The Ratatouille Principle. Yeah, that's what we're doing here with the WSJF. Every idea is on the table, and we use WSJF to help the best ideas float to the top. A bunch of them we've already dropped from the list and these have floated to the top. Let's go through this list, and I'll show you how we got to where we are."

WEIGHTED SHORTEST JOB FIRST (WSJF) – TRANSFORMATION

Job	Business Value	Enabler Value	Time Criticality	Job Size	Score
1. Open Space	5	13	13	1	31
2. Hackathon	1	8	5	1	14
3. Agile mindset improvements (AMMI)					
MVP 1: AMMI + 2 improvements	8	13	13	2	17
MVP 2: Big Room Planning	5	3	1	2	4.5
4. Customer Usability Testing	21	8	21	5	10
5. Pirate Metrics (AARRR)	3	1	3	2	3.5

Tim directed Naomi's attention back to the Transformation WSJF spreadsheet on the monitor, "We started by brainstorming around problems. Angela asked us to put all of our problems on sticky notes and put them up on the board. Linda, do you still have those sticky notes?"

"I do," said Linda. "Do you want me to go get them?"

"That would be great," Tim answered. "Thank you. In the meantime, we'll start by just recreating them as best as we can. Who remembers what the problems were that we were trying to solve with the new Open Spaces?"

"Meeting rooms!" Linda called out as she crossed the threshold of the conference room. Then she leaned back in to clarify, "It was nearly impossible to get a meeting room," and then she was gone.

Ali piped up, "Didn't we actually start by walking in with a list of changes that we wanted to make? I remember that I had some architectural concepts that I wanted everyone to learn."

"Yes, we did," said Jayson, "but Angela suggested, and we all agreed, that talking about the problems behind each suggestion would help to make sure that we had clear goals that actually tackled the most urgent problems."

"Yes, that's right," Tim confirmed. "Having ideas is great, but drawing a clear line between those ideas and the problems they solve is even better. So we have one of those problems on the table already: meeting rooms. Why was meeting rooms a big problem?"

"Well," said Jayson. "Everybody's cube assignment was based on when they joined the company, so they were scattered around the office."

Evah added, "Not everybody's. There have been a few reorganizations over the years to consolidate teams, but we've been growing so much that we still have people randomly placed. So having a discussion took about two to three days from suggestion to actual conversation, just to get everybody in the same room."

"Dedicated spaces," Tim summarized. "Get everybody together who works together, as the Designers do. Bring the collaborative spaces to the

---

4 Ratatouille Principle – structuring your process to make sure that the best ideas not only are sought, but bubble to the top. Coined in 2015 by one of the book's authors, Pete Oliver-Krueger.

people, instead of them having to waste any time hunting down space."

"Wait," Naomi interjected. "How did this get identified as a major problem? We all know it's hard to book a meeting room, but really? This is a major problem?"

"Well," Evah responded, "it started out as delays being our biggest problem. Remember how we were complaining about how long it takes to go from design to delivery?"

Naomi looked around the room feeling like she'd just been exposed. She didn't appreciate Evah revealing things from their gripe sessions, but in place of accusing looks, she instead saw a lot of nodding heads.

Evah continued, "Everybody felt like it was out of their control, so Linda did some digging. She traced back the timeline of every piece of work we did across one of our sprints, thanks to our DevOps metrics. She found that most stories entered the 'Refinement' stage and then sat there for two to three days, and if they were sent back from development for more refinement, they also sat for two to three days. So she went and talked to the Scrum Masters and the Product Owners to retrace their steps on each of those stories. Email histories for each date in question showed that almost immediately a meeting was scheduled, but that meeting was always two to three days in the future. When the meeting was finally held, then the story went immediately back to the developers with no delay."

"I love that," added Jayson. "A perfect example of DevOps-style, no-blame problem solving. Linda wasn't looking for a person to blame but went looking for the data, and we ended up identifying a bottleneck. The teams love the new response times. They just ping the Product Owner to ask their questions and continue working. I mean, I knew getting a meeting room was a problem. It was just the cost of doing business. It took Angela pointing out that it didn't have to be that way to get me to wake up to the idea that the physical space itself solves problems."

"Right," agreed Tim. "The furniture delivery was not great timing, but it ended up being the solution that we didn't know that we needed. Okay, next. What was the problem that led to the Hackathon idea?"

"We needed new ideas," Jayson stated matter-of-factly. "Ratatouille Principle again."

"Ok," Tim asked, "What other problems were solved by the Hackathon?"

Everybody shrugged and looked around. This is what Naomi was afraid of. She took the chance to redirect them back to the real problem and called out, "Intuition!"

"Right. Of course," confirmed Tim. "Intuition is our biggest problem. However, they are the competition that we cannot control. We can, however, improve ourselves.

Naomi was still thermonuclear hot about what Intuition had done and decided to bring that up, "What is the word with Legal on suing them out of business?"

Tim looked annoyed, "Don't expect Intuition to go out of business, let alone stop what they are doing anytime soon if ever. Legal has said that they are working on the loopholes in the Non-Disclosure Agreement. So far it's turning out to be a dead end."

Naomi openly groaned while Tim paused to let that sink in. "Back to the point, in order to improve ourselves, we need new ideas specifically for solving the onboarding of new customers."

"We had ideas," countered Naomi. "We just needed to get them out the door without distractions and impediments."

"Also true," Tim confirmed with a note of caution in his voice. "That was on the board too, and was covered under the next item, 'Agile mindset improvements'. So how about we just jump to that row?"

"Oo! I've got those!" Linda said, raising up a stack of stickies in her hand as she made her way back to her chair. "Let's see... it's this stack here... Okay, here we go." She held up the first sticky note, "The problem that we gave the most number of dot votes to was 'Understanding what the user doesn't like with the new account creation'."

"That's right!" said Tim enthusiastically. "We each got to place five dots, marking what we each thought were the top priorities, and 'Understanding Account Creation' was definitely top of everyone's list here."

Tim looked at Naomi, but she couldn't tell what that look was supposed to mean. He continued, "What was next, Linda?"

"Task Switching and Wasted Time," Linda said, flipping through several sticky notes that were stacked together. "We combined several similar sticky notes into a common theme.

"Right," said Tim. "First we brainstormed problems. Second, we clustered them together by common themes. Third, we did dot-voting on the biggest problems."

"Yes," Linda agreed, "and the next-biggest problem that people chose was getting a new direction every day. They never had time to finish the previous designs before they were given new ones. They felt that the time spent on each incomplete design was time wasted."

"Let's not forget," Naomi wanted to clarify, "that we were running those user tests and getting new results. Whenever we had new results, we produced new designs to solve the problems uncovered. We were just following the users."

Jayson responded this time, "I remember we talked about how to brainstorm for that. Solve multiple problems at the same time. We decided to do the space changes, in parallel with running the Usability testing, so that we could batch up several discoveries, and then solve them all at once."

"Right," chimed in Ali. "There was a dependency for the Hackathon idea that the Usability testing had to happen first so that we had a clear target for the Hackathon. So we put the Hackathon on hold and worked on the Open Spaces, the Agile Mindset, and Usability testing in parallel. Clyde and Vera volunteered to take the lead on Usability testing, Linda and Angela volunteered to lead the mindset changes, and Tim, you were going to work with Facilities on setting up the Open Space furniture."

"Yeah," confirmed Tim."They promised that they could do the setup in one weekend."

"But hold on a minute," Naomi broke in. "Who decided that Open Spaces was number one, the Hackathon was number two, and the Agile Mindset Improvement was number three? I know I didn't, and I'm the Product Manager, aren't I?"

"Need I remind you," Tim pushed back, "that had you not skipped this meeting, you would have been at the center of this prioritization from the very beginning."

"Yes indeed," Angela inserted. Naomi startled and looked at the door to the conference room.

Angela was standing in the doorway with Zach.

"How long had she been there?!" Naomi wondered.

With no hesitation, Angela just walked right in and took over the meeting. "I'd like to drill down on that point, Tim. I mentioned before that these values were temporary. No prioritization would be complete until our talented Product Manager was involved."

Points to Angela for trying to use flattery, but they were beyond that.

Angela continued speaking, "And now, it seems, is a great time to fix that. Rather than walking her through the past discussions, let's have a new discussion. Everybody's objections must be heard and addressed or else there can be no consent. So far I've heard everyone else's objections except hers. You all had quite a few objections, and each one was heard and addressed. I'd like to give the same opportunity to Naomi now. May I?"

Naomi cringed as Tim instantly buckled under to Angela and passed her the computer keyboard.

"This first column of scores," Angela began, "is almost entirely for you."

Tim jumped in to clarify, "Evah and I already gave her the introduction to Business Value versus Enabler Value."

"Thank you," said Angela, barreling on ahead. "The rest of the team filled in the Enabler Value scores, but we weren't able to do full justice to the Business Value column without you. Actually, I'm just going to delete all of these values and start over. If the numbers were right, we'll find them again."

She proceeded to go straight down the Business Value column and deleted all of the entries, much to the surprise of the others in the room too. Naomi was struck by how little regard Angela seemed to have for their inputs.

"It's okay," Linda called out, "I have the original scores in my notebook too if we want to look back at them."

Angela looked around and actually seemed a little embarrassed. "Oh, this is a great time to reiterate something I said before, but I can't say enough about WSJF. While WSJF is super helpful in setting priorities and creating estimates, it's not actually an estimating technique, and I think this is a great example of that. WSJF is actually a *conversation* technique. It provides a framework for bringing out the right conversations at the right time. WSJF is always about the conversations. That's why we use the Planning Poker cards, and why I don't let any of you enter your scores into the spreadsheet before the meeting. The point is to let the discussion about the scores lead to the right questions and bubble up the right conversations now, not weeks or even months in the future. So a score that was developed without one of the major decision-makers in the room, is an incomplete score."

"Like that game show," Linda added, "'Whose Line is it Anyway?'[5] where everything is made up, and the points don't matter!" She guffawed out loud. "God, I love that show! Have you seen it?"

"Well," said Angela cautiously, "it's not quite the same. The points do matter."

"Oh, right!" Linda said apologetically. "Of course they do! I'm so sorry." She tucked her head in embarrassment.

"It is a great show," Angela smiled, "but I just don't want to get too far away from the purpose of the exercise here. The exercise leads to the discussions. The points reflect the outcomes of those discussions, and the calculations help to balance weight and size, to make sure we're working on the right thing next. So when I say that the scores don't matter, I mean that any scores without Naomi's direct input are not the best scores that we can produce."

Naomi had to admit that it was a masterful save on Angela's part and that it was to her benefit, so Naomi decided to go along for now.

Angela redirected them back to the spreadsheet, "Ok, step one: setting our boundaries. Let's start with the least important. What's the least important thing here from the Business point of view?"

"I say the Pirate Metrics," Naomi offered. Since Roy wasn't there, she knew she wouldn't get any pushback. She wasn't sure why he was missing, but she was glad for it.

Angela looked around the room, "Any objections to setting Pirate Metrics as our one? I'll do a quick round. Tim?" Tim shook his head no. "Evah?" Evah did the same. "Linda?" Each person gave the same answer. "Jayson? Zach? Ali? Ok, we'll set the Pirate Metrics as the new baseline."

Angela moved to the upper boundary, "And what's our most important thing, from the Business standpoint? What's our twenty one?"

"Not going out of business," Naomi said matter-of-factly.

"Agreed," said Angela, redirecting, "and which of these items is the most important to make sure that we don't go under?" Everybody mostly looked at Naomi to give the answer.

---

5 'Whose Line Is It Anyway?' is a fake game show improvised entirely on the spot by comedy actors that originated in Britain. *https://en.wikipedia.org/wiki/Whose_Line_Is_It_Anyway%3F*

Naomi obliged, "Well it's not the Open Space. After all, we're in the middle of a crisis! We might not even be in business in a month. Now is not the time to try experimenting with 'mob coding', 'programming Kumbayas', or rearranging the whole office."

"Actually," Tim jumped in, trying to rescue Angela, "during the middle of a crisis is just the time to try something new. The definition of insanity is trying the same thing and expecting something different will happen..."

Naomi cut him off, "Really, Tim? Insanity?" *"How much did he tell them about her episode?"* she wondered.

"Naomi," Tim countered. "You know I'm not saying anything about sanity. It's just a saying, and a quote from Einstein nonetheless. Rearranging the office is not what either of us would have done, but we had our chance. We tried our things and they weren't working. Angela had some new ideas that worked for other companies in our situation, and some of the teams wanted to try it, so we're trying it."

Naomi reacted, "Tim, this is a mistake! Don't you trust me?"

Tim spoke clearly and with feeling, "Of course I do and we would both agree that we want high-performance teams. That's why I handed over the reins to Angela and you are expected to do the same. What we had been doing had not been working. Give her a chance. She can help us get out of this rut we are in, but only if we let her help us!"

"So you no longer trust me. I had a feeling it would come to this."

Tim looked shocked, "That's not what I said. I trust you to do your job, but you are struggling and need help with a fresh perspective. Don't you agree?"

Naomi snorted, "Well yes, I do, but this isn't the way to do it."

"How do you know?" Tim asked.

"Well," Naomi retorted, "I don't know what to do to fix this, short of bombing Intuition, but I do know this isn't the way to do it. Even Roy's ideas would be far better than having this 'adult playground' for the teams."

"And this isn't about trust," Angela added. "I don't want you to do anything based on blind trust. Every option should have proof to back it up."

Tim chimed in with an encouraging tone, "That's right, Naomi, this is an experiment. We'll let them give it a try and then examine the results. Some of the other teams were less interested, so we kept them unchanged. If it doesn't work, we will revert to our previous way of working. Angela has shown me proof from past clients that it can work, though, if applied correctly. She also worked with Linda to establish clear evidence for these changes regarding code quality and increased performance."

Linda took over, "The teams agreed. The expectation is decreased defect count and increased velocity. We have the teams' baselines and will compare that with their future performance. They understand that their goal is to improve product delivery, and they will still depend on you and the Product Owners for the work they do. It should work."

"But that's not the point," Naomi said exasperatingly. "We have work to do, and all of these changes are just distracting us from the work that we have to do! I'm sorry to get so strident, but nobody around seems to care anymore. We're just throwing anything at the wall to see if it sticks!"

"Yes," began Angela in a pleading tone, "you are very right that the stakes could not be higher. We have to get the new user counts up, and you and Vera's group are working on that, but the teams also want to help. Everybody has ideas and we want to work on those ideas in parallel with you and the designers. You are burning yourself out! I heard what happened with your eyesight and feel truly concerned for you. We have to get to the point where the teams are solving your problems to understand the user needs along with you, not just you by yourself! Otherwise, your stress level will be too high and the product will never be bigger than you!"

Naomi was fuming. How dare Angela bring up her eyesight! Yeah, sure, everybody probably already knew about it, but to rub it in her face in a public meeting was unconscionable!

Naomi shot back, "Determining what the users really want is the responsibility of the business – me and my teams, not the scrum teams. We can deliver that under my direction."

Angela pushed back, hard, "Your teammates shared that Clyde had recorded user sessions with customer feedback and that you decided to ignore that. Your peers want to amplify that kind of feedback!"

"Are you saying I'm incompetent, Angela?" Naomi asked. "I mean, I know that I'm part of the problem, and I know that Tim trusts you, but your sugar coating and empathy won't solve our problems. Experience, and expertise in banking will. So stay in your lane!" Naomi was getting so frustrated! Just because Angela reported to Tim didn't mean that she could just change anything she wanted!

Naomi kept going, "Yes, teams can help solve problems but only under proper business guidance! Haven't you read the Scrum Guide? The Guide makes it clear that Product Owners provide what is built and that teams figure out how to do it! Plus, we obtain amplified feedback as mentioned in the second way of 'The Phoenix Project'. That's why we have frequent User Acceptance Tests."

Angela countered, "Naomi, the business has an essential role, but we are not the user and we need the user's input to help solve our challenges. The original Scrum Guide was focused solely on the work of the development teams. It actually starts with a pre-defined backlog with no discussion about how that backlog gets built. In the decade since its launch, practices have evolved. We've also learned through Lean Startup, Usability research, and Design Thinking that direct user engagement is exponentially faster at producing the right results. That's why Linda and I are putting together a watch party with all the teams to showcase Clyde's recent recordings so that they can see where the user struggles the most and create new ideas to solve those problems."

Naomi was astounded by the ego and brashness of Tim's "savior". She had not been at Ares for even a month and was already talking as if she owned the product! Naomi was really trying to contain herself, but her tolerance had reached a limit.

Naomi glowered back and spat out, "Now you are going to have movie time with the teams instead of letting them work on the new designs. This has gone too far." Naomi did not appreciate being talked to like a child. Who did Angela think she was? She had no right!

She was breathing very deeply now, but to no avail. The level of arrogance incited Naomi beyond anything she had experienced in a long time. She felt that proverbial straw breaking the camel's back and keeping totally passive on the surface, said very calmly and quietly, "I see."

Naomi stood up and addressed Angela, "You have clearly won the trust of Tim and I have lost it, and I don't need to go down with this ship." She turned and looked at Tim, "I can see that you no longer need me, so I will get out of your way. I'll send you my official resignation letter later."

She took off her badge, slapped it down on the table, and walked out of the meeting room. She went directly to her office, collected her things, and headed to the elevator. She could feel all of their eyes watching.

Good.

Key Points of Learning

- Self-Awareness & Vulnerability
- Agile Open Spaces
- Campfires & Caves
- Mob Programming
- Weighted Shortest Job First (WSJF)
- Ratatouille Principle

PART 3

SHIFTING TO PEOPLE

Chapter 7

Angela – The Tipping Point to Autonomy

MALFUNCTION JUNCTION

(Earlier that same day)

As Angela hung up the phone, she turned to Zach full of hope, "I'm so excited! Naomi is finally here, in person!"

"What?" Zach didn't seem as enthusiastic.

"That was Linda on voicemail," Angela explained. "She said that Naomi came into the office today and that she was talking about listening and wanting to understand the changes! What a day to have our phones turned off," she added with regret. "While we've been watching the Usability tests, they've been walking Naomi around through the new open spaces and giving her the background on the changes. And now she wants to meet with us about the WSJF prioritization. This might be my chance to make a difference!"

"I wouldn't get your hopes up too high", Zach responded.

"You have to have hope," Angela chided him. "Without optimism, there is no change. They are two sides of the same coin."

"Right. I agree that optimism is important," countered Zach, "but if they have jumped into discussing the WSJF prioritization... All I'm thinking of is how difficult it was to walk the rest of the team through that. God, the arguments we had!"

"I know. It's not the topic I would have chosen for our next discussion with her," Angela sighed, feeling the loss of opportunity. "Naomi never accepted the invitations, though. She was always too busy."

Zach jumped in, "Yeah, WSJF requires the ability to be comfortable with uncertainty because it happens before you have all the information. Leaps of faith are not Naomi's strong suit."

"Nor any of the others either," Angela countered. "Do you remember the emotions that arose around the Open Space discussion alone?" She gave a low whistle. "We eventually all came around to the same understanding, and surprisingly it rose to the top of the list, but there were some strong emotions around 'not being disruptive'."

"That's true," Zach acknowledged. "If we hadn't stopped that one WSJF meeting and gone on that excursion to talk to those two teams, it probably wouldn't have happened. It was the passion of those team members that swayed people. They really wanted an open space! I'm worried that Naomi didn't get to hear those stories."

"What heartens me, though," Angela interjected, "is that everyone else on that leadership team has proven to be 'Movables' or 'Movers'. That helps a lot. I'm hoping they'll be able to bring Naomi around."

"Movables?" Zach slowed his walking pace, reviewing his memory. "I don't think I've heard that before."

"Oh, no?" Angela said, a little surprised. "I haven't used that term yet? I'm surprised."

"Maybe you did," Zach offered, "and I just didn't catch it. Can you say more?"

"Definitely!" Angela jumped at the chance. It had been years since she had been able to tap into this topic.

As they stepped outside and started their trek from the testing center back to the Ares Innovation Center, Angela explained. "The concept of 'Movables' comes from Benjamin Franklin — one of my favorite Founding Fathers of the American Revolution — and way ahead of his time."

"I've always been fascinated by Franklin too," added Zach with a huge smile.

Angela continued, now also smiling with that feeling of Sympatico, "Ben Franklin identified three primary reactions to change in people. As he phrased it, 'All the world has three classes of people. Those that move, those that are movable, and those that are immovable.' I was reading some writings by author Jason Little about Franklin's ideas and I think he captures the concepts quite well. He describes the 'Movers' as those who already hold the mindset for change, and are its champions. Our job with the Movers is mainly to inspire them, fill in any gaps in knowledge, and remove obstacles."

"Makes sense," Zach nodded as he waved to a couple of people crossing the opposite way on the footpath.

Angela waved too and continued, "But the second group, the Movables, it turns out are the keys to reaching a tipping point. Once they tip over, things really start to happen. Unfortunately, Franklin and Jason Little found that they cannot be directly influenced. Movables have to see results before they will believe in something, and they only trust results from people that they already know and respect."

"Okay, so we focus on the Movers," Zach recapped as he held open the door to the Ares Innovation Center for Angela. "Help them remove obstacles, and then use their successes to influence the Movables."

"Check and check, and thank you," responded Angela as she walked through the doorway. "The third and final type Franklin called 'the Immovables'. Immovables are of the mindset that change is wrong and can not be convinced otherwise. In fact, the more we push for change, the more they will push back." She glanced around to see if anyone was listening to them, and said more quietly, "According to Jason Little's study of Franklin's philosophy, the goal is to show them empathy and spend as little time as possible trying to change them since it is essentially ineffective. I have trouble following that last part, though, sometimes."

DING! The conversation was paused by the elevator's arrival. A couple of people got out, and Angela and Zach got in. Zach waited until the doors closed and then verbalized Angela's fear, "And you're worried that Naomi is an 'immovable' and not a 'movable', right?"

"Does that mean you are worried too?" Angela asked trepidly.

"What do you do with an 'immovable'? Do you have to let them go?" Zach asked.

Angela responded cautiously, not wanting to reveal that she had already had this conversation with Tim. "It's a delicate situation. It's not always possible, and sometimes people seem immovable until they suddenly move."

"So what do you do?" Zach wondered aloud, as the elevator doors opened and they stepped out.

Angela said, "Well, Jason Little agrees with Franklin that the return on investment with Immovables is very low and it's usually better to invest your time supporting the Movers and Movables. A little hope never hurts too. I've personally seen Immovables suddenly move and nobody knows why, although I suspect it's due to the collective influence of the Movers and the Movables."

THE END OF THE BEGINNING

Angela and Zach reached the door of the conference room and found the discussion was already well underway. The WSJF spreadsheet was up on the screen and Tim was walking Naomi through it.

"Task Switching and Wasted Time," Linda said, flipping through several sticky notes that were stacked together. "We combined several similar sticky notes into a common theme."

"Right," said Tim. "First we brainstormed problems. Second, we clustered them together by common themes. Third, we did dot-voting on the biggest problems."

Angela smiled as she and Zach sat down next to each other. They really cared about getting the technique right. It warmed her heart.

"Right," Linda agreed, "and the next-biggest problem that people chose was getting a new direction every day. They never had time to finish the previous designs before they were given new ones. They felt that the time spent on each incomplete design was time wasted."

Angela whispered in Zach's ear, "Good, they've launched into some social proof. Let's see if it works."

"Let's not forget," Naomi interjected to clarify, "that we were running those user tests and getting new results. Whenever we had new results, we produced new designs to solve the problems uncovered. We were just following the users." Naomi seemed understandably defensive to Angela. It was a normal reaction. She hoped that the team wouldn't get sucked into the defensiveness, and they didn't.

Jayson responded, "I remember we talked about how to brainstorm for that. Solve multiple problems at the same time. We decided to do the space changes, in parallel with running the Usability testing, so that we could batch up several discoveries, and then solve them all at once."

"Right," chimed in Ali. "There was a dependency for the Hackathon idea that the Usability testing had to happen first so that we had a clear target for the Hackathon. So we put the Hackathon on hold and worked on the Open Spaces, Agile mindset improvements using AMMI, and Usability testing in parallel. Clyde and Vera volunteered to take the lead on Usability testing, Linda and Angela volunteered to lead the Agile mindset improvements using AMMI, and Tim, you were going to work with Facilities on setting up the Open Space furniture."

"Yeah," confirmed Tim."They promised that they could do the setup in one weekend."

"But hold on a minute," Naomi broke in. "Who decided that Open Spaces was number one, the Hackathon was number two, and the Agile Mindset Improvement was number three? I know I didn't, and I'm the Product Manager, aren't I?"

"Need I remind you," Tim pushed back, "that had you not skipped this meeting, you would have been at the center of this prioritization from the very beginning."

Angela flinched. That seemed to come out of nowhere, and applying force was not going to make this right. There were very few things that would, but using force was definitely not one of them. It looked like Tim had been building up some anger internally, and it was starting to surface. She would have to act now if she wanted to avoid letting that anger control the next step of the process, so she tried coming to Naomi's rescue.

"Actually," Angela inserted without leaving any space for a reply, "I'd like to drill down on that point, Tim." Everyone seemed startled. They obviously were hyper-focused on the discussion and hadn't seen her walk in yet.

She continued unabated, "I mentioned before that these values were temporary. No prioritization would be complete until our talented Product Manager was involved. And now, it seems, is a great time to fix that. Rather than walking her through the past discussions, let's have a new discussion. Everybody's objections must be heard and addressed or else there can be no consent. So far I've heard everyone else's objections except hers. You all had quite a few objections, and each one was heard and addressed. I'd like to give the same opportunity to Naomi now. May I?"

Tim, to his credit, acquiesced quickly and gave Angela the floor and the keyboard for the conference room computer. Angela accepted both and turned her attention to Naomi.

"This first column of scores," Angela began, "is almost entirely for you."

Tim jumped in to clarify, "Evah and I already gave her the introduction to Business Value versus Enabler Value."

"Thank you," said Angela. She desperately wanted to ask Naomi if she had any questions, but she was equally concerned that if she gave Naomi the floor, she might lose this opportunity, so she pressed on. "The rest of the team filled in the Enabler Value scores, but we weren't able to do full justice to the Business Value column without you. Actually, I'm just going to delete all of these values and start over." She noticed gasps from around the table, which was unexpected. Well, if she had time to think about it, it would have been easy to anticipate, but she was still afraid of losing momentum, so she just added, "If the numbers were right, we'll find them again."

A little feeling of dread started to bubble up in Angela's chest. Things were evolving just fast enough that she wasn't sure if she was making the right decisions. While it felt a little wrong, it also felt right at the same moment, so she went ahead and deleted all of the entries in the Business Value column.

"It's okay," Linda called out, "I have the original scores in my notebook too if we want to look back at them."

Angela breathed a sigh of relief, internally. Hopefully, Linda's statement would allay any concerns at the moment, but she figured she had better address the concern directly, anyway. "Oh, this is a great time to reiterate something I said before, but I can't say enough about WSJF. While WJSF is super helpful in setting priorities and creating estimates, it's not actually an estimating technique, and I think this is a great example of that. WSJF is actually a *conversation* technique. It provides a framework for bringing out the right conversations at the right time. WSJF is always about the conversations. That's why we use the Planning Poker cards, and why I don't let any of you enter your scores into the spreadsheet before the meeting. The point is to let the discussion about the scores lead to the right questions and bubble up the right conversations now, not weeks or even months in the future. So a score that was developed without one of the major decision-makers in the room, is always going to be an incomplete score."

"Like that game show," Linda added, "'Whose Line is it Anyway?'[1] where everything is made up, and the points don't matter!" She laughed out loud. "God, I love that show! Have you seen it?"

Angela wanted to offer some words of appreciation and camaraderie for Linda's attempt to ease the tensions. She did really enjoy that show, but she was afraid the conversation would quickly spin out of control. "Well," she said cautiously, "it's not quite the same. The points do matter."

---

1 'Whose Line Is It Anyway?' is a fake game show improvised entirely on the spot by comedy actors that originated in Britain. *https://en.wikipedia.org/wiki/Whose_Line_Is_It_Anyway%3F*

"Oh, right!" Linda said apologetically. "Of course they do! I'm so sorry." She tucked her head in embarrassment.

"It is a great show," Angela smiled. "I just don't want to get too far away from the purpose of the exercise here. The exercise leads to discussions. The points reflect the outcomes of those discussions, and the calculations help to balance weight and size, to make sure we're working on the right thing next. So when I say that the scores don't matter, I mean that any scores without Naomi's direct input are not the best scores that we can produce."

Angela redirected them back to the spreadsheet, "Ok, step one: setting our boundaries. Let's start with the least important. What's the least important thing here from the Business point of view?"

"I say the Pirate Metrics," Naomi offered. Angela glanced around the room looking for Roy, but he was nowhere to be found. Why couldn't she ever have everyone in the same room at the same time? She wanted to advocate on Roy's behalf, since metrics were important, but decided it wasn't worth it.

Angela looked around the room, "Any objections to setting Pirate Metrics as our one? I'll do a quick round. Tim?" Tim shook his head no. "Evah?" Evah did the same. "Linda?" Each person gave the same answer. "Jayson? Zach? Ali? Ok, we'll set the Pirate Metrics as the new baseline."

Angela moved to the upper boundary, "And what's our most important thing, from the Business standpoint? What's our twenty-one?"

"Not going under," Naomi said matter-of-factly.

"Agreed," said Angela, redirecting, "and which of these items is the most important to make sure that we don't go under?" Everybody mostly looked at Naomi to give the answer.

Naomi obliged, "Well it's not the Open Space. After all, we're in the middle of a crisis! We might not even be in business in a month. Now is not the time to try experimenting with 'mob coding', 'programming Kumbayas', or rearranging the whole office."

Angela was about to redirect Naomi away from negative objects to positive ideas when Tim jumped in, "Actually, during the middle of a crisis is just the time to try something new. The definition of insanity is trying the same thing and expecting something different will happen..."

Naomi cut him off, "Really, Tim? Insanity?" Angela raised her hand to stop Tim. Angela could see the "immovable" pushing back harder. She thought maybe bringing up a different change could make Naomi reconsider. Immovables can become Movables and even Movers depending on the change that is recommended. Tim was too much on edge and didn't even see her hand.

Tim countered right away, "Naomi, you know I'm not saying anything about sanity. It's just a saying, and a quote from Einstein nonetheless. Rearranging the office is not what either of us would have done, but we had our chance. We tried our things and they weren't working. Angela had some new ideas that worked for other companies in our situation, and some of the teams wanted to try it, so we're trying it."

Naomi reacted, "Tim, this is a mistake! Don't you trust me?"

Angela tried again to interject, but the two of them weren't really listening anymore. Tim spoke right over her, "Of course I do and we would both agree that we want high-performance teams. That's why I handed over the reins to Angela and you are expected to do the same. What we had been doing had not been working. Give her a chance. She can help us get out of this rut we are in, but only if we let her help us!"

Angela was momentarily distracted. She didn't want the reins. She was supposed to be the coach, not the replacement.

Naomi settled in, "So you no longer trust me. I had a feeling it would come to this."

Tim looked completely frustrated, "That's not what I said. I trust you to do your job, but you are struggling and need help with a fresh perspective. Don't you agree?"

Naomi snorted, "Well yes, I do, but this isn't the way to do it."

"How do you know?" Tim asked.

"Well, I don't know what to do to fix this," Naomi retorted, "short of bombing Intuition, but I do know this isn't the way to do it. Even Roy's ideas would be far better than having this 'adult play place' for the teams."

Things were unraveling fast. Angela tried on a few different responses in her head. There was no real chance of going back to the exercise now, especially since everyone wanted to wait for Naomi to give the next answer. Naomi was not in a participating mood right now. She wanted to respond to the comment about an 'adult play place' as that seemed to have sparked anger in a few faces around the table, including Linda's. That was significant because Linda didn't often show anger, but Angela knew that that was a conversation for later.

Her mind settled back again on Ben Franklin, the Movables, and the use of social proof, so what she ended up saying was, "And this isn't about trust. I don't want you to do anything based on blind trust. Every option should have proof to back it up."

Tim, to his credit, tried to help by chiming in, "That's right, Naomi, this is an experiment. The change in layout is limited to only two teams, the two most interested in the change. We'll let them give it a try and then examine the results. The other five teams were less interested, so they were kept unchanged, and we will closely watch these two teams on whether it works. If it doesn't, we will revert to our previous way of working. Angela has shown me proof from past clients that it can work, though, if applied correctly. She also worked with Linda to establish clear metrics for these changes regarding code quality and increased performance."

Angela cringed again. She really didn't want this to become an Angela versus Naomi battle.

The anger in Linda boiled over and she jumped into the fray, "The teams agreed. The expectation is decreased defect count and increased velocity. We have the teams' baselines and will compare that with their future performance. They understand that their goal is to improve product delivery, and they will still depend on you and the Product Owners for the work they do. It should work."

"But that's not the point," Naomi said exasperatingly. "We have work to do, and all of these changes are just distracting us from the work that we have to do! I'm sorry to get so strident, but nobody around seems to care anymore. We're just throwing anything at the wall to see if it sticks!"

That's one thing that Angela loved about Naomi. She really did care about the customers and the work. That was the spark of hope for Angela, so she figured that she would try praising it. "Yes, you are very right that the stakes could not be higher. We have to get the new user counts up, and you and Vera's group are working on that." A thought crossed her mind about reframing the teams as helpers for Naomi so she pivoted tactics, "...but the teams also want to help. Everybody has ideas and we want to work on those ideas in parallel with you and the designers."

"Be helpful," Angela told herself. That's when the exact wrong thing popped into her head, and instead of realizing it was the wrong thing, she said it out loud. "You are burning yourself out! I heard what happened

with your eyesight and feel truly concerned for you. We have to get to the point where the teams are solving your problems to understand the user needs along with you, not just you by yourself! Otherwise, your stress level will be too high and the product will never be bigger than you!"

Everything she had just said was absolutely true, but also absolutely the wrong thing to say right then, in a public setting. Naomi's problem with her eyesight may not have been public knowledge. Even if it was, that was the kind of thing you said privately so that the person didn't lose face. Angela would later come to regret her choice, but things were moving so fast that it hadn't registered yet.

She saw Naomi's anger rising, and understandably so, "Determining what the users really want is the responsibility of the business – me and my teams, not the scrum teams. We can deliver that under my direction."

Now Angela felt herself getting emotionally out of control. It was almost as if she wasn't really in control of her own responses. She heard herself say, "Your teammates shared that Clyde had recorded user sessions with customer feedback and that you decided to ignore that. Your peers want to amplify that kind of feedback!" Again, correct, but an inappropriate response for this moment.

"Are you saying I'm incompetent, Angela?" Naomi demanded. "I mean, I know that I'm part of the problem, and I know that Tim trusts you, but your sugarcoating and empathy won't solve our problems. Experience, and expertise in banking will. So stay in your lane!" Naomi was also triggered. There was no going back now.

Naomi kept going, "Yes, teams can help solve problems but only under proper business guidance! Haven't you read the Scrum Guide? The Guide makes it clear that Product Owners decide what is built, and that teams figure out how to do it! Plus the Phoenix Project tells us that we have to amplify our feedback, which is why we have frequent User Acceptance Tests."

Angela tried to put Naomi's misconceptions in context and another string of facts poured out of her, that she would later recall as accurate but irrelevant to the emotional situation before her. "Naomi, the business has an essential role, but we are not the user and we need the user's input to help solve our challenges. The original Scrum Guide was focused solely on the work of the development teams. It actually starts with a pre-defined backlog with no discussion about how that backlog gets built!"

She was so tired of that old trope, that the Scrum Guide was somehow the bible of Scrum and held all the answers, that she continued, "In the decades since its launch, practices have evolved." In a vain attempt to lend credibility to her words by falling back on external authorities, she added, "We've also learned through Lean Startup, Usability research, and Design Thinking that direct user engagement is exponentially faster at producing the right results."

She thought again about how both Linda and Clyde had been hurt by Naomi's dismissal of their ideas, and her own mama-bear, protective instincts kicked in, "That's why Linda and I are putting together a watch party in our auditorium with all the teams to showcase Clyde's recent recordings so that they can see where the user struggles the most and create new ideas to solve those problems."

It had been such a great idea, and the teams were super excited about it. It was fun. It was useful. It was exactly the type of thing that she wanted to see Naomi participate in… and it was the absolutely wrong thing to say right now.

Naomi glowered back and spat out, "Now you are going to have movie time with the teams instead of letting them work on the new designs? This has gone too far."

Naomi stood up and with a very eerie calm simply said, "I see." Angela noticed the full-bodied emotion, and secretly wanted to hold it up as an example for the team, but kept silent. In fact, everybody kept silent. Nobody else in the room had actually been speaking outside the two of them for a while now, but somehow it felt like the room had suddenly gotten even quieter. Naomi became the only sound in the room. She said, "You have clearly won the trust of Tim and I have lost it, and I don't need to go down with this ship." She turned and looked at Tim, "I can see that you no longer need me, so I will get out of your way. I'll send you my official resignation letter."

She took off her badge, slapped it down on the table, and walked out of the meeting room. Everyone stared out of the conference room window into the main office space in shock. They saw Naomi disappear to the right, then reappear again with her bag and her jacket. She walked directly and confidently to the elevator, pushed the elevator button, got in without turning around, and let the doors close behind her.

A NEW JOB?

Angela remained sitting there stunned for a good two minutes, her mind rapidly replaying the scene several times over in her head... Everybody else, in sequence, very quietly collected their things and exited. First was Ali, then Jayson, followed by Linda and Evah. Eventually, it was just Angela, Tim, and Zach in the room. Tim asked Zach to give them the room and close the door on his way out.

Once the door was closed, and Zach was out of earshot, Tim leaned back in his chair and whistled sharply, "So, she finally did it. I was wondering when she would reach that point."

Angela was stunned! "So you expected her to quit?"

Tim opined ruefully, "Well, I wasn't certain, but I definitely feared she would. Remember when we talked about whether we could fire Naomi?"

Angela quickly responded, "I remember strategizing on how to reach her. I remember saying that I wondered if we could find another place for her. I don't remember saying to fire her. Please don't put those words in my mouth."

"Well I talked with Ahmed about our troubles," Tim admitted. "He said, and I agreed, that moving her anywhere else in the company would look like retribution for Intuition. And we really didn't want that to be seen as her fault."

"Good," Angela agreed, "because things like the Intuition problem happen all the time. That is definitely not her fault."

"Exactly," Tim agreed. "And because it's not her fault, Ahmed said we also opened ourselves up to potential liability if we fired her."

"Again," Angela inserted, "there are a lot more options than firing someone."

"Right," offered Tim, "so Ahmed suggested that if Naomi didn't switch over to our new way of working, she would come to the conclusion that it wasn't the right fit and leave, solving both problems. We don't have to actually do anything about it. Things will just work themselves out... That's a quote. Where does the line, 'things will just work themselves out' come from?"

"That's a quote from the movie 'Office Space', Tim," Angela answered. "'The Bobs' — the consultants — say it. It's actually not a good thing to emulate. And again, there are other ways to handle this besides firing and quitting."

Tim pushed back, "Right, and we tried those other things. I mean it's not like we didn't try, and it's not like you and I didn't collaborate on other strategies. We tried a lot of things. I just didn't collaborate with you on this specific part of the strategy."

She found herself getting really upset again, "How could you not tell me about this part, Tim? That was really stressful, and it's been a really stressful past several weeks for everyone. Your choice here seems very unfair. With that extra knowledge, we could have tried something else. We could have..."

"We tried Angela," Tim responded with a strong sense of compassion in his voice. "I really hate to see her go too, but we tried. Hard. And when it comes to the realm of firing, that's not really in your purview. Plus, this is the way Ahmed wanted to handle it."

"There are always other options, Tim," Angela insisted, "if we put our heads together. I could have helped you come up with another plan."

"You had enough on your plate," Tim interjected, obviously trying to be helpful, while also being very unhelpful, "So I prepared a contingency plan. Here is what we are going to do. You're going to take over as Product Manager. Congratulations!"

"Tim!" exclaimed Angela. "I did not come here to be your new Product Manager. I agreed to be your coach, and that's it. I could actually develop a bad reputation if it got around that I was replacing people. That's not the way I like to work."

"No, this is perfect," Tim urged. "Think about it. There's nobody here in Ares who knows enough yet to take over the job, and if we tried to hire someone from outside the company it would take months. We don't have months."

"Doesn't matter," said Angela emphatically. "I'm not taking her job."

"Think of the opportunity," Tim countered, shifting strategies. "In every crisis, there is an opportunity. There is wisdom in recognizing that there is always an opportunity inside major events. Naomi quitting doesn't have to be a crisis. Let's make it an opportunity to accelerate. Aren't you always going on about how we need to listen to the teams anyway? ...that the ones closest to the work have the best answers?"

"Yes, but-," Angela tried to interject.

Tim didn't stop, "Well I'm giving you the chance to prove it. You already have all of the managers willing to follow your lead. And without

Naomi, there'll be no distractions, and no one to be an obstacle to your empowering the teams to invent solutions. It's a win-win situation."

"This doesn't feel like a win-win, Tim," Angela contemplated. "Give me a moment to think this out loud..."

She took a deep breath with the intent to calm her emotions, slow down, and engage her logical brain. "Here's what doesn't sit right," she began again. "It's not the way that I like to work. It sets a bad precedent. I absolutely do not want to be seen as the coach who replaces people." She took another deep breath...in...and out. "But what does logic have to say? Is my response logical or emotional? ...or both?"

She tried to translate her feelings into thoughts, "It feels like we are taking advantage of Naomi and if I was in Naomi's position, I would be quite offended if I found out..."

Tim countered almost immediately, "Why should she be offended? She left of her own free will. She made that choice and knows the result. She even said it herself, she was 'getting out of your way'."

Tim was right. She wasn't really worried about Naomi's reaction. Naomi had already offered her own reaction, and there was nothing Angela could do to change that. No, this was about the reactions of the rest of the team.

Tim kept pushing before she had formed the words to respond, "Naomi's burnt out. She's exhausted all of her ideas. Frankly, she doesn't know what to do. You, on the other hand. I know you. You're just getting started."

"But I don't know this product," Angela inserted, finding a point to debate, "not as well as Naomi, or even the other Product Owners. I wouldn't even make an effective Product Manager."

"You'll only be the interim Product Manager then if that makes you feel better," Tim assured her. "We will start interviewing for a new Product Manager, but we'll interview for one that understands these new techniques, and who wants to apply them. In the meantime, you get a testbed to run any experiments that you want. Didn't you say that you already have some new ideas ready to execute with the Product Owners?"

Ding! That was when the idea really formed in her head. The Product Owners... they knew the product backward and forwards. They were the keys to success. Angela started piecing together the right things and the wrong things into a new strategy. She had been reacting emotionally to being backed into a corner, mainly by Tim's secret strategizing with Ahmed, but he was right about a few things. The teams did have the potential in them, they knew the product, they were absorbing the new techniques like a sponge, and without Naomi diverting half of their workdays, the potential was there to really accelerate.

Angela let the scenario play out in her mind's eye for half a minute. Tim did not speak this time. He just let her sit with it. Eventually, Angela re-engaged. "This might work," she said. Her brain had developed an alternative win-win strategy but on her own terms. "First," she continued, "I really hate the way you've done this, Tim." She glowered very purposefully at him.

"Acknowledged," Tim responded, finally appearing at least a little chagrined.

Angela continued, "Second, I will not be taking on the title of Product Manager, no matter what."

Tim tried to respond, but Angela held up a finger for him to be quiet and wait his turn. "What I will do instead, though, is continue to act in my capacity as a coach, and coach the Product Owners to work together as a team to bring this whole thing through to success." Tim grinned a huge smile.

Angela did agree with Tim that they could use this as a chance to prove that the techniques could work. She completed her thought, "The Product Owners are on board, and they're very excited about talking to customers. They wanted to but were prevented from doing so. It's time to unleash that intrinsic motivation and make some real change." That idea made Angela smile and made it a win-win solution for her.

"Alright, coach," Tim replied. "What should we do next?"

"Well," said Angela, thinking out loud. "My philosophy is always 'people first'. Let's give power to the people. We have a smart team of talented folks, who know what they're doing, are highly trained, and have a strong process. As Dan Pink said in his book 'Drive', the people closest to the work know best about what's needed. I have a technique that's designed for that."

"Nice," Tim said encouragingly. "What's the plan?"

Angela replied, "Do you remember that AMMI technique that I used when I got here, the Agile Mindset Mapping Index?"

"Sure," Tim replied. "It was a great way to do a gap analysis on the teams, quite comprehensive."

"Yes," Angela said with trepidation. "It can be used as a gap analysis, but if I'm speaking honestly," she said with a twinge of guilt in her voice. "I always feel uncomfortable using it that way. When I was getting trained in using it, they drilled into my head that AMMI is a 'self-tracking skills matrix'. It's supposed to be filled out by the teams. AMMI provides an external System of Record for comparison, and teams are supposed to design their own path to upgrading their Agile skills."

Tim echoed her thoughts, "So you want the team to go through the whole assessment again..."

Angela felt her gut clench, bracing herself against that word. She held up a single finger to pause him, "Please, don't use the 'A' word. Assessments aren't empowering. They set up an adversarial relationship."

"Ok," Tim acquiesced, "what do you want me to say instead?"

Angela responded, "AMMI uses the phrase, 'Choose Your Own Adventure'."

"Choose Your Own Adventure?" Tim repeated, skeptically. "Like those books from the eighties? Really? You want me to use that phrase?"

"Yes!" enthused Angela with a playful smile. "Or like Zork, the first, text-based adventure game!"

"Zork?" Tim chuckled. "I haven't thought about that in decades!"

"If you think about it," continued Angela, "It's the basis of every video game, and it's why they're fun. You're in control, maybe not total control, but you get to influence the outcome. You get to make the decisions. Video games are fun and engaging. Assessments are stilted and boring. AMMI is the world map for the Agile video game, and each team gets to pick which part of the world they want to explore next."

"We've just lost our Product Manager," Tim reminded her.

Angela doubled down, knowing that she was right in her gut, "This is exactly the time to do this because we just lost our Product Manager. We're facing turmoil no matter what we do next. There's going to be a power vacuum to fill, and if we don't fill it with something that is psychologically healthy, then something unhealthy will. Let's face it, they're going to be scared, and they're going to feel out of control. They need to know that they can do this. They need to build confidence, and they all need to take on some ownership for building what's next." Angela ran out of breath and inhaled deeply. She did a slow exhale, letting the idea settle in the air between them. She could feel it. This was the right path forward.

"Ok," Tim responded, "here's what I'm sitting with. Last time we used the AMMI assess... I mean... the last time we used AMMI, it took us over a week to get through it all. We don't have that kind of time."

"Oh, right," Angela countered, "let me clarify what's in my head. You're totally right. A week-long effort would be too much, but we don't need a week for this. We need a day and then a short one-hour follow-up afterward. In the beginning, that process was about me aligning with the teams, spending time with you all, and watching how you work, which takes time. This is very different. This is self-empowered. *They* will all be doing the work. In fact, I have a format that I've used before during Big Room Planning events as a reset mechanism."

"Well, we probably need to call an All Hands meeting tomorrow anyway," Tim added, "so that we can address Naomi's departure."

"Yeah," Angela agreed, "that will be important. Let me describe the format I'm thinking about..." She started walking Tim through the plan in her head, and it gave her a feeling of control over the chaos.

CHOOSE YOUR OWN ADVENTURE

Check-In

The next morning was a torrent of emotions, for Angela, Tim, and especially the team. Angela and Tim had established a quick agenda, and they started the day by presenting the plan to the leadership team, as usual.

Angela kicked everything off with a compassionate check-in, "So, how are you doing?" Everybody looked around at each other a little tentatively, so she added in the context for her question. We are all shaken up by recent events. Let's start today differently by doing a round-robin with a check-in of ourselves. We can start with these questions: 'How are you doing?' 'What are you bringing with you into the meeting today?' It acknowledges that we're human beings with lives. Things that happen to us just before the meeting, outside of the office, or at home all have an effect. Knowing where we are all coming from helps us to deal with the whole person and not jump to incorrect assumptions about people's intentions."

"I'll go," Linda volunteered. Angela agreed and Linda began, "I'm all kinds of nervous, and I probably couldn't stay quiet anyway, so I figured I might as well go first." She let out a big laugh, and then stifled it just as quickly, and looked around a bit like a turtle checking her surroundings. "I'm both excited to get started under Angela's new plan and petrified to not have anybody in Naomi's position. I mean... I don't know Angela's plan yet,... but I've liked her other plans so far! And I didn't know Naomi for nearly as long as the rest of you, but those are some mighty big shoes to fill!"

"There's no filling those shoes," came Evah's voice from the corner of the room. Everyone turned around to look. Linda paused so that Evah could speak, but Evah decided to hold her tongue. She gestured to Linda to continue.

Linda began again. "I agree, Evah, there's no one like Naomi," she said with a tone of clear respect in her voice. "The knowledge she could spout out, off the top of her head, was amazing! Angela can also spin out a ton of ideas, off the top of her head, too!" Angela felt a little grip around her heart. She found herself hoping that this didn't become a Naomi vs Angela thing. Linda continued, "With Angela, it's always a mixture of things I've loved from past projects and some new ideas that I'm excited to try! So I'm afraid of what we've lost, but I'm also excited to see what's coming next." Linda looked around again, and then added, "That's it. That's what I wanted to say."

"Thank you, Linda," said Angela. "You're both afraid for what we've lost, and excited for what might be waiting around the corner." Linda nodded and smiled in agreement with the summary.

Angela addressed the whole room again, "Who would like to go next?" There were no immediate volunteers, so Angela asked, "Evah, how about you?"

"You want me to go next?" Evah asked, just a little bit surprised.

"I'd like for us all to say something," Angela clarified, "but I also want to acknowledge that you're sitting with something."

"Of course, I'm sitting with something," Evah confirmed. "I've just lost one of my best friends, it just happened, and you're already taking over."

Angela wanted to respond and say that she wasn't trying to replace Naomi, but she knew from her training that there are times to reply immediately and times for just letting people express their opinions. This was the latter, so she just nodded encouragingly until Evah spoke again.

When Evah realized that she wasn't getting a response, she continued, "Naomi and I have been here since the beginning... Actually, before that.

We worked together before the Innovation Center. I honestly don't know how to do this without her... Nor if I want to do this without her." Evah paused as if to ask herself if there was anything more to say, and then concluded, "That's what I'm sitting with... for now."

"Thank you, Evah," Angela said in a soft tone. "You definitely did not want to see Naomi go, you don't like the idea of doing this without her, and you don't like that I'm 'taking over'. I think those were the words that you used, right?" Evah thought for a minute, probably to see if she actually used the words 'taking over', but then nodded in confirmation.

Angela looked around the room, "Who's next?"

Tim raised his hand as he stood up and said, "I'd like to respond to that."

"Actually," Angela interjected, "if we can, Tim, it's better if we don't respond to each other at this stage, but just talk about how each of us is personally feeling. Would you like to share what you're feeling as we start the day?"

"Oh... um, okay. Yeah, I can go next." Tim stammered a bit, trying to get his thoughts in order. "I'm sitting with frustration. This didn't have to go this way. I've also known Naomi for a long time, and I've always put my trust in her. And frankly, if I'm being honest, I don't feel like I got that same level of trust back from her. I tried to get her to open up but she didn't. And I know we're not supposed to respond to others, but I really respected what you said to me yesterday, Angela, and I want to make sure that others know what you said too."

Tim looked around at everyone before continuing, "I did offer to Angela to take over for Naomi until we figured out what to do with her absence, and you know what? Angela refused." There were a few noticeably raised eyebrows around the room in surprise. Tim continued, "She said that replacing Naomi was not the right move. I think that actually takes integrity, and that's one of the things that I admire about Angela. She's not afraid to tell me the honest truth, to my face. I hadn't actually seen Naomi, face-to-face, in weeks. How Naomi responded to this change was... okay, I'll just say it: selfish. She wasn't working through this with us. She was doing it all by herself. That's what I mean by 'selfish'. She wouldn't let me help her. And if I'm being honest, that made me a bit angry."

He started to sit down, and then straightened up again and added, "And to be clear when I say change, I don't mean Angela. Angela didn't start the change. Naomi didn't start the change either. Intuition kicked all this off and made change necessary. We weren't going to get out of this doing the same things that we had done before, to quote Einstein... or something like that." He sat down again, and settled back into his chair, to signify that he was finished.

"Thank you for sharing, Tim," Angela said. "So you're frustrated, or angry. You wanted more collaboration in the face of Intuition, and you don't feel like you got that."

"From Naomi," Tim clarified.

"From Naomi," Angela confirmed. "Okay, who's next?"

Jayson raised his hand. Angela pointed his way and he began, "You all know that I'm not for or against anybody. I'll work with you all to figure out what's next." There were some agreeing nods from the others around the table. Jayson continued, "And generally, I'm optimistic. I've seen this team do some amazing things. From Ali with his architectures," he said gesturing in Ali's direction, "to Vera and her design team," he added gesturing in her direction, "and the programmers impress me just about every single day." He paused for a brief second, and then concluded, "I feel confident going into battle with any of you." A few spontaneous smiles bloomed on several of the faces all around in response.

Vera raised her hand, and several nodded at her to go next, including Angela. "I'm also feeling confident," Vera added. "I've been very impressed with how Clyde has stepped up. He and the other designers have really been 'embracing the problem,' as Angela phrases it." That made Angela smile. Vera continued, "I've had to protect my team from Naomi's temper for a while now, and I'm happy to do it, but some days it's exhausting."

Vera was uncharacteristically dropping her guard today, which Angela was very pleased to see. It was not long-lived, however, and Vera redirected, "The UX and Design teams give me great joy. A lot of great ideas have been pouring out of them. We haven't gotten a chance to try them all lately, but there is no shortage of new solutions to test. I'm confident that we'll crack the case," she concluded as she settled back into her normal state of poise and composure.

"How about you, Roy?" Angela asked.

"It's no secret," Roy answered, "that I didn't like Naomi. To be honest, I wish she had quit months ago, but I'm not going to belabor the point. I think the only thing I'd add going forward is that people are going to have to pitch in and do things that they don't usually do from here on out. I guess that's what I'm bringing to the meeting."

"And how about you, Ali?" Angela said, coming around to one of the two people left at the table who hadn't spoken.

"Me?" Ali asked. "To be honest, I haven't been able to make heads or tails out of all the changes in direction we've been going through. Now, maybe that's because I'm closing on my new house next week, but I look forward to being able to put some order and structure around this whole process. If you make sure that you include architecture as we move forward, then I'm good."

Evah looked surprised and asked, "You're moving? That's fantastic! Where to? I didn't know you were moving. We'll have to arrange a housewarming."

"It's a little further away," Ali shared. "It's going to add about thirty minutes to my commute, but it's perfect. There's a separate, attached residence for my dad and a big yard for the kids to play in. And it's a great community."

"That's great, Ali," Tim interjected. "I'm glad you got the place. I do want to keep us on track here, but I also want to hear all about it later."

"Sorry. Sure," Ali acknowledged.

"No reason to be sorry," Angela clarified. "I asked what we're all bringing with us, whether professional or personal today, and that definitely qualifies. Congratulations!" Ali nodded in appreciation.

"Zach," Angela said after letting the excitement settle down a bit. "That just leaves you. How are you doing today?"

"I've been thinking," Zach responded, "about our purpose as an entire Innovation Center. To paraphrase Tim, we are collectively greater than any single person and can overcome these challenges by focusing on our vision NOT by 'beating Intuition', but by building the best product together as a team!"

Angela agreed, "Well spoken, Zach! Yes, let's keep our focus on achieving excellence together despite our loss!"

Tim spoke up, "Zach, that is worth repeating. Our goal at the Ares Innovation Center is to build the best damn product in the world and not 'beat Intuition'. We don't play by Intuition's game, nor by their rules. We make our own path and succeed through being our best!"

"Agreed," responded Angela. She purposely paused for a while to let Tim's insight sink in. "As for myself, I honestly feel a bit ashamed. From the onset, there was friction between Naomi and myself. I felt she looked at me as an adversary and not as an ally. Unfortunately, I let the worst of myself emerge and let my emotions drive some of my reactions. Naomi challenged me in ways that made me defensive and I let my pride get the best of me."

"Going forward," she continued, "I will double down on separating my emotions from my actions. Not that there's anything wrong with emotions. We need to feel our emotions, but that's different than letting them make our decisions for us."

"It's how we respond to our mistakes that matters most," Tim reflected, then added, "This check-in format was excellent!"

Angela sighed, smiled, and said, "Thank you! Thank you all for taking the time to check in and connect as people."

THE AMMI WAY

Angela opened her laptop and began connecting to the shared screen in the room. "Let me present the proposed plan for your consideration." While it was loading, she set the context, "I like to use 'The Advice Principle' as outlined in Frederick Laloux's book 'Reinventing Organizations'. Basically, 'The Advice Principle' says that if you're affected by something, you should be brought in as early as possible to offer your opinion about how the plan is going to affect you, to either point out potential problems or offer alternatives before you are affected." She looked around at everyone, and they all looked back at her cautiously.

"So," Angela clarified, "the teams are definitely going to be affected by whatever happens next, so I want to bring them on the decision-making for whatever happens next."

"That's your plan?" Roy said incredulously. "You're going to let the teams decide what we do next? That's not a plan."

"Yes and no," Angela responded. "That's part of the plan, but not the entire plan. The 'Yes' part," Angela expanded, "is acknowledging that we already have great teams. They're experienced Agilists, they already know DevOps and automation, the UX and design teams are doing a great job at the customer research, and the Product Owners combined know almost as much as Naomi did about the product, the environment, and our stakeholders. As Zach alluded to, we only lost one person. She was an important person, yes, and definitely central, but only one person."

Roy felt the need to confirm, "If anything, she was standing in the way of true understanding."

"How dare you!" Evah burst out. "She has been the backbone of this team and was working tirelessly for all of us!"

"Don't let him get under your collar," said Jayson, disrupting the tension. "You know that's a dead end. We all know how much Naomi was dedicated to Breeze. No one is questioning that. Okay?"

"Okay," Evah agreed.

"Also," Jayson added, "I agree with Angela. She was an important part of our team, but she was only one part, and we have a lot of talented people."

Ali piped up too, "What did we learn about bottlenecks from 'The Phoenix Project'? Our organization has to be able to survive even if one person is out, no matter who it is."

Evah didn't seem entirely convinced, but she was calming down, and she was settling back into her seat again. Angela continued with her explanation, "Well, here's my plan. Do you remember that Agile Mindset Mapping Index that I used when I got here? AMMI?" A few heads started nodding tentatively around the table.

"We're going to do another assessment?" asked Roy.

Angela felt an involuntary shudder down her spine, "No, we're going to use AMMI the way it was intended to be used. Often teams are stuck in a dichotomy. On one side, no one knows the needs of the team better than the team members. On the other side, though, teams often get stuck because they don't know what they don't know. The real power of AMMI is its 'Choose Your Own Adventure' approach."

There were several blank faces around the room so Angela added more detail. "AMMI is a self-diagnostic tool. When teams are encouraged to look through the library and choose what they want to do next, they tend to stumble upon the things that they need to learn next. They recognize their problems better than we could."

"Why?" blurted out Evah, "Why is this the thing to do now?"

Angela gathered her thoughts for a moment as they all waited for her response. "Because," she began, "we need all minds on this problem, and we don't have that right now. Our teams have not been trained to think for themselves."

"How can you say that?" Jayson objected, rallying to the defense of the teams. "Our people are very intelligent!"

"They are!" agreed Angela. "Highly intelligent. What I am saying is something different. If you've only ever been empowered to realize someone else's vision... If you have never been empowered to create your own visions of the future, then have you really been empowered?"

"We are not micro-managers here," Jayson insisted, visibly upset, and rallying this time to the defense of the leadership team.

"Let me ask you, then," Angela countered, "have we been following the suggestions of everyone on the teams in addition to Naomi's ideas?"

She paused for the response, which was not immediately forthcoming as people thought about it for a moment.

Vera was the first to respond, "No. My designers have a whole backlog of alternate ideas that have been shelved."

"No," Linda agreed. "The Scrum Masters have been complaining to me that they are so overworked that we are taking on larger and larger amounts of technical debt and the teams are abandoning our best practices to keep up."

"And don't get me started," Ali added, "on the complete disregard for the architecture. I have so much code that I have to fix."

"And metrics," Roy tossed into the mix, his arms folded and clenched tightly across his chest. "No one has listened to a single word that I've said in months."

Angela felt a wave of relief that multiple voices had also seen what she had been seeing. She built on top of their observations, "One of the core tenets of Agile and Lean is removing impediments and removing the bottlenecks. This is not just about the flow of work but is also about the flow of ideas. We have a bottleneck in the flow of ideas. We need to listen more to our teams, understand what they see as their obstacles to success, and help them remove those obstacles."

"That is why I am proposing AMMI now, at this point," she continued. "They are not used to us listening to them, and to their concerns. They have been taught to put their concerns aside for the greater good. We need to put them front and center again and let them choose what's next. They are the closest to the information. They are actually better equipped to see the possibilities than we are."

"What if they don't choose anything?" Evah asked, changing concerns. "What if they don't know what to change?"

This time Linda replied with confidence, "They'll choose something. We don't have any slackers here. These teams have been asking to make changes, but they've been so overworked that they haven't had the time."

"Yes," Angela agreed, "I don't think that will be a problem, but we can also be clear that every team must pick at least one improvement."

"What if they pick the wrong thing?" Evah asked. "You mentioned that they don't know what they don't know. Shouldn't we help them pick the right items?"

"I would propose that there is a better strategy," Angela reassured her. "Teams will be required to back up their choice by designing an experiment. They must lay out what change they expect to see by implementing the change, collect evidence to assess their success, or failure, and provide regular updates."

"It's about time we got here," exclaimed Roy with more enthusiasm than Angela had probably ever seen in him.

"If it's not the right change," Angela explained, "the team will see that. In my experience, some of them even discover that it's the wrong choice just through the process of designing the experiment."

"I'm not sure I'm on board," Vera shared rather unexpectedly. "We already have a bunch of changes in the design queue. Getting those built and tested should be our top priority."

"Yes they should, and they will be," Angela agreed. "Work on the backlog doesn't stop. It's about rethinking the way we work on that backlog. We are making changes to our process of how we work on that backlog. David Marquet refers to this as 'Blue Work' in his book, 'The Language of Leadership'."

"You don't want change just for change's sake," she added. "Teams must also be able to show a link between the change they want to implement and their ability to solve our current dilemma. For every change that they want to make, they need to tell us how the change helps us to meet the challenges of the market. Will the change help us to get work done faster? Will it provide more information? Will it increase our income? Will it help us to reach more customers?"

"That would be okay," Vera acquiesced, albeit with some visible remaining skepticism. "It's just that sometimes I see changes around here and I have no idea where they came from."

Jayson interjected, "We can make that a requirement to get approval to make the change. I'll back that up. That sounds reasonable to me."

"But won't this also waste a lot of time?" Evah added. "All of this change is going to slow us down."

Jayson replied, "No, not really. We used the term Blue Work when I was in the military too. Blue work is the strategy behind doing the work. It becomes part of the operation. We could even call it 'Operation Blue Work'!"

"I like that!" Angela enthused, "Operation Blue Work! It represents an important Agile philosophy of 'slowing down to speed up'. We have to set aside the time to slow down, look at what we're doing, and see if it is helping us or hurting us. Google has shown us that even with as much as 20% of their time spent on learning and practicing, a team working at 80% capacity is more productive than a team working at 100%..."

"Wait a minute," Evah exclaimed. "One day per week? You want us to lose one day of productivity per week from every person on the team?!"

Vera started speaking up, "Yeah that's t--"

"Now everybody, just hold on!" Tim interjected, rising quickly to his feet to command the space. "I'm really getting tired of all these interruptions. Angela and I worked on this plan together, and it's good, but you haven't even heard half of the details because you're all interrupting every two minutes. So I'm going to put a stop to all the interruptions and instead, I'm going to ask you all for three things."

"First," he said, holding up one finger, "I need you to understand the whole plan of what she's proposing before you start poking holes in it. See the entire picture before you decide how good it looks." He looked around the room and met every single one of them eye-to-eye before continuing.

"Second," he said, raising a second finger, "I learned a saying that's always been useful for me in processing new ideas, 'Rule it in before you rule it out.' I think that absolutely applies here. If you don't like that, follow Stephen Covey's 'The Seven Habits of Highly Effective People' and 'Seek First to Understand, Then to be Understood'."

"Third," Tim held up three fingers, "I need you to believe in our teams." He gestured towards the windows of the conference room and out at the main room, beckoning them to look at the teams hard at work at their computers.

Then he summed it all up, "What she's asking you to do here is to believe in our people, our own people. If those people aren't capable of solving their own problems – if Naomi was our only hope – then we might as well just pack it all up and close down the office. Angela is right. We don't need to protect our people from themselves. We need to start listening to them. That's why I approved this plan. We have amazing teams, and it's time we started letting them show how amazing they are!"

Everyone sat in stunned silence for a few moments as Tim's words settled over them. A feeling of warmth and gratitude filled Angela's heart. She felt heard... really heard... and understood, for the first time in a long time. She couldn't have said it better herself.

Jayson clapped his hands a few times as he leaned back in his chair, "Well spoken! I'm with you!"

Everyone else gradually leaned back in their chairs too and turned to face Angela. "Thank you," Tim said with a tone of honest appreciation. "When Angela is done laying out her whole plan, then we'll open the floor for questions. Agreed?"

There were nods from around the table in agreement. Some of them seemed like reluctant nods to Angela, but they were nods nonetheless. It was best if everyone was in agreement going forward, but Angela also knew that when it comes to trying something new, just like the teams, the managers also don't know what they don't know. This is not the first time that she had to ask people to do something without understanding it first. The understanding would come after the execution of the plan.

"Thank you for your support, Tim," Angela said. "I appreciate it. I was honestly a little conflicted. I knew everybody would have questions, which is why I've been answering them, but I agree that some things will make more sense after I get through the whole plan. How about this? We've got sticky notes here. I don't want us to forget those questions. Please write them down on these so that I can respond to them later."

People reached for the sticky notes in agreement as she passed them around, and Evah and Vera started writing their comments on their pads. She turned again to the monitor in the room and walked the team through the plan on the screen.

Agenda

1. Tell the teams about the departure of Naomi [5 min + time for questions]
2. Describe the agenda and the plan [15 min]
3. Introduce the AMMI catalog [15 min]
4. Teams research, discuss, and vote on one area of improvement using a smaller variation of 1-2-4-All called 1-2-All
    a. Individual Research [15-20 minutes]
    b. [Break]
    c. Discuss in Pairs [10 minutes]
    d. Vote as a whole team [10 minutes]
5. Identify how our problem connects to the Intuition problem [15 minutes]
    a. (Move on to the next-highest vote if a connection cannot be found)
    b. (Managers circulate and offer advice when needed)
6. Teams share their chosen improvement, and how it supports the overall goal.
    a. Open the floor for a round of appreciations after each idea.
    b. Continue with a second round of clarifying questions about each idea.
7. Teams spend the following hour designing an experiment, including a hypothesis of what is going to change, and how they will collect evidence to assess potential success and failure.
    a. Will you be able to work faster?
    b. Can you increase sales?
    c. Will you increase referral rates?
    d. Will it reduce expenses or eliminate wasted work?
    e. How will you know if you're successful?
8. Teams share the design of their experiment and the evidence they plan to collect.
    a. Open the floor for another round of appreciations.
    b. Continue with a second round of clarifying questions.

Teams spend the rest of the day working on building the framework necessary to collect the data that they need to test their hypotheses.

"OK," Angela began the walkthrough, "We'll kick the event off with the big news about Naomi, and not make anyone wait for it. If they have questions, I think we should address them right away. I want to leave time for emotions and show them that we care about their feelings. It is not the time to be business-like and impersonal, but exactly the opposite.

I believe in always putting 'People First' and that means we have to deal with emotions first." Nods of agreement came from almost everybody around the table.

Angela didn't get pushback, but she still felt a strong need to drive the point home. "Too often people rush into big announcements like this and expect the teams to just pull up their bootstraps and get down to work like automatons. If we really want to change our culture, change starts from within, so we have to leave space for people to be people."

"The Scrum Masters can help with that!" said Linda excitedly, raising her hand in the air. "Our Scrum Masters are really good at dealing with emotions!!!" Then she dropped her hand and covered her mouth, blurting out between her fingers, "I'm so sorry. We're supposed to stay quiet. I'll shut up." Angela smiled in appreciation.

"Thank you, Linda," Angela said to soothe her embarrassment. "I'll definitely follow up with you on that later."

"Second," she continued, "I'll walk through this agenda with them and describe what we're going to be doing for the rest of the day."

"That introduction will transition into Step Three, the presentation about the Agile Mindset Mapping Index. I'll talk about the six Points of Collaboration – People, Design, Planning, Implementation, Verification, and Operations – and describe the Range of Influence."

"Fourth," she said holding up four fingers, "we'll get ready for the breakout sessions. During those breakout sessions, the teams are to use AMMI, or any other external reference of their choosing, to research different options that might be problem areas for their teams."

Angela clarified how this process would happen. "Here I want to use a variation of a technique from 'Liberating Structures' called '1-2-4-All'[2]. First, each person individually does research for about fifteen to twenty minutes. We'll combine that up with our first break, for flexibility if people get done early. After we come back from our break, people will pair up to discuss their chosen areas. After discussing in pairs for ten minutes, they all came together as a team to share what was discussed in the pairs. After each pair finishes sharing, the teams will vote. They have up to thirty minutes to choose one or two problem areas that they want to change. I'm purposefully phrasing them as 'Problem Areas'. I want teams to focus on identifying problems and not solutions. They may need our help to stay on track with this. Everybody usually loves to gravitate towards the solutions."

"Linda," Angela said, turning to look at her, "I'm hoping that the Scrum Masters can help with this part too." Linda didn't say a word but shook her head up and down enthusiastically. "Plus, as managers, I'd like for us all to be floating around the room and also encouraging them to keep things focused on the problems. To help with that, I plan to introduce the Design Thinking Double Diamond as a way to keep them focused on the right things at the right times."

"It became popular through Design Thinking," Vera interrupted, "but the Double Diamond was actually first proposed by Bela Banathy, a thought leader in Systems Research and Behavioral Science[3] in the late nineties."

Angela was pleasantly surprised, though also caught off guard, but she took it in stride. "That I didn't know," Angela responded. "Always fun to learn new things," she added with a smile. "I had heard of the British Design Council of two thousand three, was she a member?"

"He," Vera clarified. "Bela was a man, and he actually was a linguist by trade."

"Fascinating!" Angela said with renewed enthusiasm. "Then I guess I have some research waiting for me!"

Vera smiled and agreed, "It's an interesting little nugget of history."

"Well then," Angela began again, "Bela discovered and Design Thinking championed the approach that you have to tackle the problem separately from the solution. And we are going to focus the event on just the first half, Problems. I have a diagram to help us visualize this."

She scrolled down to a graphic of the Double Diamond for clarification.

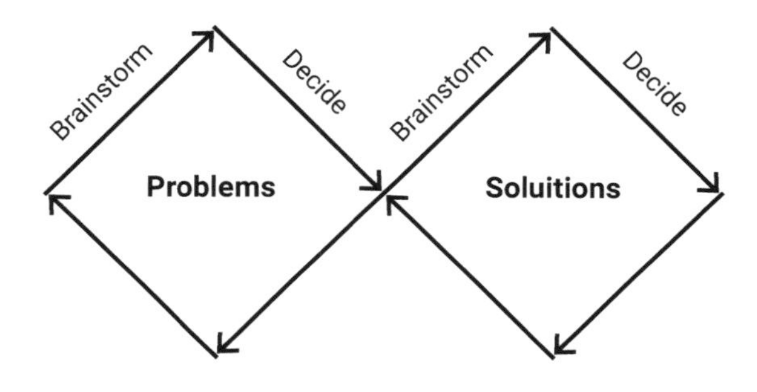

"Step Five is fifteen minutes for teams to identify how the problem they chose helps to solve our Intuition problem. This could be hard or it could be easy, and either outcome is okay. Each team will be different. We should be circulating around, asking them questions, and testing their connections. If we can't find a connection together with a team, we should encourage them to move on to the next improvement with the highest number of votes. And if the answer is obvious and they finish quickly, they can take another break."

"Once they've picked their top one or two problems, we all come back together for Step Six and each of the teams will share their chosen problems and how they believe it connects to the problem we're experiencing with Intuition."

"As for feedback for each team, I plan to employ the first two steps of the Double Aces only. After a problem is presented, I will open the floor for anybody to express any appreciations for the chosen problem, and what they like about that choice. If anybody tries to tack on any criticism, I'm going to stop them, and I could use your support. I want to apply the 'Ugly Baby' technique that Ed Catmull talks about in his book, 'Creativity, Inc.', about the management philosophy at Pixar. He shares that inside Pixar, every new idea starts off as an 'ugly baby' and needs to be protected. As it grows, it gets better, but that's up to the team. It's important that nobody comes in from the outside and judges the choices of each team until they get a chance to work on their 'ugly baby'."

"After the appreciations, I'll open up the room for a second round of Clarifying Questions only. Anybody can ask a question about a chosen problem, or its connection to the Intuition problem if it is unclear. We just have to be careful about catching veiled criticisms, expressed in the form of a question, like, 'Do you really think that's going to help?' or 'Wouldn't it be better if...?' I'm going to jump in and block those questions, and I will need you to back me up on that. Some other key phrases

---

2 1-2-4-All" is a Liberating Structure created by Keith McCandless and Henri Lipmanowicz to help facilitate better meeting outcomes. *liberatingstructures.com/1-1-2-4-all/*

3 Béla Bánáthy published what would later become known as the Double Diamond approach in his book, "Designing Social Systems in a Changing World" in 1996. *https://en.wikipedia.org/wiki/Double_Diamond_(design_process_model)*

to look out for are when people start talking about 'a lack of something' and use negative words like 'insufficient'. Oh, another keyword is 'political' as in someone starting off with a phrase like, 'Now this might sound political...' In these cases, the key is to bring things back to the concept of 'clarifying'. Jump in and ask if their question is 'clarifying' something that they don't understand."

"Then it's time for Step Seven, collecting evidence!" Angela said with enthusiasm. "Step Seven will be hard, and we're going to especially need your expertise, Roy." Roy looked surprised and snapped quickly to attention. Angela clarified, "People don't always know what can be measured. We may all need to circulate amongst the teams and offer advice on how to collect data to define their problems. If they get done early, let them start working on the technical challenges of how to collect the data that they need."

Angela continued, "And if nobody objects, I want us all to use the term 'experiments'. We don't know for certain if their choices will work or not. Even if it worked in a previous team, there's always a chance that it won't work in this context. Calling it an experiment helps us to understand that if it does not work, we can easily change it or even drop it without remorse."

"The last point about Step Seven," Angela concluded, "is to coach them on measuring clear outcomes. In scientific terms, we're looking for clear 'causality'. What do they expect to see because of this change? Finding a strong connection between the change and the outcome is the key. For example, if a team used to take over a month to get a new feature ready, but after introducing 'Customer Experience Mapping', they're getting it done in less than a week, there's a good chance that Customer Experience Mapping caused the reduction in time."

"They will be tempted to pull easy data," Roy inserted. "They may try to say, 'Look, our Cycle Time used to be a 5 and now it's a 4.2,' but that's not a big enough change to prove causation."

"Very true, Roy," Angela agreed. "The best improvements are also the ones that we can feel, like 'it used to take us the whole week but now it's only taking a couple days!' Obvious impacts help us to identify causation, that this change definitely caused that outcome."

She continued, "We'll follow that up with Step Eight, another presentation from each of the teams to the whole group. Just like before, I'll start by asking everyone to express what they like about the evidence to be collected by each team. When the appreciations are done, then I'll ask for any clarifying questions, but just like before, we'll need to be on the lookout for criticisms framed as questions."

"And that's the whole event!" Angela said with an expression of finality for having gotten through it all.

"The rest of the day the teams can start working on the technology needed to collect the data for their experiment. The first step in entering a 'Build, Measure, Learn Loop' should always be 'Measure'. Actually, I'll leave them with that. We can't have learning if we don't have data from both before and after the experiment to use for the comparison. It's just as important to collect the data now before they get started, as it is to collect the data as they get underway. Their first deliverable will be to collect enough evidence to establish a baseline, a 'before' picture." She searched her computer and found an old Lean Startup graphic that she had built previously, and quickly added it to the presentation.

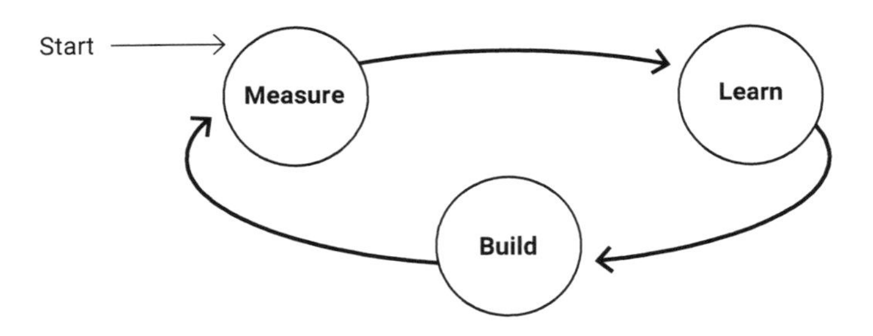

She looked around the table and saw several sticky notes full of questions and comments, so she asked, "Who has questions?"

Ali's hand was the first to go up, even though he didn't have any sticky notes on the table. "Yeah," he said, "my question is when do we decide on the solutions for their problems? I'm down with collecting evidence first, but you didn't talk about where in the process they pick which solutions to experiment with."

"Yes, you're right," Angela considered. "That is part of the plan too. It was intentional to leave it out of today's process, but you're right that I need to share my plan for that too. The reason that I'm leaving it out of today's agenda is that it's super important that they really get to know the problem and understand it."

"But knowing a problem exists does us no good if we don't solve it," Ali countered. "I mean, we know that we've got plenty of problems," he said with a knowing chuckle.

"We do," Angela responded, "but knowing our problem is different than understanding the problem... just like the backwards bicycle!"

"I loved that backwards bicycle video!" Linda blurted out. "I ordered one of the bikes by the way! They're back-ordered, though. Who knows when I'll get it. My husband's a mechanic, though, and he said that he thinks he could build me one, but he's also 'back-ordered'," Linda added with a hearty laugh. "Who knows when he'll get around to actually building it."

Linda glanced at Angela, then realized that she was interrupting and said, "But I'm sorry. You go on ahead."

Angela smiled at Linda's enthusiasm and continued, "We need the teams to really understand their problem, and the faster they switch to the solution, the less likely they are to choose a solution that actually solves their problem versus something that just sounds like it will solve their problem, but doesn't."

"That definitely sounds like our problem," Jayson added with a knowing nod, still leaning back in his chair with his hands folded across his chest, taking it all in. "We've been implementing a lot of solutions that sound like they're going to solve our problems, but don't."

"That's the real danger," she paused to emphasize. "More time is wasted on solutions that don't actually solve the problem than is spent on truly knowing the problem. As the saying goes, 'Sharpen the Saw'. The teams need to really understand the problem first before they can choose the right solution. Since our brains use the predictive circuits in the brain 95% of the time, their brains will already be trying to connect the problem with a solution. If we let them move on to those solutions before they've decided how to collect their evidence, statistically speaking they're more likely to choose a solution that doesn't actually solve their problem."

"Huh," was all Ali said in response. It looked like he was thinking it through, though.

She was about to call on someone else when Ali countered, "I might already have a solution to their problems, though. I mean, that's kind of my job as the architect."

"Right," Angela agreed. "Many of us might have multiple options for them. I haven't written this part of the plan up yet — it's only been less than twelve hours — but here's the basic idea. They're all going to present their problems to everyone, including us, right?"

People nodded.

"Well, if you think you might have a good solution, make note of it and bring it to this meeting tomorrow. Any of you. I want to compile a list of solutions for them to choose from. Here's the important part, though... In order to unlock their Intrinsic Motivation, they have to choose the solution. We give them a list of solutions tailored to their specific problem plus the list of solutions in AMMI, but they get to choose which solution to implement."

"What if they choose the wrong one, though?" Ali asked, more like a criticism than an actual question.

Angela was ready for this question, though. It was always raised by someone, and it helped her to drive home her point, "That's why taking the initial time to collect evidence is so critical. When a team is asked to establish baseline data, they usually fall into three categories: First, a bunch of the teams that get to this stage figure out they were planning to choose the wrong solution as soon as they collect the current, baseline data. They either collect the data and realize that the numbers aren't actually what they thought they were, or they realize that the solution isn't going to change the numbers."

Angela paused and then continued, "Second, a surprising number of teams actually pick the same solutions that the managers would have chosen for the team. Sometimes it's because it's been talked about in the past, and sometimes it's just the logical choice.

Angela paused again, "The third group, a minority of the teams in my experience, do choose the wrong solutions, but as they start collecting their evidence and they don't see the data changing, then they start to question their choices. Eventually, they will course correct and learn a valuable lesson about what does or does not work, and how to adapt when it doesn't."

Angela increased her speaking volume to make a point, "So in conclusion, all three of those areas are where the learning comes in. Whether it be success or failure, there is always the opportunity for learning and then improving as a result of that learning."

"There's even a chance," Angela added, "that the solutions that we would have chosen for them won't solve their problems either. If they end up using our solution because we told them to, then they won't check the experiment against the data for fear of disappointing us. They'll use the wrong solution for a longer period of time because they didn't take ownership of the choice."

"That also sounds like us," Jayson said, punctuating Angela's point, "teams implementing solutions because they were told to, regardless of whether or not it's actually making a difference." Ali considered this for a moment and then settled back into his seat without further rebuttal.

Evah looked through the sticky notes in front of her and pulled one, holding it up in the air. "We should pick a retro for them to do during the '1-2-All' event. They may not know how to pick the best problem. I know a great prioritization exercise that they can use."

"I like it!" Angela enthused. "Let's add it to a library of options for them to choose from," she suggested. "Would you consider it fair to see what the teams come up with first, and then only step in if they actually get stuck? I'd like to not assume that they will get stuck. If the teams are going to own the outcomes, they also need to pick the prioritization technique."

"Fair enough," Evah agreed. She looked through the sticky notes in front of her. "Answered. Answered... That makes sense. Oh, here's one: What if they want to tackle three or four problems?"

"We may need to save the teams from their own ambitions in this case," Angela offered. "Encourage them to focus on just one or two, max. If they get those problems solved easily, then they can move on to the next problem in the list."

Evah laughed, "Good luck with that!"

Internally, Angela agreed, though she didn't dare say it out loud. She was curious and nervous about all of the known challenges, especially in a culture where "doing more" was not only expected but demanded.

It was time to start changing that...

Key Points of Learning

- Role negotiation
- Choosing Your Own Adventure
- Liberating Structures – 1-2-4-All and 1-2-All variation
- Double Diamond
- The Build, Measure, Learn Loop

Chapter 8

Angela – Shifting Mindsets

PAIRING PROBLEMS WITH SOLUTIONS

The next day, Angela met up with Zach to formulate their plan. There hadn't been a lot of emotions following the announcement concerning Naomi, besides some private conversations that Linda and the Scrum Masters helped facilitate. Angela had expected more... she didn't know what. Something more. Anything more. She was sorting through it in her head.

Zach was the first to say it out loud, though, "That 'All Hands' meeting went more smoothly than I expected!".

"Agreed", said Angela.

"That's not to say," Zach added, "that the AMMI sessions weren't without their obstacles, but the things that teams got stuck on were so different from team to team."

Angela had felt a little uneasy. "It felt a bit *too* smooth," she shared. "I hope we got them to make the connection between their problems and actual customer impact."

"It was interesting," Zach added, "that some teams had absolutely no problem with that, but struggled with thinking about things in terms of hypotheses. And others were fine with hypotheses, but had trouble collecting evidence to back them up."

"Yeah," Angela commented, "you never know which teams are going to have which strengths and weaknesses until you really get into it. Collecting evidence can be tricky."

"You got that right!" Zach agreed.

"So," he said, transitioning, "are you ready for our 'world tour' today? I think a fair number of the teams spent some time collecting numbers like we asked. The Help Desk staff has been fielding a lot of requests for customer data."

"Fantastic!" enthused Angela. "I can't wait to see what they've been planning! Be prepared to see a lot of biased evidence, Zach, but that's okay. The first step towards learning how to collect good evidence is to learn how to collect that evidence in the first place."

"Right," Zach reflected, "then we tell them how to fix it."

"It's more nuanced than that," Angela countered. "They do need to have the power to *pick*, but any solutions that they have already chosen will probably be a bad match for their unique problems."

Zach countered, "But I thought the saying was, 'those closest to the problem know the problem best.'"

"Yes," Angela confirmed, "'Those closest to the problem know the *PROBLEM* best," she repeated, emphasizing the second use of the word "problem". Angela explained further, "Another of my life mantras is that 'If we knew the answers to our own problems, they wouldn't be problems.'"

She paused for a moment, checking Zach's face to see if the words had translated from her brain to his. She explained further, "It's a reminder of a time in my life when I was facing an insurmountable problem that I couldn't crack. At the same time, I had a good friend who seemed to be in a similar dilemma, but her problem seemed so easy to me that I couldn't understand why she was struggling. I don't want to get into details, but it wasn't until everything had completely exploded on both of us that we finally talked about it. I shared what I would have done in her situation and she said, 'I never thought of that!' Then she offered me advice on my situation and after she said it, it seemed so obvious but it had just never occurred to me."

"I see," Zach mused, "if we knew how to solve our own problems they wouldn't be problems for us. Woah, that's deep."

"Exactly," Angela confirmed with a huge sigh that expressed years of unnecessary frustrations. "We don't know what we don't know."

"Which is why we have to come up with the solutions," Zach said enthusiastically, trying to complete her thought.

"Mmmm, I'd rather say that we have to collaborate on the solutions," Angela said, hoping to fix his misunderstanding. He nodded. She let it go. This was probably something that couldn't be addressed in words. It probably had to be seen in action.

"Alright," she said, shifting focus, "the challenge for today is to make sure that each team has at least one complete improvement to carry out during the next sprint. Teams often get stuck on trying to get everything 'perfect' and risk never actually doing anything."

"Yeah," Zach agreed, "'Perfect is the enemy of good enough.' And I like how you were saying that time has to be set aside by the Product Owners for these team changes. They can't skip out on making changes that they don't like by shoving them down to low priority in the backlog."

"All too often," Angela expounded, "people want to make a change, but the change never gets approved. Always reserve a few hours in each sprint for improvement. The goal is to have a fair balance between delivering work, and getting better at delivering work."

Zach smiled, "Yes, of course. So once they have decided on their problems and evidence, do we only suggest solutions listed in AMMI?"

Angela clarified, "The AMMI website can be a good source of ideas, but good ideas can come from anywhere. Our responsibility is to find solution choices that align with the AMMI 'Points of Guidance' in each category, and then they get to pick which solution to try. That way they have a choice, but we can ensure that their choice actually has a chance to solve the problem."

"Okay, hopefully this doesn't happen," Zach asked earnestly, "but what if they absolutely refuse to try any of our suggestions?"

"That does happen," Angela confirmed. "And that's why collecting evidence is so important. Everything is 'hackable', but if they are collecting evidence that describes the problem, when they deploy a bad solution, the numbers will not move, or they will go in the wrong direction."

"We're not so great with numbers," Zach bemoaned.

"That is true," Angela agreed, "at least at the team level. Not enough practice. We will probably have to do a bunch of the work when it comes to designing good evidence collection until they can see the difference."

"Gotcha," Zach nodded, adding notes to his notebook. "Okay, we have seven teams total. We can meet with two this afternoon, two tomorrow, and I'm still checking on the timing for the other three."

THE RIVERLANDS

Angela and Zach met with the Riverlands team first to review their chosen techniques. She discovered that all the teams were named after a Game of Thrones Kingdom. Something about it being a super-popular TV show at the time. She had never watched the show nor read the books — it wasn't really her kind of thing — but she enjoyed how the teams had really bonded around their team identities.

"So how did yesterday's workshop go for you?" Angela asked them all.

"We felt it went pretty well," offered Geena, Scrum Master for the Riverlands. "I personally enjoyed getting a break from Naomi's constantly pushing us to get work done!"

Other team members nodded their heads in hearty agreement.

Angela echoed their thoughts back to them but was careful not to let the team focus on Naomi as the source of blame. "Yes, taking a break from constantly doing the same thing can help teams get some energy back!"

The Team Decides

She redirected the conversation back to the challenge at hand, "So which problems did you pick?"

Geena gestured to the rolling whiteboard in their team area, flipping it around to reveal a list of problem statements. "We came in yesterday wanting to improve hard and fast, and wanted to tackle as many of our biggest problems as possible."

Zach reviewed the list of problems, "Hmm... Let's see what you have..." He counted partially to himself, but also out loud, "Oh my, that would make it a total of nine items! You didn't choose all nine, did you?"

Venkat, the team's Product Owner replied this time, "Well, we wanted to. With Naomi not around, we expect to have a lot more free time, so we really want to get our hands dirty with some substantial team improvements."

Angela and Zach shot a concerned look at each other.

Venkat added in, "However, in doing so, the team realized that taking on too much work is one of our problems! When you said that it had to be just two, that actually led to many...shall we say...deep conversations about the prioritization. I really thought Iterative Prototyping should be in the top two, and really pushed for it."

At that moment, all eyes on the team looked up and looked at Venkat. He looked around at them, then lowered his own eyes and clarified their unspoken reaction, "Alright, yes, I'll own up to it... What I actually said was, 'I'm the Product Owner. I get to prioritize the backlog, and I pick prototyping, but you all can pick the other one.'"

There were some nods from around the group.

"Thanks, Venkat," Geena said, "I know it's not easy."

Zach and Angela looked around at the unexpected reactions. "What just happened?" Zach asked.

Venkat offered to explain. "The team – very helpfully – pointed out that I was 'dismissing others' contributions', not expressing 'appreciation', and not asking 'clarifying or confirming questions' before making that call."

This brought out smiles on Geena's and several other team members' faces.

Venkat continued, "We didn't really have a name for it before, but when we read about it in the Library..." He paused, looked over at Christina, the team's business analyst, and acknowledged her with a gracious smile, "actually, when Christina read about it in the Library, she pointed out that these behaviors were also things I complained about Naomi always doing to us, not listening to our opinions, making calls, and not being curious enough to ask questions. For all these reasons, we decided that mastering 'Connecting as Humans' should be at the top of the list."

"Besides," added Veni, a developer on the team, "prototyping is more a responsibility of the designers. We have a healthy relationship with them and they have learned not to ask us to paint the Sistine Chapel," she said with a chuckle. "So, we argued that the other two improvements were more important. We can do prototyping later."

Angela found herself desperately wanting to address Veni's statement. Outsourcing prototyping to the design team was an often-misunderstood anti-pattern, but she stopped herself. It wasn't what the team had chosen, and especially because they had chosen "Connecting as Humans", she reminded herself that had better listen and follow their lead.

She shifted back to their chosen topic, "Okay, this is interesting. Please continue."

"Sure!" replied Venkat, "Geena, you're up!"

One at a Time

"Right on!" Geena replied as she pulled up her iPad on the screen. They had already created a slideshow for their choices, and the first slide outlined their approach to Connecting as Humans.

Improvement: Connecting as Humans

Benefit Hypothesis – By actively focusing on Connecting as Humans, the team will increase productivity and morale, using the "wisdom of the crowd" to build improved solutions.

Customer Impact – Through listening, we will understand our customers' needs better and translate that into better solutions, gaining more market share back from Intuition. Through appreciation, we shall build greater trust and safety, and become more willing to take chances to improve delivery.

Evidence – Increase our user behavior metrics (Acquisition, Activation, Retention, Revenue, and Referral) through the release of one of our features.

Thank you, Geena," Angela responded after Geena recapped the first slide. "Before you go on to the next slide, though..." She turned and addressed the Product Owner, "Venkat, I want to applaud you for your willingness to be vulnerable, listen to your team, and be willing to change your mind, especially after being as forceful as you described. That is important!" She started clapping, and Zach joined her. Within a few seconds, everyone else was clapping too. Venkat seemed a little embarrassed, but accepted the applause graciously.

"I'm excited that you chose this one!" Angela enthused. "I'm also so pleased that you all felt comfortable enough to step forward and say something."

"I almost didn't," Christina blurted out. "The credit there goes to Geena. I mentioned how much Venakt sounded like Naomi as a snarky aside," she said, looking at Venkat before continuing. "But Geena said it was something that needed to be said out loud."

"Well then," Angela added, "appreciation for Geena too!" Geena held her palms together in front of her in a playful, yoga-style bow. "And," Angela finished, "great job everyone for sticking through the difficult conversation." More shy smiles appeared around her.

"Now," Angela said, shifting gears, "I'd like to ask a clarifying question. The story you told before about your team conversation was very much about Connecting as Humans, listening to each other within the team. The evidence I see on this slide, though, is about listening to customers."

She looked around at the puzzled expressions on their faces, and explained further, "Listening to each other and listening to customers certainly comes from the same place, but the Library draws a distinction between the two types of listening. Which one is the higher priority for your team? Is this more about listening to each other within the team, or listening to customers outside your team?"

"Oh no, did we do it wrong?" asked Geena, worriedly.

"No, sorry" Angela reassured her. "I don't want you to think that what you did was 'wrong'. This process isn't about right or wrong. I'm only pointing out the distinctions between the two types of listening, and you tell me which one is the higher priority."

"Oh I get it," interjected Christina. "Connecting as Humans can be done in both places, but you could spend all your time listening to customers, and not enough time listening to your teammates!"

"Exactly," confirmed Zach. "Especially when data is involved, it has to be causational."

Noticing Christina's eyebrow raise, Angela clarified, "Right, the word 'causal' here means that we want to be pretty confident that the changes we make actually *cause* the outcomes that we want." She put a really strong emphasis on the word 'cause' to drive home the point. "In this case, there are a lot of steps in between your efforts and any impact on the customer."

Angela brought it back around to her previous question, "And again, there's no right or wrong here. I just want to know which is more important to you, practicing listening to each other, or listening to the customer?"

Venkat looked around for confirmation as he answered for the team, "It's 'Connecting as Humans' within the team, right?" Heads nodded all around. "So... how do we tie that back to the customer?"

"It may not be easy to do," Angela confirmed, "but I'd like to hear from you all before I get involved."

"Isn't the answer right here in our hypothesis?" asked Sameer, one of the senior test engineers. "The 'wisdom of the crowd' will increase productivity and provide better solutions to customer problems. Whenever we've put our heads together in the past, the combined effort was always greater than the sum of the parts, and better solutions will help us beat Intuition."

"Ooh, that's good," said Geena as she started editing the slide. "I'm going to mix that in with what we already have."

"Great!" Angela exclaimed. "I like it!"

Customer Impact – As we build greater trust and safety, the 'wisdom of the crowd' will increase productivity and provide better solutions to customer problems, gaining more market share back from Intuition.

Leading versus Lagging Evidence

Angela moved on, reading their evidence out loud, "'Increase our user behavior metrics (Acquisition, Activation, Retention, Revenue, and Referral) through the release of one of our features.' Okay, how shall we change this to tie more closely to internal team collaboration?"

"Ok then," Christina tossed out, "our goal is for everybody to feel heard."

"Right," Zach added, "'heard' is the operative word there. You won't be able to do everything that everybody wants to do, but you'll never know what's truly possible if you don't listen first."

Geena chimed in, "I can take a poll at the end of each discussion and see if everybody got to express their ideas. I don't mind doing that. That could be our evidence."

"I like it," Zach confirmed. "It's a direct causal relationship between the change and the evidence." Geena started changing the slide.

"Wait," Sameer interjected, "what about the impact on the customer? I think we still need the customer metrics. I mean, I'm all for listening, but if listening to each other doesn't help gain market share, it's not enough."

"Sameer makes a great point," Zach agreed. "We could say that Geena's poll of who does or doesn't feel heard is the 'leading' evidence, and the customer metric is the 'lagging' evidence."

"What is lagging evidence?" Christina asked.

Zach responded, "'Lagging evidence' is essentially evidence that you capture after you have delivered your work. It's 'lagging' because it arrives after the work has already been done, so any changes you make in response would be counted as rework. 'Leading evidence' provides evidence that your hypothesis is working as you do your work, allowing you to make changes as you go."

Angela spoke up, "Right! Lagging evidence is necessary to confirm whether or not your hypothesis is correct, but it arrives too late. Our goal is to establish both leading evidence and lagging evidence. They work hand in hand. Leading evidence allows us to adjust our course of action with the least cost, and lagging evidence verifies if we chose the right leading evidence."

"Okay, I get it," Christina said, and several of the others nodded with her.

Angela beamed, "Splendid! Shall we talk about techniques?"

"Hold on, Angela," Zach interrupted, directing his attention at Venkat. "I didn't think we had any good customer metrics in place yet, so how were you going to baseline your lagging evidence?"

Venkat smiled bashfully, "Well actually, we were going to come to you to collect that data for us and we recognize that as a big dependency for achieving our improvement goal. Do you think you could add those by the next sprint?"

Zach's brow furrowed, "That statement also sounds a lot like Naomi..."

Angela noticed Venkat's horrified reaction and jumped in, "Venkat, we recently had a prioritization review by leadership of upcoming work to bring in and better customer metrics was a candidate, but unfortunately not selected yet."

Venkat looked disappointed, "Oh, that's unfortunate. What do we do then?"

"Do you already have some features in mind that you think will have an impact?" Zach asked.

Venkat responded, "Yes, we are working on changes to the account creation process to streamline the challenges our customers have been openly complaining about."

Zach lit up, "That I can help you with! Although the customer metrics would be wonderful to have, we don't need to have that as your lagging evidence. Since the account creation process has been producing a lot of Customer Service calls, how about we measure a decrease in the number of service tickets? I can pull the current number of calls about account creation and that can be your baseline."

Venkat and Geena responded together, "Right on!"

Zach smiled, "I really like service ticket reduction as a target since it will help free up my team's time to focus on other issues!"

Geena updated the slide again to reflect their new evidence.

Improvement: Connecting as Humans

Benefit Hypothesis – By actively focusing on Connecting as Humans, the team will increase productivity and morale, using the "wisdom of the crowd" to build improved solutions.

Customer Impact – As we build greater trust and safety, the 'wisdom of the crowd' will increase productivity and provide better solutions to customer problems, gaining more market share.

Evidence

[Leading] All team members feel heard after every discussion.

[Lagging] A decrease in the Churn Rate – the number of people who don't come back to the app.

[Lagging] A decrease in the number of service tickets related to account creation.

[Lagging] An increase in market share.

Pairing Problems with Solutions

"Wonderful!" Angela exclaimed. "Well, with this evidence, let me encourage you to take a look at 'Double Aces'. 'Reasoned Objections' from Sociocracy are also a great match."

"'Double Aces', is that what you were talking about the other day, Zach?" asked Geena.

"Yeah," Zach agreed, "Angela taught it to me a few weeks ago, and I've been working it into my daily habits. It's amazing how much of a difference it has had in everything I do! And there are many ways to work it in. It can become a formal part of daily stand-ups, sprint reviews, technical reviews, or especially sprint retrospectives – anytime there's the potential of disagreement or conflict."

"That sounds a lot like 'Yes, And...'" Geena added. "I learned that in an acting improv class. It's a powerful technique to promote psychological safety."

Christina raised her hand, "Why is it called 'Yes, And...'?"

Geena responded, "It asks you to consider how you could say 'Yes, And' when responding to another's idea as opposed to saying 'No, but'. This ties into acknowledging the other person's point of view."

Angela added, "Be sincere, though. If your answer really is a 'no', search for something else you can agree on. One great trick when you are just getting started is to practice writing down what you would say, and then read it to yourself to see how it sounds first. You can also practice with people you trust, such as family members or close friends who you can trust to give you feedback in a caring way and help you get better. If you give these a try, I think you'll be amazed by the improvements that can result in both your professional AND personal lives!"

"There's another variation on that called the 'Yes, if…'," offered Zach, "which was coined by a guy named Jim Damato, who was a coach at my last company. Instead of saying, 'No, because…' he would ask people to look for the reverse, 'Yes, we could do that, but only if…' something else happened."

"Let's do all of them!" Sameer suggested.

Venkat jumped in to slow them down, "Wait a minute! We still have to get work done in the sprint, you know. We already talked about the fact that we can't do all the things."

Geena turned to Angela and asked, "How long would it take to give us the formal introduction to Double Aces to see if we want to do more?"

"We can cover the main concepts in about an hour," Angela shared.

"Ok," Geena added, "I could teach some of the acting exercises I learned for 'Yes, And' in less than an hour too. What if we dedicated only one hour in the first week of the sprint to learning Double Aces, and one hour in the second week to learning 'Yes, And'?"

Zach jumped in, "I could show you how to do the 'Yes, If' variations without any extra time. We can just practice those during your existing Agile Ceremonies."

"What do you think, team?" asked Geena. "Should I schedule an hour? Raise your hand if you're on board with an hour each week."

The team nodded their heads in agreement and all the hands went up, albeit some of them faster than others.

All except Venkat, who insisted, "But there are ten people in this team. That's 20 hours of work! That's equivalent to one person spending half a week on this. That's a lot of wasted time!"

"*Yes,* Venkat," Angela responded, emphasizing the word 'yes' to telegraph what she was about to use the 'Yes, And' technique. "That is 20 hours total. *'And...',*" she said, emphasizing the word 'and', "the total number of hours across the whole team is ten times forty, which is 400 total hours in the week. That still works out to only 5% of your time spent on learning how to listen to each other and be more effective collaborators. Beware of pulling numbers like '20 hours' as isolated stats to make your point. Everything is relative. Compared to an entire week of work, or even eight hours in a day, does everyone think that they could spare fifteen minutes in a day to practice listening to others without impacting what you have committed to deliver?"

Most of the team nodded their heads 'yes'.

"I'll go one better," Geena inserted into the discussion. "'Yes'...," she said emphasizing the word, "we can minimize the disruption, 'If'..." she added, emphasizing the word 'if', "we group these activities with our existing collaboration time so that it doesn't interrupt our focused work time. I'll look for time in the schedule next to our other events like the Retro, or maybe right after a Daily Standup."

"Great example of 'Yes, If', Geena!" Zach said enthusiastically. "What about right before the Daily Standup, so people can practice using it during Standup?"

"Sure!" Geena agreed.

"Anything else to discuss here?" Angela asked as Geena jotted down some notes. Everyone shook their heads no.

THE REACH

A team called 'The Reach' was up next. They had chosen 'Prioritized Serial Delivery' as one of their improvements. Their Scrum Master, Natasha, had already displayed their initial improvement statement on the screen.

Improvement: Prioritized Serial Delivery

Benefit Hypothesis – Frequently switching work during delivery has impacted our team's velocity. By establishing a prioritized serial delivery, we will focus on "stop starting, starting finishing" increasing flow throughput.

Customer Impact – Through higher flow throughput, we will release more features faster, increasing our odds of regaining clients from Intuition.

Evidence – Velocity increases at least 10% within three sprints. The number of incomplete stories within a sprint decreases by at least 50% within three sprints

Benefit Hypothesis

Angela kicked off the discussion with a few questions, "Why did you choose this improvement?"

"Well," responded Natasha, "we each went through the guidance independently and made a list of the top five things that sounded like us. This one ended up on most of our lists. As we discussed it more, someone... I forget who... maybe Nic?" Their test engineer, Nic, raised his hand in confirmation, and several others nodded. "Yes, Nic, called out the line about how it's not enough to plan out the work, you must plan out how you are going to *finish* the work."

As she emphasized these words, Nic said them in chorus with her. "... and that's what stuck with us," she concluded. Others nodded their heads in confirmation.

"Yeah, as the resident curmudgeon here," added their Product Owner Joshua, "I can say that they're always constantly swiping, flipping, scrolling, and flicking through their phones."

"Okay, grumpy," confirmed Natasha as Joshua and the team laughed at their obviously common, shared joke. "Yeah, sure, it's easy to get bored with work. We admit it. We're constantly switching contexts. It's just life. It's part of being a super mom... but it also makes it hard to finish anything. We wanted to challenge this head-on."

"The realization for me," interjected Nic, "is that when you go back to work that's been set aside for too long, it takes extra time to remember exactly where you left off, costing time and effort. So we want to practice 'rewiring' our brains to not let go of something until it's done."

"It's okay to take breaks," Zach cautioned them, "even good for you, but I get it. You don't want to completely drop the task for too long."

"The trick is," Natasha said, answering Zach's suggestion, "figuring out how long is too long. I mean, definitely watch out for the weekends!" The team echoed her sentiments with knowing laughs. "You come back from a weekend, and you might as well start over! We kind of figured out that if you go more than a day before you return to something, it's hard to get back into the flow."

"I love it!" Angela chimed in enthusiastically. She redirected the conversation towards the evidence she saw on the screen. "So, how many stories do you typically accept into a sprint?"

"Usually between fifteen to twenty stories," Natasha responded, "depending on their average size."

"Okay, great!" Angela replied. "How many stories are incomplete at the end of the sprint? Do you know?"

Nic answered, "Well it used to be only three to four, but ever since Intuition hit the scenes, Naomi has been spinning the work around and we abandon about half of them."

Natasha jumped in, "Yes, it's pretty bad. Many of the stories from past sprints just never get done. They just sit there in the backlog, gathering dust."

"But now," added Joshua, closing out the thought, "with you taking over for Naomi, we're sure that you won't do that, and we can get back to locking down our sprint commitments!"

Angela nodded, "Okay... Just to be clear, I'm not taking over Naomi's job, but I can say that you are going to own your own Sprint Goals and Acceptance Criteria. Product Owners are going to be given control over the scope of the sprint."

Joshua smiled.

Angela continued, "Prioritized serial delivery is not only the responsibility of the Product Owner. It also involves the entire team. You will need to allow more time for collaboration, asking and answering questions about the backlog before you commit to work."

The team didn't agree or disagree. They just sat there listening, so Angela added some words of caution, "Please recognize that this is a very powerful team trait to master. Consider yourselves like the big, beefy bouncer to an elite club."

Sameer called out, “Like Patrick Swayze in ‘Roadhouse’!”

Veni laughed, “‘Roadhouse’?! How cheugy.”

Angela continued enthusiastically, “It fits, though! Members-only! Your stakeholders all want access to the club. Your goal is to allow people in only when you are ready. It’s like fire codes. If the club isn’t set up to handle the capacity, don’t let any more in.”

“Now,” Angela added, with a cautionary finger raised, “do not abuse that role. The bouncer has the power to say ‘no,’ but with that power comes the responsibility to always give a sufficient reason why. That’s where the Definition of Ready comes into play. The rules must be equally applied to all so there is no abuse of power. Is that clear?”

Nic asked, “Yes, as long as I can be Patrick Swayze.” The team laughed at the perfectly timed levity.

Angela smiled, “Yes, you can be Patrick Swayze,” she said before turning to look at Joshua, “As the PO, Joshua, can you commit the time to meet with the team, answer questions, and refine the backlog items?”

“Sure,” Joshua replied confidently. “Without Naomi, I will have more time to answer questions. Her market research requests and frequent backlog changes were taking most of my time. Now that she’s not breathing down my neck, I can definitely participate in backlog refinement meetings going forward.”

Angela tried to think of a way to minimize the Naomi-bashing but wasn’t able to think of anything in the moment, so she continued on. “Okay, are there any questions?”

Evidence, Not OKRs

The team’s lead developer, Susie raised her hand and asked, “I like the evidence that we came up with, but shouldn’t we also create Objectives and Key Results to track our progress?”

Angela beamed, “Oh yes, OKRs are very useful! However, they are normally applied at the Strategic level by Leadership, not at the team level for your improvement goals.”

Susie protested, “But at Amazon, they have a concept called ‘forcing functions’ that are created as a North Star used to guide a team’s direction before the team is even formed.”

Zach jumped in, “Correct me if I’m wrong, Angela, but AMMI improvements aren’t the same things as a North Star for a potential new product. The North Star metrics are more geared towards the product level than the team level."

"Yeah," Angela agreed, "and even one step higher. That kind of evidence is covered at the Organizational level in AMMI."

"That's why we picked this," Natasha clarified. Her tone suggested that they had already had this discussion as a team. "We wanted to understand our activities without spending too much time over-analyzing."

"But I've seen OKRs done at the team level," Susie insisted.

Angela paused for a moment before responding, "Did the OKRs look like a checklist of changes to be made?"

Susie thought for a moment and said, "Yeah."

"I see that a lot. Those aren't actual OKRs. Sometimes people create a checklist and put the name 'OKR' on it, but those aren't really OKRs. Unfortunately, it's way too complicated to get into here, and I don't want to take up everyone's time discussing the nuances, but if that is what you are thinking of then, yes, we do want checklists. Checklists are a great solution to help with prioritization, but let's remove the name of 'OKR'."

Prioritizing Prioritization Methods

"Okay, I'd like to set the stage for prioritization," Angela said, transitioning the conversation. "Almost everything in this category grows out of the truism that it doesn't matter how much work we do on an item if we don't get it done and out the door. Value in Agile is not measured by how much work you do. It's not like a timesheet. You only get value when the work crosses the finish line. This is the core problem addressed by Prioritized Serial Delivery."

"After the work gets done," she continued, "then, and only then, does it begin to matter how much time it took to get done versus the value to the customer. So our three core questions are, 'Is it worth doing, from a customer's standpoint?', 'Can we get it done?', and 'Is the amount of time worth it?' If it doesn't pass these three questions, we shouldn't work on it."

"But how do we answer these questions if we don't work on it?" Joshua asked, with a bit of snark and a raised eyebrow intended to raise a laugh. His attempt was vaguely successful.

"Fair enough," Angela agreed with a wry smile, "and that, Joshua, is a great definition of what we call 'refinement' or 'grooming' work in Agile, the minimum amount of work necessary to answer these questions, before we begin doing the actual work itself. The outcome of refinement should be prioritization."

"That's what is so hard about prioritization," Natasha lamented. "You don't know."

"Agreed," said Angela, "but we do know that if we split our time between multiple tasks, jumping back and forth, we slow down our ability to get any of them out the door. It's better to do a little research, and then just make a call."

"That's why," added Zach, jumping in, "in the early days of Agile, the Product Owner was given the role of prioritizing the backlog. The assumption was that the Product Owner was spending time with the customer and could put items in order based on customer need."

"Yes, but over time," Angela continued, picking up on his addition, "we discovered that it was just about customer priority. Time also matters, so refinement became a whole-team activity. So my first suggestion for you is called 'Weighted Shortest Job First'."

"I was taught MoSCoW prioritization," Joshua offered. "Does that work?"

"Moscow?" Susie asked. "Like Russia?"

Joshua wrote an uppercase 'M', lowercase 'o', uppercase 'S', uppercase 'C', lowercase 'o', and uppercase 'W' on the whiteboard. "It's that Must Have, Should Have, Could Have, and Won't Have system I give you," he said pointing to each of the uppercase letters.

"Wait," Susie asked, "is that why everything has a random 'M' on it?"

"Yeah," confirmed Joshua, "everything has been top priority recently."

"I don't think I've ever seen a 'C' or a 'W'," Susie remarked.

"Well, you shouldn't," Joshua returned. "I'm not going to send you unimportant things."

"Oh, okay... Thanks," she replied.

"That is one of the issues with MoSCoW," Angela interjected. "In teams that use it, it's actually pretty common for most things to be rated as 'M' over time, and then the ratings lose their meaning. I want to give you permission to ask for the reasoning behind each rating. That reason should be written into the description for the Feature and User Stories. Check the reasoning and make sure that it is tied to the customers. These are not our own personal Must Haves and Should Haves, regardless of our roles. These have to be customer or user-focused Must Haves and Should Haves. These have to be based on real words that came from an actual customer."

"I had to go by what Naomi told me," Joshua offered as his excuse. "I didn't get to talk to the customers."

"But now you will!" Zach countered. "We're going to add all the Product Owners to our customer testing, so in the future, you will have first-hand knowledge."

"You will also need to add something for Job Size," Angela added. "MoSCoW only covers customer value. For the size of a task, you will need a different system to pair with it."

"We could do Fibonacci estimates," offered Nic.

"We could," answered Susie, "but what if we don't know enough to score it yet?"

"Then I would suggest Assumptions Mapping by David Bland," Angela offered. "You place everything on a grid with 'Have Evidence' to 'No Evidence' on one axis and 'Unimportant' to 'Important' on the other axis." She drew the grid on the board as she explained it. "If something does not have a lot of recent evidence, then it is probably going to take longer."

"We could also use the Eisenhower Box," Natasha offered. She drew her own grid on the board as she explained a little further, "It's a system that President Eisenhower used. It's like Assumptions Mapping but it has Not Urgent to Urgent on the other axis. That way we have both an importance and a time measure."

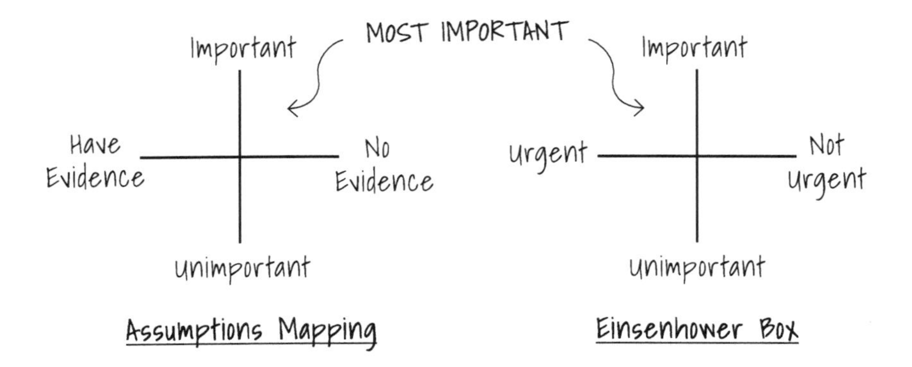

"Oh, I see what you're doing there," Angela said, starting with a quick appreciation, then quickly pivoting, wanting to spare them from her pain of decades of misused Eisenhower boxes. "The pitfall of the Eisenhower box is that once everyone knows that you're measuring Urgent versus Not Urgent, suddenly, surprisingly, everything becomes urgent!" she added with a smile.

She watched for the realization to spread over their faces, then continued, "No Evidence is less hackable as a measurement. Plus, we're less concerned here with Urgent, and more concerned with how fast something is to implement. Eisenhower doesn't solve our need for speed."

"I have the need!" called out Nic. "The need for speed!" He looked around incredulously. "What?! Nobody knows the movie Top Gun? It's a classic!"

"Cheugy," Susie simply offered in return.

"Saying cheugy is cheugy," Nic shot back, obviously annoyed.

Angela jumped in to head the conflict off with a chuckle, "I remember Top Gun, Nic! You can be my wingman any time." Nic smiled and gave her a huge double thumbs up. "Okay, great progress here, and I love the collaborations! Let's take a break before we move on to your second choice."

The Westerlands

The Westerlands were next on the list. It started with a brief recap of their selection process, after which their Scrum Master, VJ, displayed their first chosen improvement.

Mapping Customer Experiences

Improvement: Visualizing Customer Experiences

Benefit Hypothesis – Through systems thinking and Customer Journey Maps, a more complete solution will be developed, avoiding late-breaking rework.

Customer Impact – By focusing on UX, and building more complete workflows, we will find the most valuable features, and deliver them faster than Intuition.

Evidence – Decrease rework due to missed steps in our workflows.

“I think this hypothesis is great!” Angela said enthusiastically. “You’re listing the action, it looks like you’ve already chosen a technique to use from the AMMI Library, ‘Customer Journey Maps’, and you’ve highlighted ‘avoiding rework’ as your goal.”

”Wonderful!” VJ replied, while several of the other members of the team beamed with pride.

“Zach?” Angela asked. “Any notes?”

“Not on the Benefit Hypothesis. If we can switch, I’d like to look at this phrase about the ‘most valuable features’. How are you planning to determine which pieces are the most valuable?”

“MVPs!” exclaimed Enuma, their Product Owner. “By mapping out the customer flows we’ll also be able to identify what’s most important to the customers, and then we can deliver those parts first.”

“I was wondering if ‘most valuable features’ might take us into another category,” Zach mused.

Independent Variables

He turned to direct his thoughts out loud to Angela, “Are these really separate categories? Visualizing Customer Experiences is about identifying Value, and so is Prioritizing, and Minimum Viable Products. Maybe they should be combined together into one category about ‘Customer Value’.”

Angela had been expecting this question at some point. She had been warned by her own trainer that it was very common for people to want to change the AMMI categories, but not to do it.

“I’m going to ask that we not worry about the categories,” she explained. “The categories were designed after decades of scientific experimentation. Changes require scientific rigor, experimentation, and peer reviews, and I’d rather not get into that whole process. We are allowed to skip individual guidance points that don’t apply, though. We can also change the names of the categories so that they are easier to remember. That should be enough flexibility for our needs.”

Zach screwed his face up a bit in obvious skepticism so she expanded, “When you think about it, most things that we do are focused around ‘Customer Value’. That or team happiness. The categories are not about the goals, but instead about the obstacles between us and those goals.”

“AMMI”, she continued, “was designed around clear, tangible changes that can be done independently of each other to remove one obstacle at a time. You can prioritize without mapping and still see a boost in productivity, or you can map very effectively without prioritizing. You can prioritize without using Minimum Viable Products, or you can use MVPs even if you don't prioritize the order in which you build them."

"If you want to get super-technical," Angela continued cautiously, "as I was told, the categories are considered *independent* variables, meaning you will see a noticeable difference in performance, even if you only implement one category. *But* the Points of Guidance inside each category represent *dependent* variables – practices that are so intertwined that they all affect each other."

She looked around the room at glassy eyes and apologized, "But that is way too much detail! All we really need to remember is that every change requires time and effort."

She slowed down to emphasize the next point, "If you try to change too many things at once, it can quickly become overwhelming. When you're overwhelmed you skip steps or mix up instructions. If you make a big mistake, you may not solve an important problem, and then you won't see the intended benefit. It's better to make a couple changes at a time until you've internalized them, and then layer on the next improvement."

Angela let them ponder that for a while.

Zach eventually broke the silence, turning back to the team, "So, if you only get two, the question for the team is whether or not you want to choose both Visualizing Customer Experiences and MVPs as your two chosen improvements?"

"Works for me," enthused Samuel.

"No," interjected a voice from the back of the group, which had been silent until now. Bisby, whom Angela had met before as a member of Evah's testers, evidently had a concern.

Angela encouraged her, "Go ahead, Bisby."

Bisby began with a low intensity, "The point of this choice was to stop the rework. Stopping the rework is going to stop all of the retesting that is wasting our time." The intensity grew, "If we add MVPs, we're going to go back to delivering half-solutions, which will then have to get reworked and then we're stuck with double and triple testing. It's not what we agreed on."

Given Bisby's obvious courage in speaking up, Zach decided to back her up, "Sounds like a good discussion already happened here. I'm glad I brought it up. Would anybody object if we removed the part about most-valuable pieces? That would quickly bring us back in line."

Samuel acquiesced quickly, "Ok, ok. Focus is important. I think we can do it, but I won't object."

IMPACT IS ABOUT CUSTOMERS

Angela picked up a new thought, "I'm noticing that the impact statement is focused on internal impact. For this category in particular, I think it's important to center the description on the customer."

April, one of the developers, sheepishly raised her hand, "How is that not focused on the customer? We can build better products faster if we understand the user's full workflow before we start working on it."

"Yes," Angela said with a smile. "That's getting closer to customer impact."

"Wait..." April asked, perplexed, "how is what I said different from what's up there?"

"Great question," confirmed Angela. "I'm going to turn that back around to the group before I weigh in. I'm betting at least one person here sees it." She turned to the Scrum Master, "VJ, can you add April's version up next to the one that's there?"

"Sure," VJ agreed, "if she can repeat it."

April recapped her statement and VJ wrote it on the screen next to the original.

Customer Impact – By focusing on UX, and building more complete workflows, we will find the most valuable features, and deliver them faster than Intuition.

Customer Impact – We'll build better products faster if we understand the full workflow of the user before we start working on it.

Angela let the question sit out there as the team read through the two statements again.

Samuel, the team's Product Owner, took the bait after about fifteen seconds of silence, "I think I know what you're looking for. In UX we spend a lot of time rewriting things from the customer's point of view."

Angela smiled and encouraged him to keep going. The wheels in his brain were turning in the right direction.

Noticing her silent prompt, Samuel continued, "It's not just about building, either. Building things is our work. Through mapping the process — their process — we will not only design better experiences for our customers, but by eliminating rework, we'll be able to do it faster. That will decrease their frustration, and increase retention and growth."

VJ added Samuel's version next to the other two.

Customer Impact – Through mapping the customer's process we will design better experiences for our customers, and do it faster by eliminating rework, thereby decreasing customer frustration and increasing retention and growth.

"That's what I was thinking," Angela confirmed.

"So," April added in, "the point is more that we rewrote the Impact section from the customer's perspective?"

Angela confirmed April's summary, "That actually makes a huge difference! The Impact section should be directly traceable in some way to our customers. Writing it from the customer's point of view is critical here, or else you might fail to satisfy their needs without even realizing it." Angela let the thought settle in for a bit.

As some of them started to refocus their eyes on her, she moved on, "Okay, as for evidence, how could we measure progress building features faster and with less rework?"

VJ answered, "Higher customer usage?"

Samuel caught on fast, "Yes, we should expect better customer survey results for those features that use User Story Mapping."

"That would fit," Angela agreed. "Are you all familiar with leading versus lagging evidence?"

"We are," Bisby offered. "Leading comes before the work is done, and Lagging is measured afterwards."

Angela smiled, "Great! This is lagging evidence. Do we have any leading evidence?"

Initially, nobody answered. After a moment, though, April raised her hand.

Angela pointed at her and April offered, "Naomi and the Design team started doing monthly 'feedback loops' with customers back when we were studying the Phoenix Project[1]. Perhaps we could collect their feedback and look for improvements?"

"Yes, April, that's right!" Samuel responded. "We could track the number of changes they approve, change, or reject and see if they approve more of the features that have been mapped."

"First," Angela said, starting with appreciations, "great job at finding a way to directly interact with your customers! Second, fantastic idea to use this opportunity to get ahead of problems! Third, I think that would actually make this inverted data," Angela added. "You actually want the number of changes and rejects to be higher, earlier in the process."

Samuel and the rest of the team looked at her with a quizzical look. "I'm not sure I understand 'inverted'," he responded. "Aren't we supposed to find the mistakes before they do?"

"Yes," Angela explained, "we can uncover mistakes earlier, but only the customers can tell us if it solves their problem and if they love it. Maps are the fastest way to get this feedback, but they don't have a lot of detail. As we add more detail, like with mockups, prototypes, and proofs-of-concept, we get better feedback, but our effort keeps increasing. And all of these are easier to do than changing code, architectures, and databases."

VJ, who had been typing away at the computer, brought them back around the task at hand, "Okay, I took a stab at updating our evidence based on the conversation. Does this look good?"

Evidence

[Leading] An increase in changes to the workflow maps after early customer feedback.

[Leading] Decrease the number of rejected demo items.

[Lagging] Increase customer survey feedback scores for those features that used User Story Mapping.

"These are great!" Angela replied. "Plus the data here about rejected demo items, and customer survey scores will be useful for many of our teams!"

VJ smiled as everyone nodded in agreement.

THE CROWNLANDS

Meeting in the Middle

Angela found herself a little uneasy as she and Zach planned their next session. "This is the team that tried to cancel, right?" she asked Zach.

"Yeah," Zach confirmed. "Their official response was, 'We're good.'"

"Just a little resistance, huh?" Angela said jokingly.

"When I explored further," Zach expanded, "they said that their biggest obstacle was Naomi, and now that she's gone, they think they're doing just fine."

"Hmm... There's always something to improve," Angela mused as she pondered their best approach.

"I know, right?" agreed Zach. "No team is perfect."

"Even staying away from the word 'perfect'," Angela expounded, "there are three levels to the AMMI catalog and almost one hundred points of guidance in each level. There are lots of places to explore."

"Yeah," agreed Zach, "well we have often had problems with this team thinking that they're better than everyone else. And they're really good technically, but not so great at people skills. But they also don't have enough people skills to see that, so it's hard to get them to focus on learning better people skills, which creates a paradox."

"Aaah, that kind of team," Angela commiserated. "Not everybody is ready for change. If we're not successful here, don't let it weigh on you."

"Moveables versus immovables, right?" confirmed Zach. "No, I get it. I am afraid that they're immovables."

"Let's hope they're just skeptics," Angela said optimistically. "I can work with skeptics."

---

1 "The Phoenix Project", by Gene Kim, *https://itrevolution.com/product/the-phoenix-project/*, 2013

Angela figured that she better collect as much information as she could before walking into the room. She sent messages to Linda and Jayson to gather their insights.

Happily, there was time after lunch to get together and brainstorm. "My goal by the end of this session," Angela began as they all sat down together, "is to make a list of problems that we may have heard expressed by the Crownlands team at some point in the past."

Linda and Zach nodded their heads in confirmation.

"What if," Jayson countered, "we score the team ourselves to see if we can identify their biggest bottlenecks?"

"I could meet you halfway," Angela offered in return. "Two problems that I want to make sure we keep in mind with AMMI, especially when we have a team that is resistant, are Intrinsic Motivation and that we don't use AMMI as a weapon."

"Whoah," Jayson replied defensively. "I only proposed filling out the assessment ourselves, not turning it into a weapon."

"I know," agreed Angela, instantly dropping into an appreciation to help reconnect with Jayson. "You have a great reputation for being on the side of your teams. The developers love you here, and I bet you could present your version of the spreadsheet and they would accept your insights and try their hardest to live up to your expectations."

She paused. That had given her a thought. "Say, that's a good point. Could you join Zach and me for this session? I think that would help them to really take this seriously if they see you taking it seriously."

"Sure," Jayson agreed, cautiously, "if I'm not in a meeting that I can't get out of. Now back to this weaponization part?"

Angela clarified, "I am not at all talking about your actions here. It's only about their perceptions. There is nothing in what you are doing or what you are proposing that will be weaponizing AMMI. When a team is potentially resistant like this one, usually... not always... but usually, we find that they have adopted a mindset of 'us versus them' and no matter what we do, they will see everything that we do through that mindset. It's like wearing a pair of blue-tinted glasses. We might have the best of intentions, but those good intentions will be like red light which cannot be seen by someone wearing blue lenses."

"To stretch that analogy further," she continued, "what I want to do is to make sure that what we are presenting is based on their perspective, in the color blue, so that they can see that we're trying to help. After we are all seeing the world in the same way, then we can help them see new things."

Jayson pondered this a moment and then tried to put it into his own words. "So I have a friend, Keith, who's color-blind. He has a special pair of glasses that help him to see a wider range of colors. This is like Keith's glasses?"

"Clever analogy," Angela replied, "but what I'm proposing is that we put their blue glasses on first, and that we do *not* try to decide what glasses they should wear. We start by seeing the world the way they see the world, by changing our glasses first. After they learn to trust that we see what they see, then we can offer them a different pair of glasses so that they might see our point of view. But it starts with us putting on their glasses."

"This reminds me of someone I used to know," Linda chimed in. "Her name was Ellen. She struggled with understanding other points of view. Her way of helping was to put herself in their shoes, figure out what she would do in their situation, and then help them do that."

"Heaven forbid, though," Linda continued, "if they wanted to do something different than what she came up with. She would get *soo* angry." Linda modified her voice and did an impersonation she had obviously done many times before, "'Why won't they let me help them?!!' she would mutter, but she never actually cared about learning why. Others would ask me to intervene, but there was nothing I could do. Eventually, everyone would just cave in and do it Ellen's way so that she'd be happy and go away. Then they'd go back to redo it their way."

"I learned a lot from her," she added, with a wistful sadness, "about the line between good help and bad help. It's not helpful if other people don't see it as help. You have to understand what kind of help they want, from their point of view, or else they will just go around you."

Angela smiled with sadness in her eyes at what seemed like a hard-learned lesson.

After a few moments of silence, Zach asked, "Wasn't Ellen your mom's name?"

"Good memory, Zach," confirmed Linda. "Yeah. That was my mom." She touched the corners of her eyes a little bit but then took a deep breath and instantly bounced back to her cheery self. "Anyway... So, I agree with Angela. There's no guarantee that it will work, but it's probably the best strategy we've got."

"Thanks, Linda," Angela replied, "and I'm sorry about your struggles."

"I appreciate it," Linda replied warmly.

"Okay. Understood," Jayson chimed in. "What do you want us to do then, Angela?"

"Well," Angela clarified, "I'd like to brainstorm some problems from their point of view – problems that are happening ***to*** them. It could be a problem that's been around so long that they've stopped trying to solve it. Maybe they brought up the problem in the past, but nothing was done about it, so they stopped bringing it up. I want to know what they complain about, and how they talk about it in their own words."

"From their point of view..." Jayson mused, thinking deeply about Angela's challenge.

"They don't like estimating each other's work," Zach offered. "Sometimes I'll sit in on planning sessions and the dev will offer a size of five, QA will offer a size of three, and then they'll just add up the score and call it an eight. There's no discussion, no alignment, and no cross-learning. One day when I called them on it someone said, 'Who am I to tell QA how long it takes to do their job?' If you want words, those are the words they used."

"That is definitely a problem," agreed Linda, "but they are not going to see that as their problem."

"They hate being told what to do," Zach suggested as an alternative.

"There are too many meetings," Jayson added. "They are often very frustrated with how many meetings they have to go to. I try to instill in them the importance of collaboration, but you can tell that they don't really want to be there."

"That's a good one," Angela said enthusiastically. She added it to her list of candidates.

"They don't have a good Definition of Ready," Linda offered, but then retracted. "That's what I want, though. Hmm... How about... there's a lot of rework because there's no Definition of Ready. No, again, they see that as the designers' fault, not theirs."

Angela took note of it anyway. They might be motivated to do less work.

Jayson picked up on Linda's comment about the designers, "Sometimes they complain about the designs that they get from the Designer Den. They say that they're 'ridiculous', 'stupid', and 'over-complicated'."

They continued brainstorming until they reached the end of their timebox and it gave Angela some optimism about what was coming up next, but she still had some lingering dread. She didn't have a guess as to which problem was going to inspire the team... if any.

Working Sessions, Not Meetings

Angela kicked off the Crownlands session with enthusiasm, but it quickly ground to a standstill. "There's nothing in all three levels of the AMMI catalog that looked interesting?" she found herself asking the team.

"No, there really wasn't," confirmed their Scrum Master, Omar. "Like we told Zach, our main obstacle was Naomi, and she's gone now. And the other areas didn't apply to us. The designers handle the Design category. Product takes care of Planning. We already do everything in the Implementation category, and all of our Verification and Operations are automated. We're good."

"What about the practices in the Product and Organization levels?" Angela asked, prodding them further.

"What about them? They're not our job," Omar countered. "That's your stuff, right?"

Angela knew this wasn't true, but she also knew well enough that this wasn't about whose job it was.

"What problems would you like to see solved?" Jayson asked, wading boldly into the conversation.

"You want to help us with something?" sniped Cory, one of the developers. "How about the meetings? I have so many meetings I don't have time left to do my actual job."

The other developers and the PO chimed in, agreeing with Cory. Angela got excited and a smile crept across her mouth without her realizing it. *"Is this the problem? The one they've given up on?"* she wondered.

She tested the idea a little further, "What if we could get rid of a bunch of meetings? Between the three of us," she said, pointing to herself, Zach, and Jayson, "I bet we could eliminate a few unnecessary meetings."

"Sure," Cory said noncommittally.

Angela clarified, "How many hours do you think you spend in meetings now?"

Omar started counting them off, "There are Daily Standups, Sprint Planning, Sprint Retro, Sprint Review, Backlog Grooming, Scrum of

Scrums, Jayson's Tech Talk CoP, Product Sync, the Weekly Status Review meeting..." He continued counting meetings, making a list of over fifteen meetings before he was done, most of them lasting more than an hour each. His final tally was about fifteen hours of meetings per week.

Angela was astonished, as were Zach and Jayson. "Fifteen hours of meetings every week?" she confirmed. "That's an average of three hours of meetings per day!"

"You don't have to tell us," Cory quipped.

Omar jumped in to give further insight, "We had decided a while back not to have meetings in the afternoons so that everyone had time for focused, uninterrupted work. We also designated Fridays as 'meeting-free Fridays.'"

"Nice," Zach replied.

"Seemed that way, until it wasn't," Cory shot back. "'Meeting-Free Fridays' gave us a chance to skip the commute and work from home uninterrupted, but then everyone just started joking about us taking a three-day weekend." Audible grumbles of frustration percolated around the room. "Eventually no one else respected our reserved time. They just treated it as available and kept inviting us to things."

"Yeah, and when we protested," added their automation tester, Saima, "they would just go to the managers and say that we weren't being 'collaborative' and force us to go." Saima punctuated her remarks by sitting back in her chair, folding her arms, and staring at the three leaders. She seemed to be particularly staring at Jayson, though he didn't register a response.

Omar jumped to the team's defense, "We even tried setting up a policy to not disturb us when we have our headphones on, but they didn't respect that either. After a while, they would just come up and tap you on the shoulder. When you're in a groove, no one likes being jarred out of it by someone banging on your shoulder."

This prompted Guilford, another developer who had tucked himself into the corner, to unexpectedly break his traditional silence, "I've told them before. 'Don't touch me.' But nobody listens."

"To be fair, Gil," Jayson said, challenging him. "I don't think I've ever seen you with your headphones off."

"That's because no one respects my time!" spit out Gilford, angrily.

Secret AMMI

Angela saw an opening to reach the team but also saw it slipping away as they started to get carried away by reliving the emotions of past battles in vivid detail. She decided to jump in and test the opening that they had given her, but first, she had to get them back on track.

Three concepts immediately jumped into her head as she remembered similar situations from the past: "amygdala hijacks", Double Aces, and problems-first. Several people in the room were already in "amygdala hijack" mode. They were hurt, and their reactionary emotional brains had taken over. This reminded Angela of the work of neuroscientist Jill Botle Taylor[2]. She knew she needed to give them time to cool off, and according to Taylor, that was going to take about ninety seconds for the emotions to process themselves through the brain. So she needed to use up ninety seconds without getting them upset with her. Not an easy task.

Double Aces recommended starting with appreciations. A lot of opinions had just been expressed and then skipped over by the other people in the room. Spending time letting people know that they had been heard and that someone was taking them seriously seemed like a good use of ninety seconds.

Thirdly, being there as part of the AMMI process reminded her that we usually fight over solutions, but find common ground through hearing each other's problems. At that moment Angela made a quick mental calculation and decided to review the conversation up to that point, appreciating each of the views expressed, and reverse-engineering their statements into the problems that they were feeling.

She quickly began with a framing, "This is the struggle here, isn't it? Balance, trust, and respect..." She spoke calmly and slowly, but without leaving gaps that might encourage people to jump in and try to take over the conversation.

"I'm also frustrated on your behalf at how your needs have gone unheard for so long. If you've given up on asking for changes, I understand, but I think it's important to capture them as we go. Zach, do you

---

2 "Whole Brain Living" by Jill Bolte Taylor: *https://www.drjilltaylor.com/whole-brain-living/*

mind writing these things down as I review them?" She pointed him towards the whiteboard so that it would be visible to all.

"Oh, uh, no," confirmed Zach, caught off guard at first, but then grabbing a whiteboard marker.

Angela continued, "First, Gil, no one should touch you without your permission. I want to put that problem at the top of the list. Especially after you have asked that others respect your personal space. I'm sorry that happened, Gil, that it has *been* happening to you, multiple times." Guilford nodded in acknowledgement of being heard.

Angela carried that back a step, "After all, you were just wearing your headphones so that you could have a chance to focus, get in the groove, and tackle some big problems. Do you know that it can take almost thirty minutes[3] to get back on task? That's why we built campfires and cave spaces in the office in the first place. Reserved, dedicated, sacrosanct time to focus on work is important. Some work cannot get done without large blocks of uninterrupted time." She pointed to Zack to make sure to write that down.

She went further, "What I'm hearing is that you all tried out various different approaches to carve out a balance, and one by one each was dismantled by the other teams. I, for one, admire your flexibility and creativity in testing out multiple approaches! Great job!" She nodded at Zach and Jayson as she said this, encouraging them to join her appreciation, but didn't wait for them to add their voices.

"Let's forget the AMMI stuff," she tossed out, testing a revised approach. She wasn't really going to abandon the AMMI approach, but she was going to abandon the formal AMMI assignment. "I want to help you find that right balance, and I promise to work with the other teams to respect that balance once we find it. So the question is 'What is the right balance?'"

She moved right along from her rhetorical question without giving them a chance to respond. "Zach, can I borrow the marker?" She took over from him at the whiteboard. "I'd like to start by rewriting everything as problem statements. On one side we have personal and physical bound-

---

3 "The Cost of Interrupted Work" by Gloria Mark, Daniela Gudith, and Ulrich Klocke: *https://ics.uci.edu/~gmark/chi08-mark.pdf*

aries being broken without consent." She wrote the problem statement next to Zach's notes.

"We also have team norms being ignored, but why is that a problem?" She continued, thinking out loud without pausing as a way to demonstrate without turning it into a formal lesson. "This sentence is essentially saying that we shouldn't ignore team norms, but that's really a solution statement... Let's see... We want people to respect team norms. Why? What problem does establishing team norms solve? Well... you form them together. It's about consent. It's actually not very far off from this original problem statement. The problem is forcing someone to do something without their agreement, right?" She turned to write that on the board.

Over her shoulder, she heard Jayson reply, "In the military, you often don't have the luxury of getting to talk it out."

Angela cringed a bit. That was not going to help. "True," she countered, "but we're not in a life-or-death situation here, so time is on our side. That gives us more options."

"Well, this is kind of life-or-death," Jayson answered, "for the company. If we don't figure out how to combat Intuition, that could mean the death of Breeze, or Ares, or ABS."

"Not really," shot back Zach. "Breeze might die, but then we'd just work on something else. Let's admit it. Nothing we do here is going to take down ABS Bank."

"Agreed," asserted Linda, with a nervous laugh. "We're not talking about physical death here. The stakes aren't that high."

Angela could feel them starting to get off track again, but she remembered her training. She needed to write down every problem that came up so that people felt heard. They could address the relative severity of the problems later.

"But a problem is a problem," she said out loud. "Let me add that to the board. Without a solution for Intuition, ABS might shut down the Breeze app. It's valid, and that problem doesn't go away, but I also think we're getting away from the team's immediate problems," she added as a reminder to Jayson, Linda, and Zach of the approach that they had agreed on.

"Right, too many meetings," Linda offered, bringing them back on topic.

"Yes, too many meetings," Angela confirmed, "and what I heard behind that was not enough unbroken time to concentrate, get into the flow, and solve big problems. What else sucks about meetings?"

"Having to sit there," offered Cory, "and listen to things that have nothing to do with you."

"Good one," Angela replied. "When the agendas aren't well planned out, people don't know if they're needed or not."

"If there even is an agenda," sniped Saima.

"Ah, yes," agreed Angela, "not having an agenda is a big problem. I'll write that down as wasting people's time listening to things that don't apply to them."

"What if it does apply to you?" asked Zach. "Would that mean that the meeting is okay?"

"Not when it could have been an email," Omar offered.

"That's a good question," Angela proposed. "When is a meeting appropriate and when is it not? What's the dividing line?"

"When we've got questions," Gil answered.

"What about if the other team has questions?" asked Linda.

Gil answered, "Send us the questions and if we can send you the answers we will."

"And if you can't," Linda clarified, "then we might need a meeting?"

"I guess," reluctantly offered Gil.

"What if they have questions about your answers?" Linda asked, pushing him further.

"Now we're getting into endless message chains," said Zach with exhaustion in his voice.

"Sounds like a problem," Angela called out, writing it on the board.

Problems

- Forcing someone to do something without their agreement.
- ABS might shut down the Breeze app.
- Need unbroken time blocks to concentrate.
- Wasting people's time listening to things that don't apply.
- One-way meetings that could have been a message.
- Endless message chains.

There was a momentary lull in the brainstorming so Angela jumped in, "Let me see if I can sum things up here. You'd like people to send you a message first outlining why they need your time. If you can answer them in a message you'd prefer to do that first. If it can't be settled in a couple of messages, then that might be a reason to get together, but it needs to be scheduled so as to not interrupt your unbroken concentration time."

There were no immediate protests from the team, and a few heads nodded, so Angela nudged them for a verbal confirmation, "Any more?"

"Seems about right," Omar offered. No one else resisted.

"Ok. Good," Angela replied. "This reminds me of a technique: 'Working Sessions'. The philosophy behind Working Sessions is that meetings are bad and to be avoided as much as possible."

Some heads nodded in agreement as she continued on. "Now they define a meeting as any time you get together to talk about something without actually doing anything. That means you then have to leave the room and go do the thing that you were just talking about. In a Working Session, by the end of the time block, you must get something done so that you don't have to think about it anymore. If you can't get something done in the time block, then don't schedule the session."

"Makes sense," Omar offered.

"Does that rule out brainstorming sessions?" asked Saima.

"How do you mean?" clarified Angela.

"Well," explained Saima, "If we're brainstorming, we're just coming up with ideas to work on in the future."

Angela turned the question to the team, "What do other people think? Is brainstorming a Meeting or a Working Session?"

Their Product Owner piped up, "Isn't making a decision an outcome if we don't have to think about it anymore? For example, prioritizing and choosing tasks could be an outcome, or designing a spike or proof of concept, even if we don't work on it. Each of those can be decisions that we don't have to think about again."

"Yeah," countered Cory, "but do you need us there to prioritize? Just tell us the order that you want things."

"But that order," Hal protested, "depends on how long it's going to take."

"I see where this is going," Jayson offered. "Hal, you could present your prioritized list to the team and ask for size estimates. They could send you sizes and if it doesn't change your order, no meeting. If the sizes do make a difference then it could become a Working Session, but your job is to do the first two steps before the Working Session. That would respect all of the problems in this list."

"So," echoed Saima, "a brainstorming session is a working session if it can't be handled as an email, and if we can make a decision by the end?"

"I think so," Zach agreed with an encouraging smile.

"Huh," was her noncommittal reply.

While they had been talking, Angela had been writing out their thoughts on the board.

Proposal

- Meetings: Daily Standup, Planning, Retro, & Review.
- Working Sessions: Anything else:
    1. Request Information (message)
    2. Team replies to request (message)
    3. Omar schedules a working session outside reserved time (if needed)

"Here's my proposal for you," Angela suggested, walking through the items in her list. "If you're up for it, we can try an experiment for the next couple of sprints. I will work to take you off as many meetings as possible. The only meetings you will have to attend will be the Daily Standups, at fifteen minutes per day. Then the Retro, Planning, and Review sessions for one hour each, every other week. And Refinement for one hour each week."

She clarified, "That works out to only seven and a half hours of meetings per sprint, an average of forty-five minutes per day, a fraction of the three hours per day that you currently spend in meetings. That's the first half of the deal.

"The second half," she continued, "is that if anyone else wants your time – the other teams, the managers, myself – we must first tell you why, give you a chance to respond, and only if it requires further discussion will we schedule a Working Session with a clear agenda and list of who needs to be there. And we will work with Omar on the schedule so that we respect your dedicated working hours."

"Linda? Jayson? Do you think we can do that? Does that sound like a worthy experiment to see how it goes for at least a couple of sprints?"

Jayson didn't look happy but reluctantly agreed. Angela made a mental note to follow up after the session.

She asked the rest of the room, "Team, does this sound like a good experiment?"

They looked at each other for a while and shrugged back and forth, but no one objected.

"I'd like to do a formal poll, please," Angela responded. "Can you please give me a thumbs up if you're willing to support the experiment, a thumbs down if you're not, and a thumbs sideways if you'd rather abstain."

Fists slowly raised around the room as they looked at each other. Some thumbs started up, a couple down, then moved sideways. Others moved from sideways to up. Only Gil's thumb stayed as a thumbs down.

"Why a thumbs down, Gil?" Angela asked.

"I don't think the other teams are going to respect it," he responded.

"That's our job to work with them," Angela countered. "In fact, we should have some way to measure that." She wrote the word "Evidence" on the board and asked Omar for help, "Omar, if we work on getting everybody to go through you, can you track how many meeting requests have clear asks?"

"Also ask how fast they want an answer," Zach added. "Like Customer Service, some things need a quick reply and others don't."

"Okay," agreed Omar. "I'll get a goal from everyone and their urgency. Say, I could announce them at the daily standup and see who has the time to respond."

Angela captured it as 'Evidence' on the board.

Evidence

- No more than 5.5 hours of meetings per sprint.
- Meeting requests have clear goals and urgency.
- All requests get a response depending on urgency.
- If multiple messages are exchanged, schedule a Working Session.

"Does that help, Gil?" she asked.

"Sure," Gil reluctantly agreed, adding, "but I still don't want to go to the Sprint Review and the Retros."

"Come on," Jayson asserted, a little fed up, "it's a better deal than you have right now. If you're only willing to work by yourself, I'll find you something else to work on."

Gil pondered it for a few moments, then reluctantly pointed his finger to the side.

"Thank you, Gil," Angela said appreciatively.

"Thanks, Gil," Jayson echoed. Gil nodded.

Angela turned and added the title "Working Sessions" above her notes.

Working Sessions

Problems

- Forcing someone to do something without their agreement.
- ABS might shut down the Breeze app.
- Need unbroken time blocks to concentrate.
- Wasting people's time listening to things that don't apply.
- One-way meetings that could have been a message.
- Endless message chains.

Proposal

- Meetings: Daily Standup, Planning, Refinement, Retro, & Review.
- Anything else:
    1. Request Information (message)
    2. Team replies to request (message)
    3. Omar schedules a working session outside reserved time (if needed)

Evidence

- No more than 5.5 hours of meetings per sprint.
- Meeting requests have clear goals and urgency.
- All requests get a response depending on urgency.
- If multiple messages are exchanged, schedule a Working Session.

Angela felt her whole body relax and breathed a sigh of relief for the hard work they had just accomplished.

THE NORTH

After leaving the Crownlands, the final two teams were the team of designers, which was called the "Dorne" team, and Jayson's system team, which was simply called "North", or technically "The North", supposedly another name from the Game of Thrones that was foreign to Angela.

Jayson was with Angela and Zach again for this session, since he acted as the Tech Lead for The North. He kicked things off by explaining the team's decision process, "Since our job is helping other teams complete items in their own backlogs, 'Shared Better Practices' from the Product level seemed like the perfect fit for us. We've been itching to do these kinds of improvements for a long time and have a lot of energy to push it through."

Improvement: Shared Better Practices

Benefit Hypothesis – Teams will increase their rate of improvement through collaboration if techniques are shared through a centralized location and managed by a single responsible party.

Customer Impact – By eliminating less-efficient and less-effective practices faster through knowledge sharing, we will accelerate our delivery of solutions and get ahead of Intuition.

Evidence – At least one new improvement is adopted every month from the knowledge base. At least two new entries are added to the knowledge base each month.

"Okay, this should be exciting!" Angela said enthusiastically. "Just beware," she added, "that the time spent is worth the time saved. Set up a time budget for each idea. If you think you're going to recoup two hours of time each week per person, then only spend two hours of time each week implementing it. If not possible, then the payoff may not be worth the time invested."

"I really like that idea," Jayson volunteered. "I'll add that to our evidence section."

Sharing Benefits

Angela noticed that she had been talking too much and Zach seemed to be itching to join in, so she passed it over to him. "Zach, would you like to lead this review?"

Zach's face brightened and he picked up the cue. He dove in immediately and kicked off with some appreciations, "I see a great statement of the parameters of the experiment. I see a centralized location and responsible parties. My main question on the hypothesis is how will we know that the shared practices are improvements? What if we share practices that don't make us better?"

This surprised everybody, even Angela. It was a great question and she smiled broadly, eager to see how they would respond.

"Well," a developer named Benita offered, "Angela gave us the answer when she presented us with this challenge."

Angela found herself puzzled.

Benita clarified, "The answer is good evidence. We are not going to just share better practices. We are also going to share metrics that teams can use to report their evidence before and after, just like we're doing with these improvements."

Zach, looking impressed said, "That would do it for me, Benita! Thanks! What about you, Angela?"

"That's a great idea!" Angela agreed. "It fits perfectly. Great job, Benita!"

The Scrum Master, Taneesha, updated the hypothesis to match and asked for feedback, "What do you all think of this wording?"

Benefit Hypothesis – Teams will increase their rate of improvement through collaboration, if techniques are shared through a centralized location and managed by a single responsible party, along with metrics that are both shareable and comparable.

Everybody nodded their heads in agreement so Zach read the next part out loud.

Customer Impact – By eliminating less-efficient and less-effective practices faster through knowledge sharing, we will accelerate our delivery of solutions and get ahead of Intuition.

"That looks pretty good to me," he added. "Angela, anything you want to add?"

Angela used the Double Aces technique and started her feedback by outlining the positives, as Zach had done with the hypothesis. "I like the stated goal of faster improvement through knowledge sharing. It also clearly calls out that in order to get ahead of Intuition, we need to get a lot faster at delivering solutions. I can't actually think of any improvements right now."

So Zach read out the evidence section.

Evidence – At least one new improvement is adopted every month from the knowledge base. At least two new entries added to the knowledge base each month.

Benita raised her hand. "Go ahead," Zach prompted her.

Benita suggested, "I think we need to add a reference to the use of shared better practices. Maybe, 'At least one new improvement adopted every month from the knowledge base along with comparable metrics,' and 'At least two new entries added to the knowledge base per month along with repeatable metrics.'"

"Plus," Taneesha added, "I'm going to insert the part about the time budget."

Zach nodded his head, and Angela too, followed by the rest of the team. Taneesha updated the description on the screen.

Improvement: Shared Better Practices

Benefit Hypothesis – Teams will increase their rate of improvement through collaboration, if techniques are shared through a centralized location and managed by a single responsible party, along with metrics that are both shareable and comparable.

Customer Impact – By eliminating less-efficient and less-effective practices faster through knowledge sharing, we will accelerate our delivery of solutions and get ahead of Intuition.

Evidence – At least one new improvement is adopted every month from the knowledge base along with comparable metrics. [Leading] At least two new entries are added to the knowledge base per month, along with repeatable metrics. Every improvement has an estimated time savings and the implementation can not take longer than the time savings.

"Remember, this requires recruiting other teams to participate, but your team shall be the catalyst. The lion's effort of work to progress this improvement will be on you. Make this as easy on them as possible."

Everyone agreed.

Communities of Practice

To wrap things up, Zach asked, "What made you decide to address Shared Better Practices?"

Taneesha responded, "I was recently talking to one of the Scrum Masters and realized she had some great tips on managing the backlog and the flow of work I had not considered. That got me excited so I shared some of my practices with her in gratitude."

"And when Taneesha mentioned that," a tester named Nathan interjected, "I shared how Jayson holds similar 'Tech Talks' every other week that are essentially the same thing. We realized that a lot of great practices are getting lost between teams. We need more collaboration."

Angela felt invigorated, "Yes! Shared Better Practices is a great way to address that! I would suggest starting by establishing a Scrum Master Community of Practice. I don't think you have one yet, right? I've only heard about Jayson's Tech Talks and Evah's Quality Engineering CoP. It's important to have one for each key discipline."

"I wonder if we could add that to Linda's monthly meeting," Taneesha asked out loud. "She already holds a session for all of the Scrum Masters."

"Great idea, Taneesha," Angela agreed. "We can go talk to Linda about it. I bet she'd enjoy that."

"Wonderful!" Taneesha happily responded. "What else do we need to do?"

After a long pause, Benita spoke up, "Per our hypothesis, I highly recommend having a centralized system of record that is separated by department: Design, QA, and Development."

"And leadership," Zach offered. "I already built one for our leadership team. We already have a growing collection of blogs, references, tips, anti-patterns, and even short videos."

"Can I offer one slight adjustment?" Angela quickly interjected.

Benita and Zach paused, and the others turned and looked at her as well.

Angela explained, "The folks behind AMMI discovered that Agile frameworks can have vastly different roles, to the point that roles don't actually matter when it comes to classifying practices. What they discovered was that it's more important to focus on points of collaboration: People, Design, Planning, Implementation, Verification, and Operations. Would you all be comfortable using the AMMI taxonomy as your organizing system?"

"Well," Zach offered, "now that you say it, that does make sense. Any objections?"

Taneesha and the Product Owner Enuma shook their heads no, and no one else in the room offered any objections.

Nathan instead redirected the conversation, "Can we do knowledge-sharing sessions? Like brown-bag lunches or guest presentations? Maybe each time we add to our library we do a brown bag. It will help keep the flow of ideas going!"

"I love it!" Angela said, delighted at the energy.

Enuma jumped in, "Angela since you're guiding the Product Owners, let's propose a Product Owner Community of Practice too!"

"Great minds think alike!" Angela agreed enthusiastically.

"Great!" Enuma added. "It will be fantastic to learn from each other! One other question."

"What's that?" asked Angela

"Well, we are still looking for a single person to handle organizing our centralized repository. We were thinking that would be you, Angela."

Angela looked surprised, but chuckled, "While I fully agree we need a single person dedicated to keeping that repository organized, I'm not the best person for that as your coach. Zach, Jayson, maybe let's talk afterwards and determine who could take on this responsibility? We will need someone with the knowledge to organize the content, plus the energy to keep it fresh." Jayson nodded in acknowledgement.

Zach added, "Any final comments or questions before we close?"

Enuma wearily said, "Not here. I'm exhausted! And it's lunchtime!"

Zach laughed, "Okay thanks, everyone! That's a wrap!"

EXPANDING AWARENESS...

The next day, Angela and Zach reviewed the results of the "Problems World Tour" in her office. Zach had already sent a short survey to the teams. The initial results naturally varied from team to team, but overall the feedback was promising.

Angela was very proud of how Zach had led during the sessions. He was encouraging but without forcing them to do anything. Angela could tell that he had the "heart of a coach".

"How do you want to tackle the remaining people in Ares that aren't directly on teams?" she asked.

"Well," Zach answered, "Quality Engineering is already embedded into our existing teams, so no need to meet with them separately, and we already met with all the Product Owners."

"Speaking of the Product Owners," Angela added, "I am planning a meeting with them to discuss how things are going to shift with Naomi gone."

"I think that just leaves the Design team," Zach concluded. "I intentionally scheduled them *after* the other teams. Unfortunately, they are like 'herding cats', so we will have to meet with them next week."

"Ok," Angela agreed, reluctantly. "We also need to stop by and talk with the non-team team members like Sales, HR, and marketing."

"Oh, I hadn't planned for them," Zach admitted. "Do we have to have a special session with them since they're not technically part of the Ares Innovation Center? Well, by that I mean they're covered under the general ABS budgets..." He paused before continuing, "I mean I guess that makes sense now that I think about it."

"Yeah," Angela responded. "We are in a unique situation. We're a blend of Agile teams, immersed in an entrepreneurial culture, and nested within a traditional hierarchy. But we want to understand and integrate everybody that works with us."

"Of course," Zach agreed, checking his watch. "Okay, I have to head out. The Crownlands scheduled their first 'working session' and Omar asked me to make sure that everything goes as planned. See you next week in the 'Designer Den'?"

"Of course," Angela confirmed. As he left, she scanned her notes for references to the design team. The overall theme was a lack of integration. It was a common pattern she had seen with every organization that used an "internal design agency" model. She considered an approach strategy to use with Vera. This was going to be a big change for her group.

"Maybe they're already aware!" How great it would be if they had chosen "Cross-Functional Teams" from the AMMI library as the improvement area. *"Maybe?"* she hoped.

Key Points of Learning

- Focus First on Problems
- Giving Teams Control Over Their Future
- Connecting as Humans
- Lagging and Leading Evidence
- Benefit Hypotheses
- Evidence, Not OKRs
- Prioritized Serial Decisions Versus Context Switching
- Dependent versus Independent Variables
- Customer-Centered Impact
- Dealing With Difficult Teams
- Secret AMMI
- Working Sessions, Not Meetings
- Shared Benefits & Communities of Practice

Chapter 9

Vera – Popping the Creative Bubble

BUBBLE-WRAPPED FOR SAFETY

Vera was pacing back and forth in her spacious, multi-colored office. She was in front of her Parota-wood desk, looking back and forth between it and the cherry and walnut coffee table that formed the focal point for her mini-conference area. They didn't exactly match. It had never bothered her before, but today it was glaringly obvious. She wondered why she hadn't really noticed it before.

She shook her head to dislodge the thought from her mind. This was not the time for redecorating. She dropped instead into one of the plush chairs encircling the coffee table and stared at the Kandinsky poster on the wall. Her gaze drifted from it to the Raku-style Japanese tea bowl on the bookcase next to it. Both were beautiful, but they also didn't match.

"What's wrong with me?" she thought to herself.

Obviously, she was nervous about Angela's visit to the 'Designer Den'. They had delayed for as long as they could, but now it was here. It's not that they didn't like Angela. She and Zach had been spending a lot of time lately in the Den, assisting with the usability testing, but today's visit just made her nervous. Now that Angela had the "temporary" role of Product Manager, Vera couldn't shake the feeling that something bad was waiting just outside.

She stood up abruptly, opened the door, and left her office.

Vera stepped out into the Designer Den and smiled as she looked around at the space with all of its beautiful, bold colors. Normally it was her safe haven. She had spent years crafting it so, not only for herself but for all the creatives. Each and every one of them felt like her children. No matter what happened "out there", they could always escape "in here", and that had to be preserved at all costs.

Vera turned towards the Espresso machine and started having this nagging feeling that Angela was already there. Her "spidey sense" was on all alerts! She was certain that Angela was there!

"I can't wait to see the two areas of improvement that your team chose," she heard Angela's voice say enthusiastically.

Vera started walking around the den and as she turned a corner, noticed Angela walking over to the conversation "campfire" area with Clyde. *"When had she arrived?"* Vera wondered. She shook herself clear of her feelings, walked over to the counter Angela had just left, and grabbed herself an apple from the fruit basket.

"Sure, no problem," said Clyde. He connected his laptop to the screen and pulled up a virtual whiteboard from their brainstorming.

Vera felt so proud to see Clyde stepping forward into a leadership position. He had been so underappreciated under Naomi, and she knew that he had such potential. It just made her heart swell to see him get to exercise it.

By the time he was ready, the other designers had settled into the eclectic mix of bean bag chairs, chaise lounges, comfy chairs, and couches that circled the conversation pit. Vera grabbed a stool on the outside edge and sat down, bracing herself for whatever was destined to happen next.

"Our top priority," Clyde began, "has to do with reducing the number of unnecessary changes that we are asked to make, by following Lund's Usability Maxims and measuring completeness by customer impact, and not internal preferences. So we chose 'Outcome Verification'." He read through the accompanying team Hypothesis, the Intuition impact statement, their goals, and how they were going to collect their evidence.

"Before we discuss this one," Angela asked, "can I see the other area of improvement that you chose?"

"Of course," Clyde said as he navigated over to the sketches for their second improvement area. "For our second improvement, we chose 'Integrating Multiple Points of View'. We figured that if we were asking the Product Owners to put aside their biases, we had to be vigilant to check our own biases as well. Through the wisdom of the crowds, and ensuring that we have diversity, equity, inclusion, and access for all." He read through the matching pieces of the template for their second choice.

"These are great choices!" Angela said earnestly. "I love where you are going, and can't wait to work with you on getting there." She paused, obviously thinking through her words, and then continued, "There is one more problem, though, that I'd like to ask you to take on. I was hoping to see it on your list already. It's a problem that may or may not be felt by you, but it is being felt by almost every other team that Zach and I have collaborated with over the last several weeks."

Vera felt a sense of dread starting to clench in her stomach. She felt it before she understood it. Something about how Angela was giving signals that were not supportive of the Designer Den. Vera knew deep down that Angela did not approve, but was not certain what exactly Angela was going to do.

Angela continued, "How can I say this the best?"

Another pause. Vera's stomach clenched a little tighter, and then Angela said, "The teams miss you."

Vera was momentarily puzzled. She was not expecting those particular words.

Angela explained further, "At multiple times during the discussions that Zach and I have had with the other teams, they would be having a great discussion and then someone would say, 'But that's a decision for the design team,' and since no one from the design team was in the room, the discussion would have to be put on hold."

Vera wondered at that moment where Angela was going with this, but deep in her gut, she already knew.

Angela added, "They have great respect for you, and the work that you do. That's obvious. What they don't consciously recognize, though, is that their work gets blocked every other day by a design decision that can't be solved on the spot, because no one from Design is in their meetings."

"What do you mean?" asked Isabella, a graphic designer, quickly rising to the team's defense. "If they ask for our input, we always send somebody over to answer their questions."

"Here's the pattern I've been seeing," Angela clarified. "A team is working out a problem. Maybe there's a data change, or maybe it's a structural change, but it affects the design. It could be as simple as a new field added, or it might require rethinking the flow of the user experience. Someone says, 'That's a design change, let's add it to our list,' and then all conversation stops for a few days."

"We do not take days to respond to their requests," Maxwell, a UX designer, retorted.

"Very true. Let me clarify," Angela countered. "It really is lovely to see. They reach out and you are all very responsive. You schedule time on the calendar that very same day."

Maxwell settled back into his seat, satisfied at defending the team's honor. Vera felt proud, both in how well she had trained her team to be helpful and responsive and in how they had internalized the design team's ethos so that they were able to defend themselves.

Angela pressed on, though, "But while you schedule the meeting within twenty-four hours, the actual wait time before the meeting occurs has a minimum of one day and a median time of two days, with the maximum going as high as two weeks. So, comparing the actual meeting time with the date when the request was logged, we find that the entire wait time has to do with scheduling."

"What's the median time?" Vera heard one of the younger designers whisper to a friend in the back of the room. The other shrugged, so Vera decided to solve the problem by raising her own hand.

"Oh, yes, Vera, did you have a comment or question?" Angela asked.

"Yes," Vera answered, "could you define 'median time', just in case anyone needs it?"

"Of course! I'm so sorry," Angela replied apologetically. "When I say the 'median time' was two days that means that half of requests take two days or less, with the other half of requests taking longer than that." Heads nodded and the designers smiled in satisfaction.

Angela continued, "To be more precise, if you lined up all the data in order by size, and looked at the value of the item exactly in the middle, that's the median. So let's round up to say we had one hundred requests. I grabbed request number fifty-one, in order by the response time, and it was two days. Since its response time was two days, that means that the fastest fifty requests were all two days or less, which is why I can summarize that the majority of requests were two days or less."

"So," Sandy called out while raising her hand. Angela nodded and the designer continued, "You're saying that the shortest design meeting request was twenty-four hours? That can't be true. I know, for example, that Bisby has called me many times to ask some of those quick questions you describe. If the answer is obvious, I tell her right away."

"Right!" Angela returned, "And I guess I need to acknowledge that as well. Now I'm going to be guessing here, but I bet that the other teams aren't logging those kinds of quick answers, only the ones that require a scheduled session. So first, it's great that you have that relationship with the teams, and that you are so responsive when you can be! Thank you!"

Sandy gave a cautious smile. Vera also felt that this was going to be followed up with "but..."

"And," Angela countered instead, "there are still plenty of design requests in the system that fit the category of requiring a scheduled review session. Then..." continued Angela, "after you determine what has to be done, each request waits at least one more week in the queue to be assigned, with some lower-priority requests waiting for up to two months before they are worked on."

"When you look at the data from end to end," Angela continued, "except for the quick responses, every other change that requires input from the design team takes at least two weeks to complete, and some take months."

"That's impossible," Maxwell shot back. "We always complete all requests within five days... unless someone is not upholding our agreed-upon response time." He looked around the room at the other designers but they all shrugged and denied responsibility.

"Sorry, not trying to imply that either," Angela interrupted. "Response time to a request is great. I looked into it. I started with the data about how long it took to close a design request. The smallest time was one day, and the longest was five days, just as you said, but after that initial meeting, the majority of requests spend at least one week in the queue waiting to be assigned, with some lower-priority requests waiting for up to two months."

"Yeah, that's kind of the point of improvement number one," Clyde interjected. "There are too many requests!" Vera and all of the other designers verbally agreed in support of Clyde. "And," Clyde continued, "we have to spend a lot of time getting their request into a format that we can take action on." Vera started snapping her fingers multiple times in support of Clyde's comment, a common response that the designers used. Someone had picked it up from poetry competitions.

Clyde continued with his explanation of design policy, "When the requests become too much, we batch the requests and force the teams to make a list of their changes, and then we tackle the whole list altogether."

"Yeah," Sandy chimed in, "life has gotten so much better since we started doing that." More snaps arose from all the designers.

"No doubt," Angela agreed. "I've seen the situation you've described many times, and it sucks. I definitely don't want to increase your workload. I'm going to be one of your biggest allies in eliminating unnecessary rework!" It was a nice gesture, Vera thought, but did Angela really get it?

Angela continued, "It's just that I'm also responsible for the bigger picture, and what I'm seeing is that the DevOps metrics says when you look at the total delivery time for any change — from idea to customer delivery — we can't get anything out the door faster than two weeks. Sometimes the wait times are built up across multiple small delays, but sometimes the majority of the wait time is clustered around teams waiting for design changes. I'd like to see if we can work together to find a solution that works for the entire process, end-to-end."

This time there were no finger snaps, and Vera knew why. She stood to address Angela on behalf of the team. She had seen this enough times through the years. It was the standard operating procedure in American Banking Systems outside of their incubator. Different Product Owners had tried doing this inside the Ares Innovation Center several times before. Sacrifice the designers in favor of the greater good, or to serve the "needs of the customer", but it wasn't about the greater good.

"Angela," Vera began, "people don't even fathom what they don't know about design. They only know that they don't like something, and very seldom can they explain why, and that intangible personal preference is death to the artistic process and poison for great design." The finger snaps returned, along with a few verbal words of support.

Vera pressed on. She knew that it was time to nip this talk in the bud. She needed Angela to understand the uniqueness of their situation and the beauty of the system that Vera had designed to protect her people.

"I do believe you want the best outcome, Angela," Vera continued, "and we would love to work with you, but I feel I need to share the history of how we developed our internal consulting model because we are NOT going back to the way it was before." The designers agreed wholeheartedly, snapping even louder than before.

"This is what we used to deal with," Vera said, stepping onto her proverbial soapbox. "In the past, usually we would only see the scope of their plans at a system demo. No consultation, no input from Design."

A few snaps of agreement arose from the designers as Vera set the stage.

"If we were lucky, some of the teams understood that we needed to be involved, but they never really understood what we did. They constantly talked down to us with demeaning requests to 'make it look pretty', the design equivalent of 'you should smile more'."

Snap, snap, snap.

"Seldom were we asked for an up-front design," she lamented, "and when we asked why, 'Emergent Design' was always their excuse. I learned to hate that phrase." Several of the experienced designers muttered in disgust at the mention of Emergent Design, matching Vera's own sentiments.

"Regardless of how it got to us," Vera continued, "when it got here, we would start the real Design work." Everybody was snapping now.

"For example," she said, punctuating her point with a single finger in the air, "the first of Lund's Usability Maxims is 'Know thy user, and ***YOU*** are ***NOT*** thy user,' so we would conduct interviews of representative users associated with the process, internally and externally, and map the current processes of everyone involved."

Snap, snap, snap.

"Then we began work on maxim number two," she added, along with another finger in the air, "'Things that look the same should act the same.' Through competitor research, we would identify the interface conventions being used and adapt our sketches accordingly."

"Then we would continue on down the list and design for ease of use, and ultimately..." Here Vera paused for effect, "...ultimately it fell on deaf ears." Silence fell over the group, including Angela, replaced with obviously frustrated, nodding heads.

Vera continued, "It didn't matter because when we presented the designs to the teams, or to the Product Owners, or Sales, they did not follow the same rigor that we did. Instead, they relied on their gut opinions. They wanted a drop-down menu instead of checkboxes, a different color, or to move some of the fields to an entirely different part of the screen, or even a different screen altogether! We explained why what we had designed was better for the users, but mostly we just got blank stares, or outright disbelief, like 'I don't think that's true'."

Vera felt herself ramping up in intensity as she re-lived her frustrations.

"We tried showing them our research," Vera continued, the tension building, "but there was always some reason why it had to be their way. Then a week later, after we made the changes, it would be shown to the execs and other stakeholders, and they would contribute their own list of changes that they wanted, and half the time, their idea would be to put things back to the way we originally had it! It was infuriating!!"

The rest of the team nodded in agreement. Vera could feel their teeth clenched just like hers.

She took a couple of deep breaths to calm herself before going on. "Eventually, we realized that we had to respect ourselves and establish clear boundaries. I negotiated a truce. We simplified our design process so that each project could be finished within one week. We then agreed to make two rounds of design changes only. They could put whatever they wanted in both lists and we would do it. The only exception was if the change was too drastic. Then a designer could come to me, and I would make the call, yes or no, and live with the consequences. Recently we've been bending the rules because of the emergency situation, and everybody here has been paying for it with their sanity!"

One final round of snaps from the designers, as Vera brought the story around to a close, "It works for us, and we will not go back," she said indignantly. "It may look like our process is a waste of time, but the alternative is so much worse! Trust me!"

Vera noticed that she had not really been looking at Angela. As she took the moment to do so, expecting to find opposition, she found instead a look of sadness in Angela's eyes.

Angela smiled and began her reply, "I'm so sorry, Vera. It can be so frustrating to be disrespected by your peers like that. It doesn't matter if it's intentional or not, or if they even know what they're doing to you. It still hurts to have your hard work and your expertise brushed away as if it has no value at all. I'm sorry that happened to you all."

"I'll be honest," Vera added, "it's not uncommon for creative types, and *women* in particular!" Finger snapping arose spontaneously, first from the female designers, and then from the men. All of them were nodding their heads in recognition of this oft-unacknowledged fact.

Angela expanded, "As a female coder I had to work twice as hard as the men, and they still never really took me seriously. When they disagreed, they automatically assumed that with enough 'time and experience', I would eventually learn to see it their way." Angela used air quotes to emphasize their condescension.

"I was so insecure at the time," she confided, "that I believed them and doubted myself." The women in the room automatically shook their heads in recognition, Vera included.

Angela continued, "That's actually what got me into user testing in the first place. I had gotten so insecure that I wanted to figure out what I was missing, why I couldn't see what they were seeing. I started with a friend of mine who was a user of the system I was working on. I asked her to walk me through her experience so that I could learn what I was missing, and do you know what I learned?"

"That you were right all along?" Sandy responded with confidence. Vera smiled with a supportive, knowing smile.

"Yes!" Angela agreed. Satisfied smiles brightened the faces of the group. "Yes, sometimes I was totally right! I shouldn't have just accepted the beliefs of the men that they knew better. That was my first learning. I had to learn to trust myself. I went back with renewed vigor and ran some more user testing with additional users, and do you know what I found out with those users?"

"Right again!" Isabella called out.

"Actually no," Angela added, causing the smiles to dampen with furrowed brows. She explained. "I actually credit that moment with changing my career — though I didn't know it at the time. Had I also been right on those follow-up tests, I'm not sure I would have learned what I was destined to learn. I probably would have gone back, confident in being right, and pushed my ideas on my male coworkers with zeal, but what I discovered instead was that in those other tests, I was wrong, and so were the men." The women designers in particular were noticeably struggling with this unexpected turn in the story.

Angela held up her hand, prompting them to wait with their responses for a bit longer. "That was the moment where I had my big revelation, one that Vera called out earlier — Lund's first usability maxim, 'Know thy user, and ***YOU*** are ***NOT*** thy user.' That was an eye-opener for me! Sometimes I was right, sometimes the men were right, and sometimes none of us were right. But none of that mattered," she continued, "because we were not building the software for ourselves. I had reached the same realization that you all had reached, and I was so excited to go back and share my new insight with my team!"

The furrowed brows had disappeared and had been replaced with honest interest. That's when Angela took the designers, *and* Vera, in a new direction. "I went back and shared my experience with the other developers..." Angela paused for effect, "and none of them believed me."

"Ugh," Sandy exhaled. "Figures," Isabella added.

Angela explained, "I tried to share what I knew, but they all were sure that I had missed something. Nothing I said could convince them, but I wasn't going to give up. This time I knew what I knew. We had many fights, and several of them were pretty bad, both on my part and theirs. I almost gave up. Finally, out of exasperation, and without realizing what I was about to learn, I decided to go back and do more tests, but this time I was going to record them, so I could show them that I was right and that these weren't my opinions, but the users', and do you know what happened?"

No one responded this time to her rhetorical question. They just waited for Angela to answer. "As they watched the recorded videos," Angela said with a sarcastic chuckle, "being both men and engineers, they stopped arguing with me, and they went straight into problem-solving mode. I mean, many of them couldn't believe their eyes, that the users were actually behaving the way that they were. It was illogical, to them and to me, but it was also undeniable. It was right there in front of them. And right there, at that moment, I had the realization that I had gone through a journey that they had not yet taken. Up to that point, we had been working in two different realities."

"I had a lot of emotions about that fact," Angela admitted. "As I processed it later I remember feeling angry that they had never sought to do user testing on their own, and that they had made it personal, my ideas versus their ideas, me versus them. But then I realized that I had also done the same thing. I had also presented it as the users' ideas versus theirs and as the users and I versus them."

"But that realization wasn't even the game-changer for me," Angela exclaimed. "In reviewing the experience in my memory, I ultimately realized that none of it mattered. All of the macho, ego-driven power struggles could just be side-stepped by showing them the videos. All I had to do was show them what I had seen, so we were all looking at the same problem, and then we automatically started collaborating on solving the users' problems."

"Now I'm not saying," Angela clarified, "that we stopped having differences of opinions, but each time I would mock up all of the solutions, put them in front of users, and show the guys the resulting videos, and each time we skipped the arguments and moved straight on to the next idea."

"So I offer you all this proposal," Angela said in conclusion. "I promise you that we will not go back to the way it was before." She held her right hand to her heart, and her other hand up to offer a solemn swear. "As you may have noticed, I've been training the organization to integrate user testing at the heart of their process, and Clyde has been leading the way with that. Because of that, we have tools that you all didn't have before. And while I couldn't get Naomi to watch Clyde's videos, Tim has put me in charge of the Product Owners, and they will watch them." Vera noticed a big smile spread across Clyde's face. "They will also help to create them."

"I'd like to try an experiment," Angela added. "I'd like each of the UX designers here to pair with a Product Owner, both for you to guide them when it comes to the user experience, and for you to follow their lead when it comes to the business model. I believe that by partnering with a dedicated Product Owner and their team in collaborative problem-solving around concrete user testing, we can get the best ideas out the door faster, while also reducing the churn and making your lives easier. I also think that each of the teams will be exponentially better by having a designer's point of view to give instant feedback on everything they do. To that end, and as part of this experiment, I'd like to ask you to join the planning meetings, standups, and retros for that team along with your Product Owner, and help make sure that they're doing things right."

Maxwell's hand went up, "We had decided not to attend team meetings. It was just too many meetings. We have our own team meetings, then depending on which design changes we were assigned to, if we attended all of their team meetings, plus all of the discovery sessions with the Product Owner, most of our life was just meetings!"

"Nobody wants a life of all meetings!" Angela agreed. "That is not what I want for you either. No, what I am proposing is only one set of meetings each. Fifteen minutes a day for a standup, up to two hours every other week for planning, and up to two more hours every other week for demos and retros. In General, no Agile team should have more than five hours per week of required meetings. That's less than 15% of any typical 40-hour work week! How you spend the rest of your time is up to you and your Product Owners, as needed to get the work done."

Maxwell astutely responded, "That sounds like we're disbanding as our own team and joining their teams."

Concerned looks and objections arose from all the designers.

"We love working together," Vera added. "We've built a wonderful family here, and we do not want to lose that." The designers nodded and snapped their fingers in agreement.

"That's wonderful," Angela agreed. "What you have here truly is lovely, and I don't want to break up the family. In the industry, the term for what you have here is a Community of Practice, and as I said, after those five hours in the week, how you spend the rest of your week is up to you all here, whatever you need to do to best collaborate with the teams."

"You said UX designers. What about the graphic designers?" asked Isabella. "There aren't enough graphic designers for all of the teams."

"True," Angela responded, "but that's often the case, isn't it? With user experience design being so closely coupled with the mockups and daily interface choices that teams might have to make, it's more critical that there be a UX designer paired with each team. By contrast, as I'm sure you know, the graphic design work of creating the artwork, design briefs, templates, pattern libraries, etc., really crosses between teams. You'll still collaborate with the UX designers, but you don't need to be embedded in the teams. It is often better for graphic designers to work directly with Product Management."

"That's what we do already," Isabella countered.

"Then it may not actually feel different to you," Angela acquiesced.

The designers all looked around at each other, noticeably wary, but not in opposition.

Vera exhaled deeply and realized that she had been largely holding her breath during Angela's story, afraid of where it was going. She wasn't convinced of this idea, but she had to admit that it was new. It was different from the hell from which they had escaped, but also different than what they were doing now. She ran through multiple scenarios in her head, trying to anticipate how it might fall apart, but ultimately decided not to interfere. Even though life was much better than it had been in the old days, the designers were still overloaded. If Angela thought that this might actually reduce their workload, she would see how it was going to play out.

Angela doubled down on her request, "I'm asking you to give two sprints to try this out, and if it doesn't work, I promise that we'll reset back to the way you're working now." Angela followed that up with one more appeal. "To provide the best possible results, let's have you choose your Product Owners." That made all the designers noticeably happier. They were buzzing with a cautious, but growing, excitement. Vera was still feeling very cautious herself, but at least she was also feeling a little hopeful.

"Oh, and there's one more thing," Angela inserted.

"Wait, are you pulling a 'Steve Jobs moment' on us?" Maxwell blurted out with a spreading smile on his face.

"Maybe," Angela said slyly. "There's even a stage, a presentation, and an audience built right in. I'd like to shift the organization's thinking from product-centered to people-centered. I plan to do that by holding an event I call 'Usability Theater' where we show all of the current usability testing videos to our teams like I used to do with my old team."

She continued, "And I'd like to ask you to help me lead the brainstorming activities that will follow. I need your help to keep them focused on the customers. The teams are going to naturally want to pull towards talking about solutions, and I need people in each team to advocate on behalf of the point of view of the users. I'm thinking that's all of you... should you choose to accept that mission."

"I'm in," Maxwell instantly agreed.

"Me too," Clyde confirmed.

"I like that idea," Sandy and Isabella added, almost at the same time, followed by several more nods and agreements in a cascade from the rest of the designers.

"Well played, Angela," Vera thought to herself, smiling.

USABILITY THEATER

Vera was sitting on the stage in American Banking's main auditorium. She had gotten there early to center herself and get mentally prepared before everyone arrived. She had taken her assigned seat on the stage, a plush, comfy, but boringly designed sofa-chair, and settled in for some light meditation.

Before too long her attention drifted to Naomi. It had only been a little while since Naomi's departure, but Vera could already feel a lightness in the air throughout the whole office. There was more laughter heard around the office, more talking, everyone could breathe easier. Maybe it was all in her head, but other people had remarked about how "the vibe" was different. Nobody mentioned Naomi's name, but nobody had to.

Vera hated thinking about anyone as responsible for slowing the entire office down, but experience had shown her that it happens. She hated thinking about it being Naomi in that position. Naomi was her friend. They had started the Ares Innovation Center together with Tim. Before that, they had known each other for... how many years now?

Vera's brain started spinning off, following threads of doubt in her mind. The recent months had been hard on all of them, and Naomi had taken it the worst. Was she really to blame? Was her approach really at the center of what was keeping them back? Naomi was the reason that Ares had grown! She was awesome! Vera couldn't reconcile the difference.

Angela kept insisting in her one-on-one meetings with Vera that it wasn't anyone's fault, that the times were just changing, and that it required new approaches, but Vera couldn't help shaking one thought. What had worked in the early days of Ares was that she got to run the design. Naomi ran the business and trusted her to run design. In the past several months, with the whole Intuition thing, that had changed. Naomi had been trying to run design, and doing it by micromanaging. Was that how she had been running the business side of things all these years and Vera just hadn't seen it or was it just the pressure from Intuition?

Vera knew that she had run her group collaboratively. Had Naomi? She realized that she didn't really know. What Angela was proposing sounded completely normal to Vera, but the way Angela presented it, it seemed like a whole new world order on the development side of the house.

Her thoughts were interrupted by a few excited exclamations from some of the team members who had started to filter into the auditorium. It snapped her out of her recollections and anchored her back in the present moment. Tim had the great idea to wheel the old movie theater popcorn cart over from the Designer Den for the occasion. The early arrivals were lining up for little bags of popcorn and buzzing with conversation about what they were going to do.

It must have been near the time to start. More teams were starting to arrive now, lining up for popcorn or settling into their seats. Linda and Angela entered the auditorium, grabbed some popcorn, and started making their way towards Vera.

As they reached the stage she heard Angela ask, "Ready?"

"I think so," said Linda.

"Ready whenever you are," Vera added.

"Just remember to start every comment with appreciation," Angela reminded her, "just like we rehearsed with the Double Aces."

Angela and Linda put their bags down on the two seats to her left as the auditorium techs came on stage to test the microphones and finish their last-minute checks. Vera sat back down on the edge of her sofa-chair and watched the team members settle into their seats. Clyde entered and waved at her as he made his way to the stage to join them.

One of the technicians reached out with a handheld microphone. Vera stepped up to accept it. She looked for the microphone's switch and flipped it on. "Welcome, can you all hear me well?" Vera said, checking the volume of her voice echoing back from the monitors on the wall.

Linda, surprised by the sudden change in volume, stammered out, "Oh, I guess so!" and gave a nervous little chuckle.

"Go ahead and get settled in," Vera continued, "enjoy the popcorn, and we'll start in a minute."

"Where's the butter?" called out one of the programmers from the back. The whole auditorium laughed at the joke.

"I know, right?" Linda said, then added, "Actually, Vera, can I borrow that microphone for a moment? I want to make sure they know the rules of the auditorium."

Vera handed over the mic.

"I know, right? Popcorn without butter?" Linda said again into the mic. She chuckled along with the group before continuing, "Just in case that was a serious question, though, the facilities people were nice enough to let us bring popcorn in here, but they were very clear about no butter. Sorry. Oh, and no sodas!" She gave a clear "mom" look, sweeping across the whole auditorium, then added, "And clean up the area around you before you leave! Everybody! Don't just leave it for the staff, and don't just leave it to the ladies."

"Ok, mom!" the programmer called back in jest.

"That's a good boy," Linda said with a smile while handing the mic back to Vera. Everyone had a good chuckle.

Tim had just arrived on the stage. He was the last person that Vera had been waiting for. She raised the mic and began, "Welcome! Would you look at us! Two years ago there were only a handful of us, but now we fill an auditorium! Let's take a moment to congratulate ourselves on our explosive growth!" She tucked the microphone under her arm and started clapping. Everyone else joined in and applauded enthusiastically in recognition of her compliment.

Vera continued, "We've defined a new product category, so much so that big players in the market have decided to copy us. That's really flattering if you think about it." People looked at each other with a bit of surprise at first, but then tacitly acknowledged Vera's reframing of their current crisis.

"Intuition loved what you built so much that they decided to follow your lead. Let's not lose sight of that. Come on, give yourselves another round of applause for being market leaders!"

After the applause subsided, Vera continued, switching gears, "Okay, so many of you think this is a break from work. It's not. Yes, we do mix pleasure with business because happy workers are more productive workers, but this is not just for fun."

She put on a dignified expression and clarified. "The people you are going to see on this screen are our real customers, and I love the symbolism of giving them center stage here. They are the reason we all have jobs, and the goal here today is to get into their heads. Now what we're going to see here is what we call a 'closed' test. To give you the context on what I mean by 'closed', I'll briefly describe the three core types of usability tests. They are called 'directed', 'closed', and 'open' tests."

"The first type of test, the 'directed' tests, are the types of tests you all do every day in User Acceptance Testing. In a 'directed' test there are a specific series of steps outlined in a script, and we follow those steps to make sure the software works as expected and doesn't have any bugs. This kind of test puts our software at the center of focus. As such, it can only tell us what we already know. It's valuable, but its value is finite."

"The second type of test is called a 'closed' test. This type also centers around our existing software, but instead of giving people a list of steps to execute, we give them a goal. In the examples you are about to see, their goal is to create a new account. They receive no other instructions beyond that, no directions on how to do it, and no help videos. The purpose of this kind of test is to see how intuitive our software is. Can people figure out how to accomplish the goal of creating a new account without help?"

"The third type of test is called the 'open' test, and it's actually one of the most powerful tests that we can perform. It's called an 'open' test because it is completely open. We let the test subject completely drive the test. We don't tell them what we want to learn. We just give them a generic prompt like, 'We want to follow you as you go about your day and learn what it is like.'"

"Each type of test is useful in completely different circumstances. For example, when we want to collect ideas for new features, we use 'open' tests, but when there are problems with existing features, we use a 'closed' test. What you are going to see today will be 'closed' tests."

"Are there any questions?" Vera paused and peered out into the crowd for raised hands.

Venkat, Product Owner for the Riverlands raised his hand and called out, "What are the customer demographics that we chose for these tests?"

"Great question," Vera agreed. "For those who are not familiar with the term, demographics refers to how many users are male vs female, income brackets, education levels, locations around the world, etc. That kind of stuff. Honestly, the demographic here was whoever was willing to sit through the tests with us! You know how some of our users can be!"

"Ain't that the truth!" Don guffawed from the front rows.

"When we have the luxury of more willing participants," Vera clarified, "we'll be particular about our demographics, but for now we will test with what we have."

Venkat shrugged and nodded in reluctant agreement.

"Any other questions?" Vera asked. No hands could be seen, so she continued. "On with the show, then. As I was saying, these will all be 'closed' tests. We asked each one of these people to create a new account because that is the place where we are losing new customers, but for the rest of the time, we tried not to say anything at all. We just watched and took notes. Those rules have been lifted for today, though. Today we want to hear your thoughts, as you're thinking them."

"Now the reason we're doing this is because while creating a new account may seem completely intuitive to us, for some reason it is not easy for our users. The prospect of creating a new account is causing them to leave in droves, and go use Intuitions' product instead. This has to stop. Thanks to these tests we have a pretty good idea of why they're leaving. What we need from you are ideas on what we can do about it."

Vera paused for a moment. "So please watch these videos created by Clyde very carefully and take notes. Consider what you can do to correct or improve anything you notice about the client's reactions. Clyde, is there anything else that you'd like to add?"

Clyde leaned forward in his seat and said, "Not really." Vera pointed the mic at him anyway so he added, "I... I don't want to bias anyone's reaction. All I will say is that if you have any questions, raise your hands and ask them as we go along. I don't want to miss any opportunities for learning."

"You heard him, folks. Don't be shy!" Vera added. She gestured to the control booth in the back, "Can you reduce the lights and start up the first video?" The lights dimmed and the projector started glowing. On-screen the projector brightened into focus until they could see the words, "Usability Test #3".

She looked at the screen above her and gave a quick introduction. "These videos were the first usability tests that we ran on the new account creation workflow. We've made a lot of changes since then, of course, but they're really great representations of the problem at the start. As you'll remember, our early users had no problem with the software, but originally you could only sign up through a bank account. We couldn't add new users directly through the app, so Intuition ate our lunch in capturing new users. So we added our new account creation process and this happened." She pointed at the techs in the back of the auditorium and the video started playing.

As the usability test started unfolding on the big screen, Vera turned off the mic and walked down to sit on the edge of the stage, positioning herself under the glow of the projector so that she could still see the faces of the teams. Clyde followed her cue and came up to sit next to her. Angela and Linda followed suit and sat on her other side, their legs dangling over and swinging with nervously hopeful anticipation.

After the first video ended, the second recording started playing, "Usability Test #5". The room watched as the user struggled to locate the account numbers, passwords, routing numbers, and answers to the security questions, including the name of the street where he owned a house. Vera could see the teams getting restless and a hum of side conversations started to rise in the auditorium.

Tim appeared over her shoulder and said, “Can I have the mic? They’re starting to talk over the video. I’m going to try to get them to settle down.”

“Nope,” Vera countered. “It is part of the fun. We *want* to hear them express their thoughts out loud. Actually... why are we waiting for the end of the video? Let’s pause the recording and encourage them to talk out loud. We want to use the same principles as usability testing — thinking out loud.”

Vera got back up on her feet and turned the mic back on. “Can you pause the video and turn up the lights?” she called out to the control booth.

She looked out over the rows of people munching popcorn, “So, what do you think?”

There was silence.

“Come on,” Linda shouted as she struggled to her feet and joined Vera by her side. She grabbed the mic and leaned in, “We are using ‘Rocky Horror Picture Show’ rules here.” This got a smile from Vera and a few more from some of the designers over on the side who chuckled in surprise as they realized that they had something in common with Linda.

A hand raised in the third row. Linda pointed to her. “What’s a ‘Rocky Horde’?” the business analyst asked.

“Really?! You don’t know ‘Rocky Horror Picture Show’?” Linda said, a little exasperated. “You all are so young! Okay,” she added, changing references, “Think horror movie house rules.” Some people were getting it now, though there were still some remaining blank stares. “We want you to talk to the screen. Say what you’re thinking! It’s okay.”

The programmer who called her ‘mom’ blurted out, “You mean like asking how in the world can that woman not know her own home address?! I mean, seriously!” The tension started to crack. A few snickers here and there.

“Right?” called out a female voice.

“That’s a clear case of PICNIC!” Most of the programmers and testers burst out laughing, almost involuntarily.

“Yep! The problem is definitely between the keyboard and the chair.” Now the laughter was flowing, and the crowd was starting to loosen up.

“What are they saying?” Tim whispered into Linda’s ear.

Linda looked back over her shoulder and explained, “P-I-C-N-I-C. ‘Problem In Chair, Not In Computer,’ and ‘Between Keyboard And Chair’ means...”

“Oh, I got that one,” Tim said, connecting the dots and beginning to glower angrily. “These are our customers,” he interjected. “They should be more respectful.”

Angela grabbed his arm, “I know the guy is one of your friends, but don’t take it as disrespect,” she said. “They need to blow off steam. Remember what we prepared for,” Angela reminded him. “No matter what they say, use ‘Yes, And...’ thinking from the acting improv exercises we explored. They’re testing their ability to be free thinkers. Whatever they say, try embracing it first and then building on top.”

“Yes,” Vera agreed, picking up the cue. She turned back to address the auditorium. “Not what we were expecting, right? And... what can we do about it?”

“Get new users,” a different voice called out from somewhere in the middle.

“If you think about it,” Vera acknowledged, “that is what we’ve been trying to do. What other options do we have?”

Clyde leaned into the mic from the side, “You’d be surprised how many of them have a similar experience.” Vera held the mic out for him. “It turns out that when you get above about five houses, people start to lose track of addresses... and our wealthy users own a lot of real estate.”

“So what’s the answer?” Linda added again, leaning in from the other side and prompting them to dig deeper.

“Seems like we need better training,” added one of the testers.

“No,” answered someone from the customer service desk. “We have online training videos. Nobody watches them. They just call us up, all pissed off, and force us to walk them through the process.”

Angela asked Vera for the mic, “That’s one of the challenges behind any product. Once it’s out the door, we have no control anymore. We don’t get to sit down with every user and lead them down the right path. The more productive outcomes come when we ask ourselves, ‘Why does this user think that they are right?’”

"In fact," Angela continued, "everybody believes that they are right, or they wouldn't make the choices that they do. Everyone chooses to do what they do because they think it's the 'right' choice. Even when they do something that they know is 'wrong', they do the 'wrong' thing because they think that doing 'wrong' is the 'right' thing to do. Uncovering why that person believes they are doing the 'right' thing is the key to understanding another person's perspective."

"Yeah, give her a break," a new female voice added. "She's obviously an important businesswoman," she said, referring to the woman in the first video. "She wouldn't be where she is if she was an idiot." The laughter was subsiding and people were getting a little more serious.

"True, did you hear what the guy said? He flips houses for a living. I mean, when I was testing account creation, I couldn't remember the address of the apartment I was in five years ago."

Tim got up and went to stand next to Angela and Vera. "I see what you're doing," he said to them. "Can I have the mic? I think I can help." Vera cautiously passed the mic to him.

"Hey folks," Tim said into the mic. "I'm going to say something obvious but to bring home a point. We're not building a product for ourselves. We're building it for our customers. We need to solve this from their point of view, not ours. Many of these people don't manage their own finances and bank accounts. That's actually one of the reasons that we partnered with other banks at the beginning. It saved us time and money because we didn't have to build our own account creation, and the partner banks took care of the security verifications for us."

"So why don't we go back to that?" a voice called out from the back. Vera gestured to the booth in the back and one of the technicians brought another handheld mic into the audience.

Since Tim still had the mic in his hands, he raised it to respond. He began, in a matter-of-fact way, "We're not going back. In order to stand a chance against Intuition, we have to be able to create new accounts inside the app. That's non-negotiable."

Angela tapped him on the arm and said into his ear, "Be careful not to block their creativity. Say less and leave room for them to reach their own conclusions."

Tim nodded and immediately pivoted. "I'm sorry, though," he said. "I interrupted you. Please say what you were going to say."

The woman in the back continued her thought with the mic now in her hands. "Well, I'm not talking about going back," she clarified. "Maybe this isn't directly relevant, but you tell me. When I used to work in wire transfers, we asked them for their bank, and if that bank was in our trusted network we just opened up a login window on our computers and had them enter their username and password." She paused and took a deep breath to continue.

"I'm thinking," she continued, "and maybe I'm wrong here, but if that's good enough for our partners, shouldn't that be good enough for us? I mean, it won't work for everyone, but probably 90% of our customers have an account with another bank in our partner network. Plus we have to connect to those other accounts anyway in order to be able to transfer funds. Let's kill two birds with one stone."

"Naomi nixed that idea already," one of the UX designers called out from the other side of the auditorium. Someone rushed over with another handheld mic. He clarified, "She said that it was important that we weren't dependent on the other banks anymore."

"Actually..." responded a different programmer, gesturing for the mic to be brought to him. "I was never comfortable with that answer. I tried to bring this up at the time... Think about it... All we really care about is that they are who they say that they are, and we already figured that part out. We already jumped through all the "zero trust" hoops with our original authentication and authorization code. So much so that our partners allowed us to take money from their accounts. We could just leverage that trust and create a new account for the user after a successful partner login."

"Yeah," tossed back a tester, "but what if they forget their password and have to reset it? We won't have the security questions and answers already established to verify their identity."

"But that doesn't really matter," the programmer responded, "When that happens, and if that happens, we just give them the financial history questions we're using now to verify their identity again or ask them to re-authenticate with the partner bank and then send them a password reset email to the email address we have on file for them."

"This sounds like great stuff," Linda interjected, leaning over Tim's shoulder. "Is anyone able to write this stuff down?"

"Already on it," came Clyde's voice, still sitting on the edge of the stage but furiously typing away on this laptop.

"These are great ideas!" Tim agreed. "Keep it going!" The programmer in the back looked to be smiling in appreciation.

"Great!" Angela interjected, gesturing to Tim for the mic. "Let's brainstorm more ideas! Shall we keep moving? We'll play the next video. Remember... Horror Movie House Rules. Think out loud, raise your hand, or call out a problem that you see."

Vera asked Angela for the mic and added, "If you can phrase it from the customer's point of view, even better. You should have gotten a pad of sticky notes when you walked in. Write them down on sticky notes, and then do you see those whiteboards in the aisles? That's what they're for. Post them on the whiteboards."

"After we've collected all the problems," she added, "we'll go back through the problems on the board and brainstorm around possible solutions."

"At the end of all this," Linda interweaved, leaning in and pulling the mic temporarily closer to her, "pick someone from your group. We'll go around and ask each team to report on their discussions."

"I'm in! Let's do it, 'Mom'!" called out the programmer who spoke up earlier.

Vera gestured for the booth to start playing the next video as the excited crowd started munching on their popcorn again.

"We're already getting great suggestions," Linda said enthusiastically off-mic to the others on the stage.

"Yeah," agreed Vera, turning to Tim, "What do you think of that idea of using our old account creation code in that way?"

"I'll need to run it through the Risk Assessment team," Tim responded, "but it's a clever solution. If it's that easy, and the lawyers are okay with it, I'd love for that to be the solution."

"Alright, another win for the Ratatouille Principle!" Linda exclaimed.

"Shhh," the others had to remind her. "They're still watching the movies."

Linda sheepishly apologized.

"We should do this every week!" Clyde added with quiet enthusiasm.

"Let's start with quarterly," Tim advised in a whisper. "We don't have the budget to pay for this place every week."

"How about once per sprint while we're in crisis mode?" Vera countered. "Weekly might be too quick of a turnaround, but we can't afford to wait an entire quarter."

"Monthly?" Tim returned.

"We could do it monthly," Vera acquiesced. "And we can also use the Designer Den. We don't have to make it a big production each time."

"How about our main room?" Tim asked.

Vera wasn't sure what was wrong with the Designer Den, but she agreed. "With the new layout, we could do it in the main campfire space."

The videos kept rolling and the audience kept learning. When the last video finished and the audience had their final feedback, Vera announced to the theater that it was over and there was a loud collective expression of disappointment. *"Good!"* Vera thought, *"They were enjoying the interactions!"* Up until that point she hadn't really been sure.

Clearly, this had been a success. Vera was impressed by the entire arrangement and had to admit that Angela's idea was a good one. She found herself looking forward to what was going to come next.

THE WALLS COME TUMBLING

Vera paused as she crossed the main floor from the elevators and looked out towards the giant picture windows on the opposite side of the lobby. Linda and the Scrum Masters had lined up all of the whiteboards from the Usability Theater beneath the windows, and from a distance, the bright, multi-colored sticky notes looked like a field of wildflowers. Above them streaked the thick clouds outside in vibrant hues of orange and flamingo, like brush strokes on an oil painting, cresting over a row of rich green trees under a pale blue canvas.

Vera took a deep breath and took it all in. She loved discovering art in the most unexpected places. She was starting to see why Angela kept referring to that Ratatouille quote of hers. While not every sticky note contained a great idea, they had found several gems that were definitely worthy of further exploration.

She and Angela had agreed to come in early the next day to finish sorting through the results. They were both energetically eager to continue digging through the mountain of little paper squares to find those gems.

As Vera walked over to the conference room called "Winterfell", she could hear Tim talking in a strong, but hushed voice, "...leadership team to figure out the best way to do this!"

Angela's voice came back, "How much do we need to reduce the budget then?"

Vera stopped at the doorway, frozen mid-track by Angela's question, unable to do anything but listen. The sun outside drifted behind the clouds, and the room appeared to darken on cue.

"A flat 20%," Tim responded., "That translates to about four million dollars. Pretty deep! ...but I suppose it could be worse. I was inspired by all your recent changes around here, and my thought was to brainstorm how to reduce costs in a more democratic way. It will take more work, but the results will be worth it. After all, people's jobs are on the line here!"

Vera's jaw was agape. She was obviously not being subtle about her listening in, and Tim and Angela had noticed. Both were now looking straight at her.

"How long have you been standing there?" Tim asked.

"Long enough...," Vera responded.

Tim whistled, "That's what I thought. Well, everyone will know soon enough!"

Angela sighed.

Tim waved for Vera to enter the room and closed the door before continuing. "One absolute certainty is that I want to keep the teams intact as much as humanly possible. They have a growing synergy with each other that must not change! We can do a little pruning, but I want minimum team impact and more empathy."

Angela started to nod her head, but it gradually morphed into a slow, side-to-side head shake, "Tim, I'm a bit stunned."

Tim agreed, "That's natural." He looked at both Angela and Vera. "Do you both need time to process this?"

Angela shook herself, "Of course I do, but I'll be okay."

Vera merely nodded her head in agreement, feeling like she was watching herself in a movie.

Angela brought Vera somewhat back into reality, "I recommend we get our leaders together and openly discuss the options for reducing costs."

"Ratatouille Principle?" Vera asked knowingly.

Angela smiled in agreement, adding "We may have to start treating our Innovation Center as a true startup. Shoestring budget and no money to waste!"

Tim smiled, "Yes, I'm thinking the same. What should we do?"

Angela paused for a moment... "We can use an ideation process, come up with the rough amounts that can be reduced in each category, and then execute a 'kinder, gentler' budget cut."

"I like that, Angela," Tim agreed. "A 'kinder gentler' budget cut. Cut the extras, not the people! No mandatory RIFs allowed!"

"RIFs?" Vera asked.

Angela answered, "RIF stands for Reduction in Force. When Tim and I used to work together, our management did it so often that we nicknamed them RIPP's as in 'Rest In Peace, People'!"

Tim gave a slanted smirk, "Yeah, we always swore that when we took over, no more RIFs. I'll have an emergency meeting scheduled by lunchtime. All hands on deck!"

Tim asked again, this time just to Vera, "Are you okay?"

Vera snapped out of her daze and said, "Not really, but what choice do I have?" She wasn't ready for this, she realized.

"So," she added, "I guess sorting through the Usability Theater sticky notes is on hold."

"For now," Angela agreed, "but hopefully not for too long. Things were just starting to pick up momentum!"

SHIFT: FROM BUDGETS TO PEOPLE

A few hours later Tim had managed to collect all of the directors, managers, and leads in the King's Landing conference room. Vera got there ten minutes early, not wanting to miss anything, and found herself as one of the later arrivals, missing only Roy, Ali, and Tim himself. There was a lot of buzz going on, each one asking the others about the nature of the meeting. Tim had asked Angela and Vera to keep it quiet until he could deliver the bad news himself to everyone at the same time.

Tim came into the room five minutes early with Ali in tow. Ali had obviously been trying to pull some early information from him during the walk. Tim deflected his questions with calm confidence and determination. This was the Tim that Vera was used to, unflappable. He had obviously let down his guard earlier, and it was nice to see his vulnerable side, no leadership mask, but this was the Tim they needed in this particular moment, emboldened, and ready to lead them into danger.

Vera felt a sudden longing for Naomi. She, Naomi, and Tim had always tackled these kinds of challenges together in the past. It wouldn't be the same without her. Vera was starting to trust Angela a little more, and it was obvious that Tim trusted her, but Vera felt that she had every right to be cautious.

Tim began with a smile, "I see everyone came early for the first time. Maybe I should start labeling all of my meetings as 'urgent' going forward!"

There were a few nervous chuckles from the room.

"Well, most of you are wondering why we are here and can conclude it isn't good news. I don't schedule urgent meetings for good news. So I'll just say it. The last quarter at ABS was a poor one. A very poor one. The company is doing some restructuring, and as a result, the Ares Oversight Board has dropped a budget cut on us."

People groaned and Ali vocally swore out loud. "How bad is it?"

"I talked them down to 20%, but it must be implemented within one month," Tim admitted.

"God damn it, Tim!" Don blurted out. "Why didn't you stop them? If ABS ever wants to grow out of the traditional box they've built around themselves, our innovation center is the 'tip of the spear'! If you cut off the head of a spear, all you have is a stick!"

Tim held up his hand, "Believe me, I tried. It is actually much worse in other parts of ABS. Complete offices are closing. Leadership is taking major salary cuts. Business expansion plans are being cut back. Layoffs are expected for over a thousand people. We are actually getting off much easier than most of the company."

"That said," Tim continued, adding context, "our recent challenges from Intuition Bank and with our Breeze app have certainly influenced their decision. They have given us an additional ultimatum that if we don't show increased revenue and user count by at least 5% in the next three months, there will be further cuts."

Don immediately reacted, "That's bull crap, Tim! How are we supposed to run faster when they cut our legs out from underneath us?! This is the first nail in the coffin for Ares! Time to brush up my resume!"

The room erupted with frantic, nervous talking in response to Don's outburst.

"Quiet please!" Tim called out, bringing the noise to a rapid close.

"You have a solid point, Don. This is a raw deal. That doesn't mean we have to take it lying down, though, and this is certainly not the time to quit! I do have one silver lining for you. We get to determine how we do the budget cuts."

Roy made his usual late entrance at this point. Everyone took a silent moment as he found an empty seat. Vera could see uncertain, skeptical looks on several of the faces as they pondered their fate.

Tim gave Roy a look and then picked the conversation back up again. "We have been operating with many extras over the past few years and I believe that with some creativity and group thinking we can minimize the impact from this and be leaner, meaner, and more competitive as a result!"

Jayson calmly inquired, "So how do you propose doing that, Tim?"

"Glad you asked," Tim said as he held out a stack of paper. "First, let's put this in context. I have here from Accounting our entire budget broken down by each of your divisions. It adds up to a little over twenty million dollars right now."

"Now if we were an actual startup," he continued, "our budget would probably be half that, so I think this is doable. If you consider that a 20% budget cut is four million dollars. That's still millions more than many start-ups have to spend. If they can do it, we can too!"

Roy decided to add his two cents, "So are you saying we all just take a 20% salary cut in the gut and move on?"

"Not at all," Tim replied. "Angela, what techniques do you have in your toolbag for this dilemma?"

Everyone in the room turned to face Angela.

"Yes, salary reduction is an option, and even layoffs," Angela began, "but before that, we have many more palatable choices! Plus, salary may be non-negotiable for many of the people on our teams. There are many other places to cut a budget such as software licenses, training expenses, entertainment, amenities, and so on."

She continued, "I, for one, appreciate that Tim brought us here together to brainstorm on creative ways to cut the budget, instead of simply passing along a mandate from the Board. I propose that we determine high-level categories and targets for these cuts today and then take the next week to determine more precisely how we will carry them out within our teams. We can then come back to review and finalize our plan and submit that to the Ares board."

Vera noticed that everybody was one hundred percent focused on Angela. She wondered how Angela could be so cool under pressure when she wasn't even working here three months ago...

Tim added, "A week isn't much time, so I'm going to also ask you concurrently to reach out to all of your direct reports. I want you to find out which of them would be willing to take a salary cut, a furlough, or early retirement. Clear?"

"Hmm, actually, Tim," Angela interrupted, "while I do think there are some good options in your ideas around voluntary reductions in force, I'd like to focus this workshop on suggestions that are less likely to inspire fear in the teams."

"Oh, yes, please," interjected Linda. "Talk of furloughs and salary cuts makes me very uneasy. I'm sure I'm not the only one."

Tim started defending himself, "All I am saying is that we may get some volunteers to leave and that would save us a lot of headaches."

Angela jumped in pretty quickly. "If I could just do a quick reminder. You've all learned Double Aces now. These conversations are going to be very intense, very difficult, and very emotional at times. I would encourage you to please take the extra time to slow down and first acknowledge the intentions of others. Check and see if they are really disagreeing with you, and which parts of their statements you do agree with."

Angela got up and walked over to the whiteboard and started writing.

"I do agree with you, Tim," Linda clarified, "that voluntary exits would be a great help. I also like Angela's suggestion that we need to work on the language that we use to present it to the teams to minimize fear. Not that we can avoid fear." Linda chuckled nervously and self-consciously. "Let's be clear. This is going to cause fear. There is no getting around that, but there are steps we can take to minimize the fear." Vera nodded her head in agreement and noticed that she wasn't the only one doing so.

Angela stepped away from the board where she had written, "**Appreciate or Acknowledge**," "**Clarify or Confirm**," and "**Enhance or Evolve**" as a visual reminder of the steps in the Double Aces.

Vera could see Angela's point, so she decided to try and help out. "If I could summarize what I heard, I heard a suggestion from Tim to ask for voluntary exits or reductions in salary, plus a suggestion to brainstorm around the language that we use to present the idea to the teams. Angela, might I also suggest, while you're up there at the board, that you start a running list of ideas that starts with 'Voluntary Salary Reductions and Retirements'?"

"Great idea, Vera!" Angela said enthusiastically as she started writing. "Okay, our target is four million dollars, and our first potential category is employment."

$4M
Employment – voluntary early retirement, sabbaticals, salary reductions

"I know a few engineers that would love to retire early," Jayson added. "They're largely just waiting to earn a little bit more money for their retirement fund. If we can offer them a retirement bonus, I think they'd volunteer for an exit."

"Well," Tim responded, "spending more of our budget now to remove a recurring expense later is definitely helpful."

Jayson countered, "Actually, some of them would also be fine with just going part-time, until they hit their Medicare and Social Security limits, as long as they don't lose their benefits. Is part-time an option?"

"Ooh," Linda interjected, "I've got a few new parents who would also be interested in reducing hours, as long as they don't lose benefits. I like that idea! Is that possible?"

"Anything's possible," Tim replied, "That's why we're here, to think of new ways to solve the problem."

"And," Ali interjected, "if we prorate their benefits based on their part-time hours we can save even more money!"

Linda scrunched up her face. "Actually, that's not going to work. Sorry. Acknowledge: I acknowledge your enthusiasm, Ali, to find more opportunities to save. Clarify or Confirm: You are proposing, Ali, that anyone who goes part-time also gets a reduction in benefits, right?" Ali nodded and Linda continued, "The people I'm thinking of, though, still need the benefits. They have new families, after all."

"If you calculate it out," Roy added, "and think about the expense on benefits separately from the expense on salary, we are still saving money if they take a reduction in salary while maintaining the same benefits."

"Great point, Roy!" Angela said. "It seems like the main question here is about productivity. I think that's the right question for each of you to determine for each person who wants to go part-time. What's the lower threshold? At some point, they won't be as effective at their jobs with limited hours. It's the same experience as people allocated to multiple teams. We've all seen that when a person doesn't have enough hours available, they start to become a bottleneck." A lot of heads started nodding in recognition and agreement.

"Now that makes sense," Roy agreed, "but I've got another question. Who in their right mind is going to volunteer to continue working the same number of hours but take a reduction in salary when they could just go part-time?" he blurted out sardonically.

Vera jumped in to defend the idea but noticed the Double Aces prompts on the board as she did so. "Great modeling of a clarifying question, Roy," she said with a wry smile. "I remember a story about an organization faced with cutbacks. I can't remember which company, but when the employees were presented with the prospect of losing their friends, they all volunteered to take a pay cut so that no one had to lose their jobs."

"There are some stories about that in the book 'Reinventing Organizations' by Frederick Laloux," Angela added.

Linda added her voice, "I know that I would reduce my salary if it meant that I wouldn't have to fire one of my Scrum Masters."

"Me too," added Jayson. Nods came from Evah and Zach as well. Vera raised her hand in solidarity. She would do anything for her hard-working designers. It would be unfair to kick them out on the street after all they had done to try to keep Ares afloat.

Tim jumped in, "Let's make salary reductions our last resort. I'll take a salary reduction myself to help keep people on board, but if we can avoid it, let's look for other ways to reduce expenses first. Please keep the teams together as much as possible."

"Power to the People!" Linda called out, pumping her fist in the air.

Vera chuckled despite her melancholic mood. Linda was so delightfully goofy sometimes that she couldn't help but smile.

Ali raised his hand and Tim pointed his way. "Some here don't have many direct reports and don't really manage a budget. Why include us?"

Zach's hand shot up in the air, "You have oversight over our software licenses and cloud fees, Ali. That's not nothing."

Ali nodded, "True. I've already worked pretty diligently with Jayson to reduce costs." He pondered a little harder and added, "We also have a rather liberal playground of tools that we could trim down. I guess that could easily go into the hundreds of thousands."

"Excellent!" Tim belted out. "Now, that's what I'm talking about!"

Evah added, "Yes, I can also honestly say that the teams, especially our Quality Automation Engineers have been playing with many different copies of competing automation tools and we definitely don't need them all."

Zach added, "Right on! Let's make a list of all the things we can potentially go without, and then we compare and collectively determine the best options."

Ali called out, "Zach, can you add 'Cloud tools and usage costs' for the second line? For the third line add, 'Non-essential software – recurring revenue, purchases, rationalization.'

"What about our non-cloud servers and clients?" Jayson asked.

Ali mused, "We primarily use the cloud, so hybrid is a thing of the past for us. However, we do have three servers remaining, largely because we haven't finished their migrations to the cloud. If we finish those and stop using those old legacy licenses, that could save us between five and six figures. Honestly, we've been procrastinating since they're working fine and the budget wasn't a big concern before. It really isn't that long of a migration effort. Yeah, go ahead and add 'physical servers and legacy licenses'."

"Great! Everything counts!" Zach responded, writing on the board. "What else?"

$4M
Employment (voluntary early retirement, sabbaticals, salary reductions)
Cloud tools and usage costs
Non-essential software
Physical Servers and Legacy Licenses

Zach spoke up, "Amenities – room space, lunch meetings, free food, alcohol, snacks."

Don coughed, "Designer Den!" in a very unsubtle way.

Vera's eyes widened and her pupils dilated suddenly, anger welling up inside her. *"How dare he!"* she thought, especially when his expenses per month cost more than her entire team!

She gave Don a stern look, "Yes, the Designer Den will be reviewed along with everyone else when it comes to amenities, Don." She felt herself getting angrier and flushed in the face. "While we're at it, let's also add 'Training and Conferences – Attending, hosting, sponsoring' and 'Sales' too!"

Tim nodded, "Let's include Marketing in that. That's really two parts. Part of conference participation is to get the word out about Breeze, but the other half is about education, personal growth, and development. We should weigh those separately."

Don reacted, "Okay, but don't include 'Sales'! If we can't sell the product, nothing else matters."

Tim quickly countered, "Sales is definitely critical, Don. However, don't think we will ignore those expensive golf outings you and I go on with our clients! We can reduce our 'business events' or ask our clients to pay for themselves. They are rich after all!"

Don looked betrayed, "Really, Tim? But that's how we get our top users!"

"That may be true," Tim responded, "but not very scalable. We can't expect to get most of our clients by 'wining and dining' them to join. That was fine for our proof of concept, but not a viable nor sustainable business model!"

Don continued, "You know that word of mouth spreads quickly through fancy events. With just a few key contacts, word can spread virally! We really should be talking about expanding sales and bringing on a few more salespeople to support me."

"True, but still not viable," Tim insisted. "Jeff Bezos was packing books himself over twenty-five years ago at Amazon, but do you think he's still doing that? It's time to move on, Don, and make the app so good that it sells itself."

Don groaned but remained silent.

Vera couldn't help but feel a little satisfaction. *"Go, Tim!"*

$4M
Employment (voluntary early retirement, sabbaticals, salary reductions)
Cloud tools and usage costs
Non-essential software
Physical Servers and Legacy Licenses
Amenities
Training and Conferences
Marketing
Sales

Angela stepped up, "Rather than make decisions here and now, I wonder if we can resolve them all through the next exercise that I had planned. It's a technique called 'Participatory Budgeting'[1], but since we're cutting the budget instead of building a budget, maybe let's call it 'Collaborative Cutting'. I don't want you to think that this is exactly the same technique, because instead of forecasting what we're going to work on for the next several months, we have to do an expedited process to cut down our existing budget.

"We have four million dollars," she continued. "And we want to collectively determine the budget for each section. So we'll tackle that in three phases. In phase one, we split the money evenly between our areas. Since we have ten people here, that makes the math simple with each person getting $400,000 of money to cut. Go through your *own* budgets only and find $400,000."

"That sounds fair, but it's not," Evah offered. "If we have a limited budget compared to another area, cutting $400,000 is a bigger percentage. For example, Jayson's budget is probably three times larger than mine."

"True," Jayson said, "but the vast majority of my budget is people, and since we're trying to not cut people, that actually leaves me with very few options. This is going to be tough for me too."

---

1 *https://en.wikipedia.org/wiki/Participatory_budgeting*

"It's going to be tough for all of us," Tim insisted. "Nothing about this process is going to be easy. Do what you can within your own budget. If you are willing to cut more than $400,000, please do. If the $400,000 is too deep for your area, outline the cost impact for each cut, and then you'll have a chance to negotiate in the next phase."

"Tim is spot on," Angela added. "This is just phase one. The other two phases will balance out the entire amount in a more holistic manner. None of us are an island. Every decision in every group affects the other groups, and that's what phase three is for, to deal with cross-impacts."

"What's phase two?" asked Roy.

"Yes," Angela agreed, "let me finish explaining the three phases, so you can all start to see how it fits together, and then we can discuss." She started writing on the whiteboard. "During Phase One we make the difficult choices necessary to cut $400,000 from each of our budgets. If you can't find $400,000 in cuts, the remaining balance will be allocated to salary reductions, either through voluntary retirements or voluntary salary cuts."

Phase 1: (30 min) Everyone find $400k in your own budgets

Groans went up from almost everybody in the room.

"Everything is still up for negotiation, though," Angela quickly clarified. "And that's where Phases Two and Three come in. Phase One is about your budget only, but Phases Two and Three are about cross-collaboration. For Phase Two we are going to break into groups of five. For group A, we will have Don, Ali, Vera, Jayson, and myself. For group B, we will have Roy, Evah, Linda, Zach, and Tim." She wrote the names on the board for easy reference.

"I will facilitate group A and Zach will facilitate group B. During Phase Two we will each be given five minutes within our smaller groups to share which cuts we identified and how much is left over for salary cuts. Keep the readouts brief, because that five minutes is also the time for the rest of the people in your group to help you brainstorm other ways to cut funds without cutting salaries, if possible."

More groans as Angela wrote the instructions for Phase Two on the board, along with the lists of names for each group.

"Remember your Double Aces," Angela reminded them. "When it is your turn, remember that the other people are making suggestions to help you avoid losing people or reducing salaries. That is the goal of Phase Two. Help each other out. Also, remember the Ratatouille Principle. Not every suggestion is going to be a great idea, but consider each one honestly before eliminating them."

"That brings us to Phase Three," Angela said, bringing it back around the topic everyone was waiting for. "By the end of Phase Two, each group should have about two million dollars in potential cuts, bringing us to our total of four million dollars, but the cuts at this point probably are not fairly balanced, as Evah and Jayson correctly pointed out before. Phase Three is about making the final impact fair."

She continued, "We'll start Phase Three with a minute per person for each to present their list of cuts to the entire room. After all the cuts are on the table, then we start negotiating." She added the instructions for Phase Three to the whiteboard.

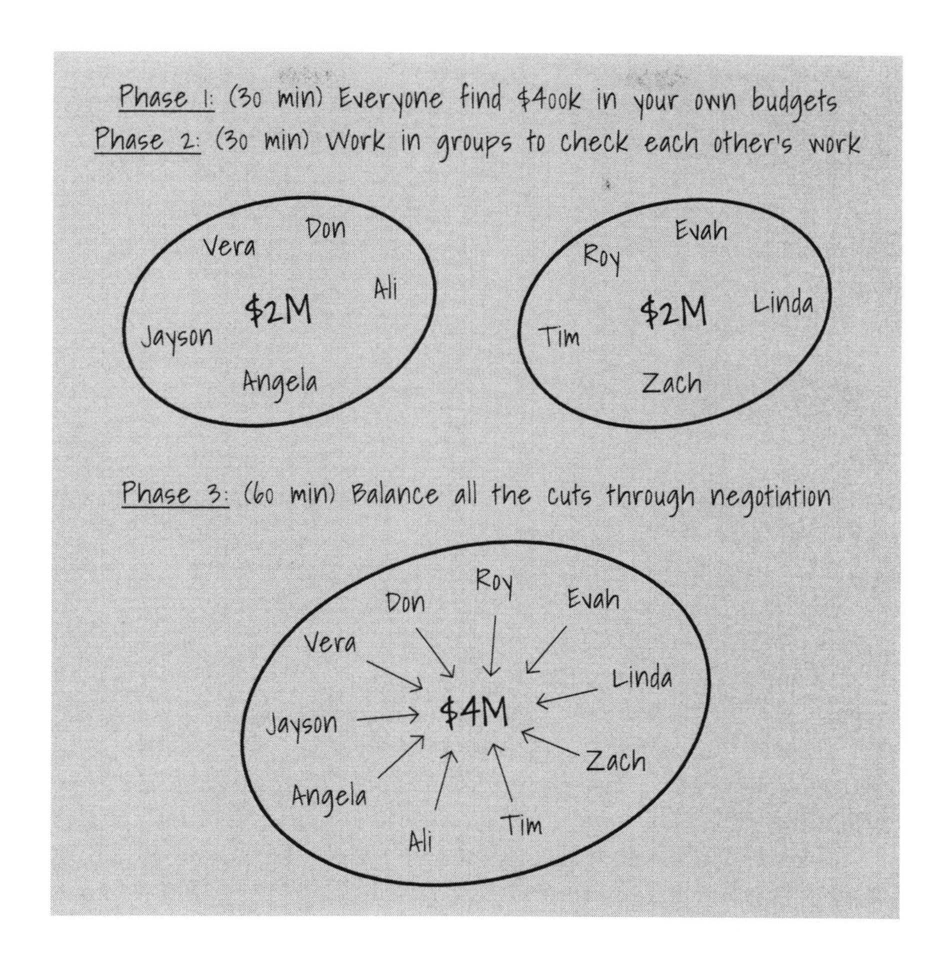

Angela continued, "By the time we're done here today, everyone should have your primary expenses and a rough amount for cuts. Focus on those and you will have more time to refine after today." Some members of the board emitted sighs of relief.

That helped reduce the tension some...

She moved on to an example, "Let's take a less-contentious example as a simulation — the snacks. Assume that we have to cut the entire food budget."

"Not the food!" Don called out, jokingly. The others laughed.

"Well," Angela clarified with a smile, "one of the rest of you could offer to cut an equivalent amount from your own budgets so that we can add the food back into the budget. Any takers?"

There was complete silence in the room.

"Exactly," Angela said, driving home the point. "We wish we could keep it all, but when we compare them against each other, we cut the ones that hurt less. To help us fairly determine the impacts of each potential trade-off during this stage, we'll follow the technique of Reasoned Objections which I've borrowed from Sociocracy. Anyone can propose a trade and we'll post each of them on a sticky note. We'll do a quick show of hands after each idea to see if there are any objections. If there are no objections, the trade is done and the cuts are adjusted. If there are objections, then we'll hear each reasoned objection in turn and debate."

Tim jumped in, "The really hard negotiations will probably be around the resulting salary reductions. Be as generous as you can in identifying operational cuts so that we can offset salary reductions. I know I'm going to be checking your work and offering additional ideas for cuts aimed towards this goal."

"Let's face it," Angela asserted. "We are going to have some tough discussions over the next several hours, and Zach and I will keep pointing you back towards the Double Aces to help soften the blows and keep things collaborative."

"One more thing," she said in conclusion, "we are not going to be using a majority vote for proposed negotiations here. These choices are too important. We're going to use "consent" — not consensus, but consent. Consensus requires that everybody has to agree, but we don't have to all agree here. Consent, instead, asks that we keep going until we all can agree to live with the consequences. If we start to get bogged down in an endless discussion, we'll table it and move on to the next cut so we have sufficient time to go through all of the ideas."

There were nods of agreement.

Angela clapped her hands. "Okay, are there any questions?"

Don raised his hand, "I still say that reducing the sales budget is going to hurt us more than you realize."

Tim responded, "Well then, start preparing your sales pitches to convince everyone else to cut money in other places. But first, you must identify your initial $400,000. No exceptions."

BUT WHO GETS THE BLAME?

Roy raised his hand. "I like the idea of figuring out the numbers here, but this really seems like an effort in desperation. As Geoffrey Moore might say, we need to accelerate to become profitable. I don't often say this, but Don is completely right."

"We don't have a choice about this, Roy," Tim answered. "May I remind everyone that we fumbled the ball when we allowed Intuition in? What we are experiencing here is karma, and we are paying for our own mistakes. But as Simon Sinek says, this is an infinite game. We can choose whether we want to stay in the game and I want to keep playing!"

"Naomi was our problem, not Intuition." Roy countered. "At least she's gone now, but a little too late."

"There it is again," thought Vera. *"Someone is putting the blame on Naomi."* This was Roy, though. Roy was always blaming Naomi. *"Is he right? Is he wrong?"* She had always been so sure that he was wrong before, but now she was starting to question herself.

Vera heard Angela jump into the discussion, "As Tim said, let's keep focused on the long term. We aren't out of the game yet. Okay, you'll have two hours to set out a preliminary budget for each group and we will review the results together. Let's get started!"

Vera couldn't shake the thoughts in her brain, though, and went ahead and said it out loud, "Was it Naomi's fault?" Her voice was very matter-of-fact, reflecting her honest curiosity. "I've been rolling this thought over and over in my brain. Was it really Naomi's fault?"

"Now," said Tim, "let's not blame someone who's not here to defend herself. I mean sure she..."

Angela interrupted him, "Can I jump in here, Tim?" He paused and let her steer the conversation.

"It's not about blame," she continued. "Let's focus on what we can change given where we are now. This is not the best time to do a retro."

Vera couldn't help herself. She switched to her confident voice that had worked so well with Naomi and took back the floor from Angela, "No, this needs an answer. You all know Naomi was my friend," she insisted, barreling ahead without stopping. "She was instrumental in getting us where we are today and I supported her completely, even though she was difficult at times... And, honestly, who among us isn't difficult at times." Roy nodded in agreement.

Vera continued, "But now I'm wondering if I was wrong to put my faith in her. As we saw in that usability session, she missed some really important clues and ignored some really great insights from the team. I don't want to make that same mistake again."

"It's not about Naomi," Angela said, trying to wrestle back control of the conversation. "It's about choices, and it's about the system. That's the caution I want to put in front of all of us before we start down the road of analyzing Naomi. That's Naomi's job, to analyze Naomi. Our job is to analyze ourselves. The responsibility for this is not on any single person's shoulders. It is a ***system*** problem. It is ***always*** a system problem. The system here was set up such that Naomi was making the call because most companies are set up that way. And Naomi made the best calls that she could."

"So," Roy said, seizing an opportunity, "we should have replaced her with someone better, who could have made better decisions."

"Like you, Roy? Is that what you want?" Evah burst out, the energy lifting her to her feet.

Angela physically stepped in between them and held out her hands. "No, that is not the answer. Someone else would have just made different decisions, not better decisions. Again, it's not a people problem, it's a system problem. This is one of the many reasons why I refused to take over Naomi's job. Handing decision power over to a single person is a problem, regardless of who it is. There are other ways to solve our problems, like the DevOps concept of 'No Blame'."

"Sounds like a clever way to avoid responsibility to me," quipped Don, snarkily.

Angela raised an eyebrow, "Don, you know this is not about responsibility. I mean, come on. If we can't turn this around, I'm the first one out the door. The coach is always the easy choice, but I know that. That's the nature of my job. But replacing me, or replacing Naomi, or replacing anyone won't solve the problem because the problem is with the system itself. The old system has to go."

"Wait, so you want anarchy instead?" Evah blurted out exasperatedly.

Angela sighed with her own exasperation, "Why do people always jump straight from hierarchy to anarchy? There are so many other ways to run a company."

"You know, you're lucky," Angela said, switching gears and catching Vera off guard. Angela explained, "Usually this fact is invisible, but you actually have the proof right in front of you. Most organizations are actually designed for this exact moment in time. The whole point of a traditional hierarchy is to give one person decision authority so that if something goes horribly wrong, they take on the blame, and the company ejects them from the system along with all the blame. Well, Naomi left, but the problems sure didn't go away. Assigning blame does not fix problems."

"So it's just nobody's fault now?" quipped Ali. "Oh, great. Nobody gets the blame and everybody gets a participation trophy. There goes career advancement."

"I wonder if you notice," Angela responded, "how many times people go to extremes around here. The words 'everybody', 'always', and 'nobody' get tossed around a lot. It's often a battle of 'all or nothing' around here. Nothing is ever 'all or nothing'."

"We need 'accountability'..." Ali began, but Angela cut him off.

"Blame," she expounded, "creates a culture of fear. If everyone is afraid of being singled out as ***'the'*** person to blame, then it will never be safe enough for anyone to own up to what they could do better. If no one can acknowledge their mistakes, then they can't openly work to fix them. We want people to say, 'That didn't work' instead of 'You were wrong'. We want to hear, 'We tried that and it didn't work,' so that we can also hear, 'What if we did this instead?' We have to openly practice making different choices or else we get stuck or even regress. A better definition of accountability is one that takes responsibility for doing something new in the future, not forcing someone to take the blame for the past."

"So..." Evah challenged Angela, "how would you rewrite Naomi's accountability in this situation?"

"I choose not to focus on Naomi's accountability," Angela clarified. "Here's what I would say using the principles of 'no blame'. We had a system in the past that placed an unfair and unrealistic burden on a single decision-maker. We switched to a system of user testing, collaborative problem-solving, and experimentation which has since produced much better results. Naomi chose to leave instead of participating in the new system. Some people do that when a system changes. No blame. It is just what she did. Had she chosen to remain instead, she would have been welcome as part of the new system."

Vera decided to attempt crafting a summary of the discussion. "So it was ***not*** Naomi's fault, but she ***was*** applying the wrong solution for our problem. That sounds like Albert Einstein's quote, 'We cannot solve our problems with the same thinking we used when we created them.' So actually, it wasn't even that she was applying the wrong solution or the wrong system, but that we were ***all*** applying the wrong system in letting her make the calls."

She paused and rearranged her thoughts, "I was going to say that we were all wrong but to use your words, our new approach is working better than our old approach, and trying new things is more important than assigning blame."

"Yes," confirmed Angela.

There was silence in the room for a while as everyone let it sink in.

"But we have gotten off-topic here," Angela said, breaking the silence, "but now that we've talked about it, I'm hoping that we can carry that new system into this exercise. It's going to take our collective wisdom to figure out how we can cut the budget, ***and*** accelerate the Innovation Center the way Geoffrey Moore recommends, ***and*** save our friends from losing their jobs, ***and*** solve the Intuition problem, ***and, and, and*** so many other things."

SHIFTING THE SYSTEM

Angela nudged them back into the exercise, "Let's start individually determining the cuts to our own budgets, and then return to this spirit as we form our groups for Phase Two and see what magic we can work."

Tim passed out the sheets of paper with the budget items on them and everyone quietly started working on their budgets for the allotted thirty minutes.

When the thirty minutes were up, they slowly started conversing again as they rearranged themselves into their two separate groups.

Vera volunteered to go first within her group. She began, "When Tim invited me to join the Innovation Center, he enticed me with plenty of perks, and I passed that same generosity on to my designers. It was how I have been able to attract and keep the best talent, but that time is behind us now. It is time for new thinking. Tools are one example. We have often splurged on multiple tools for the 'spirit of experimentation' and everyone has their favorite, but not everyone needs licenses for all the tools. Many of them could be eliminated without the team losing their ability to experiment. Overall, not a lot of money will be saved, but it's a start." When she was done with her readout, she had identified about $250,000, including cutting the entire budget for all of the food and drinks.

Vera concluded, sadly, "That leaves me with $150,000 remaining for unavoidable salary cuts. About $15,000 per person. I'll probably take a $50,000 cut myself to bring it down to only $10,000 for each of my designers."

"I'm sorry you had to dig into the salary budget, Vera," acknowledged Jayson. "It's tough to find things. Can I ask a question to see if we can reduce that?"

Vera nodded and Jayson continued, "Why do we have separate Agile management tools? I've noticed the designers use their own system that has a monthly fee and we use another one that has an Enterprise license with the company, so we only pay a small fraction of that cost."

Vera countered, "But the designers love the look and feel of our system and have streamlined it where we use it very effectively! That software has more than paid for itself in keeping all of our activities focused. Removing it would be a big hit to our productivity."

"I'll be honest," Jayson replied, "it would take a little work, but we can reproduce in our system just about every feature I've seen in yours. It might require a couple of plugins, but it's possible. We can also set you up with your own custom space so that you aren't affected by our configurations. Plus, since we are moving towards more integrated teams, wouldn't it make sense for all of us to be using the same system for tracking all work?"

"To be honest right back," Vera said, vividly remembering past frustrations and letting it coat her words, "having to wait for a system admin to get around to making changes when we need them is too much of a headache."

Jayson pushed a little more. "When it comes down to the wire, wouldn't you want to cut out that system rather than cutting designer salaries?"

"Or," Don added, "maybe leave it up to the team members. They could choose to keep their system and take an equivalent cut in their salaries."

"I can ask," Vera offered, "but based on the last time we talked about this, I am pretty sure the team would rather take a salary reduction than deal with all of that again. It was that bad!"

Angela piped up, "Let's deal with each Reasoned Objection in turn. The first objection was about the productivity the designers find in their system. Jayson, are you offering to help Vera transfer to the other system?"

"Definitely," Jayson confirmed. "You will have my personal attention," he said directly to Vera.

"Vera," Angela asked, "would Jayson's solution work for you?"

"Well," Vera considered, "it depends really on just how close he can get. I can make a list of the must-have features and then we will see how far he can get. That's the best I can offer right now."

"Ok. Makes sense," Angela agreed. "The second Reasoned Objection was around the lack of a timely response by the system admins. Let's consider all aspects and make no assumptions. Does the system have to be centrally managed?"

Ali jumped in to answer for Jayson, "When we let people do whatever they wanted to in the past, there was no consistency, and workflows were all over the place!"

"Hmm," Angela began in response, "so there was a significant, measurable decrease in productivity because of the differences between the workflows?"

"Well, no," Ali admitted, "we weren't tracking that kind of data back then. It was just a nightmare to centrally manage."

"Ok," Angela said, then added, "One of the requirements of a Reason Objection is that it has to actually affect you. Does this meet that standard? How did all of those different configurations affect the system admins?"

Ali thought for a moment and then said, "Well, the system admins had to manage all of those different workflows."

Vera picked up on that thread and pulled at the strings, "But did they? The choice was made to centrally manage all the workflows which, yes, created a bunch of work for the admins, but before that, we managed our own workflows, and we manage our own workflows now. If you didn't take it upon yourselves to manage our workflows and let us do it, then you wouldn't have had to do all of that work."

"But we were getting requests by people to make changes," Ali clarified, "and when we went in, it was a mess, and it took a lot of time to clean it up and fix it."

"Are you talking about my team?" Vera asked Ali. "Was my team one of the teams that messed things up and asked the admins to fix it?"

Ali thought for another moment, but Vera already knew the answer. Ali eventually confirmed her thought, "No, you weren't. I remember that your configuration was unusual and very non-standard, but it wasn't one of the areas that we were asked to fix."

"So why then," Vera insisted, "were our admin rights taken away?"

"It was the new policy," Ali said defensively. "Everybody's admin rights were taken away. It wasn't personal."

Angela pushed back this time, "I have always struggled with that justification. It should be personal, shouldn't it? We are dealing with 'persons' after all. I think Vera's point is why did her group need to lose their rights if they were not causing a problem? Why did every group have to be centrally managed? Was there a valid reason? And remember, there is 'no blame' here. We are only looking for the accurate circumstances of what happened." That stopped everyone in their tracks for a moment. Angela let the silence linger as Ali thought it through.

After some thought, Ali agreed. "Decisions were not made on a person-by-person basis," he confirmed. "It was a blanket decision made and applied to everyone."

Angela finished her thought, "I think we should try an experiment and give them admin access to their own area."

"Hey, I like that experiment," Jayson exclaimed in enthusiastic support. "Anything is worth a try, especially if it means we can cut more items! You and me, Vera, we'll get that space set up however you need it."

"Sounds like a worthy experiment," Vera said, then took a deep breath and let it out. "And in return I will admit that you are right about the importance of cutting wherever we can. If you're offering personal support, we can experiment with migrating our content to your system. If we can get close enough, remove our system, and save money, let's do it."

"You will be happy," Jayson said with a big broad smile. "And, once you all switch over, I have some additional thoughts that I think you will really like that I couldn't do with two systems before."

"Great examples of the spirit of this section!" Angela said in summary. "Thank you for slowing down and sticking with the process. It's important to address each Reasoned Objection in turn without chaining multiple objections together. The consequences of not doing so could cause some real harm. In this case, saving people and salaries is more important than just about everything else."

After a few more ideas, they had found another $45,000 in potential cuts, much to everyone's surprise, before moving on to Jayson's budget and the others in their group.

They went a little long in both groups, but after more than an hour, they had determined all of the initial breakdowns.

REBUILDING

After a short break, they reunited as one group and compared their breakdown lists, beginning the merge process and sorting through the differences from their combined perspectives. Being personally invested in the welfare of the Ares Innovation Center, everyone was quite vocal and there were even some raised voices at times, yet the conversations were pursued earnestly with respect.

The biggest surprise of the day came from Roy.

"Half of my cuts," he said, "are going to be my salary. I guess now is as good of a time as any to tell you that I found another job." Everybody seemed shocked. Vera wondered what had taken so long. He obviously was not happy there.

It was his comment after revealing the news, though, that was the bigger announcement. "You don't need my salary in this budget. Let's be honest. Save yourself the headache and don't hire a replacement for me, or at least not for a while. The data collection can be done by Jayson's team. Ali also knows how to design the reports. The complex data analysis that I've been trained to do, you're not ready for it."

Tim backed Roy up saying, "I think data is invaluable for the phases of growth that we are about to enter, but thinking like a startup, we do already have other people who can execute the immediate tasks that we need. Over the past several months, I have come to agree that we are not quite ready for someone of Roy's caliber when it comes to data analysis. We will be soon, but let's take our expert's advice," he said gesturing towards Roy, "and hold off on hiring a replacement for several months."

Tim then surprised the group by announcing that he was going to take a massive cut to his salary for at least six months. "I have stocks I can sell and family money to carry me over, so I'm going to take a cue from Steve Jobs and take a one dollar salary until we are back on track and generating revenue again."

"That will mean fewer trips to exotic locations," he added, "and fewer photos to share and stories for me to tell, but I think you all will survive." He smiled. "I've been thinking about doing this for a while, but frankly, I wanted to see first if you all were willing to make the hard decisions too, and you did not disappoint me. Thank you for your dedication, your caring, and your hard work today!"

He started applauding them, and they all joined in, to applaud his choice. It had been a long afternoon, but they had a high-level list. Angela placed the results on the whiteboard.

$4M
Employment - $1.1M
Cloud tools and usage costs - $0.5M
Non-essential software - $0.65M
Physical Servers and Legacy Licenses - $0.05M
Amenities - $0.15M
Training and Conferences - $0.3M
Marketing - $0.3M
Sales - $0.15M
Salary - $0.8M

When she was done tallying the updates, Angela spoke, "Okay, we now have a starting guide for our budget cuts. We all believe these are realistic estimates and still have to validate them through our teams, but we can share these guidelines for transparency that we did all that we could. Zach's going to create a shared spreadsheet on our secure server. Please update it with the results of your individual efforts."

"Also," Angela added, "if you have reason to believe we won't hit a budget target, please reach out to each other to determine what additional adjustments are needed and from where. On the flip side, if you think you can exceed your budget cuts, then please show that also so we can reduce the cost-cutting in other areas. Tim, do you have anything to add?"

"Yes", responded Tim. "Be hyper-transparent here. Think carefully about your decisions and share these with your teams. Remember the Ratatouille Principle, that a great cost-reduction idea can come from anyone! We are determining the future of not just our careers, but the entire Innovation Center!"

"Anything else before we return to our teams?" Angela asked one last time.

"There is one more thing, I hate to say," Tim added.

Tim turned directly towards Vera and she felt her stomach clench.

Tim continued, "You know how the Designer Den is on the border between our space and accounting?"

"Oh no!" Vera thought, instantly recognizing the writing on the wall.

Tim kept going, "Ahmed told me directly that he wants that space back. With all of the other consolidations happening elsewhere, they're closing down a couple of the other offices and they need to make room to consolidate all those people."

"Tim, no!" Vera pleaded. "That's the room where we all started. We have history there. What other space can we give them? Maybe we can find some other places to cut if we keep looking. What will it take to keep that space?"

"This one isn't about the money," Tim said sadly. "It's next door to Accounting, and Ahmed used it as a bargaining chip. He was willing to agree to reduce our cuts to only four million and let us figure out how to cut the budget, but ***only*** if we gave him that space. I didn't really have a choice."

"No!" Vera exclaimed. "Where will my team go? That's our home!" She felt both devastated and guilty at the same time. After all, Tim had just slashed his own salary down to one dollar. She knew she didn't have a choice, but this hurt. This hurt so much.

"You can join us," Linda offered sympathetically.

Vera could start to feel tears building, but she fought them and stuffed them down inside. *"How could Ahmed do this to her?"* she asked herself.

"I'm so sorry, Vera," Angela said.

"Did you know about this already?" Vera snapped. She could feel herself losing control.

"I didn't," Angela said in a soft voice.

Vera felt mistrust in her answer, but at the same time, it didn't really matter. She had to get herself under control. Now. Everyone was staring at her, and it looked like Don – that jerk – was fighting off a smile, poorly.

"Excuse me," was all she said. Everyone stayed silent as she walked out of the room. She had to get out of there. She felt abandoned. *"Didn't anyone understand the significance of that space?" she thought. "It's not just a room. It's a haven, a haven for art, and design... for artists and creatives!"* Without that space, Vera honestly wasn't sure if she could deliver the quality of output needed to maintain her reputation.

She looked around for a private space, but they were all too public. Eventually, she found herself outside one of the quieter bathrooms. She entered and sat down on the couch just inside. She let herself curl into a ball for a little bit, slowly regaining her confidence, while simultaneously fighting back the fear that someone else would walk in at any minute.

She got a couple of minutes of peace before the door opened. She quickly straightened herself out as best that she could.

Linda entered, followed by Angela. "We're so sorry to intrude," Linda said apologetically, "and we can leave if you want us to. We were just worried about you and wanted to make sure that you were alright."

For a moment, Vera couldn't believe that anyone cared enough to come to find her. Tears jumped to her eyes, but she fought them back. "I'm fine, no really," she offered instead, dabbing at the corner of her eye with her pinky. She desperately wanted to maintain her outer veneer of composure but was sure that she was failing.

Angela offered an attempt at conciliation, "You just found out that you're losing your home of the last several years, your home that you lovingly built and furnished from scratch. You have every right to be upset."

"It's just an office," Vera acquiesced, straightening her outfit.

"It is not just an office!" exclaimed Linda. "It's beautiful! I wish I could work in a space like that! With the art and the pottery and those sculpture thingies, and those drawings you do every day! I mean, every day, a new work of art!"

"You're too kind," Vera said, blushing a little. "After all, it's just white-board markers."

Linda countered, "No, you're painting in, what would you call that... ink? Watercolors? No, but it's watery and colorful... whiteboard marker chemicals? Ha! You paint with whiteboard marker chemicals. I don't know what they are, but whatever it is, the result is art."

Vera allowed herself to smile a little. Linda's gushing made her feel important.

"In fact, if I can be honest," Linda admitted, "I really do want your team to move in with us so that you can make our space as beautiful as yours. That would be heaven! We actually started by trying to recreate your space. We failed miserably," she laughed, "but we tried. I bet you would have great ideas on how to make that space feel more... alive, and less, just, open."

"Thank you," Vera said, her chest growing warmer with the compliments.

"I think that's a beautiful idea," Angela added. "What if you thought of the rest of the office as a fresh new canvas?"

"No, my team will need a quiet space," Vera countered. "I'm not sure they would thrive in that open space."

"You know," Linda answered, "we had that same conversation when we put our space together. I can appreciate the need for quiet. Boy, engineers, let me tell you. You do not want to bother them when they're in the zone," she guffawed. "We know how to 'do quiet'. We have designated quiet spaces, places with walls, whatever you need. We could even give you one of the big conference spaces to do with as you please."

Vera had to admit that Linda made a good sales pitch. Linda also seemed to be willing to do whatever it took to help her team feel comfortable.

"Only one request, though," Linda asked. "Please don't hide away in a conference room, okay? We want to be one big happy family. A weird, quirky...oddball...sometimes contentious family... which if you think about it, is not that far away from a real family... but I'm getting off-topic! ...A family nonetheless. The point is... whatever you need, we'll figure it out together."

Vera smiled a big, warm, genuine smile. If she was the type to hug, this would have been the perfect time for a big bear hug. She imagined what it might be like for a moment, but didn't follow through.

Instead, she started to wonder. With all these changes, what was going to happen to her designers and the Ares Innovation Center? And she started to worry again...

Key Points of Learning

- Lund's Maxims
- The Mechanics of Lean Flow
- Wait Time and Hidden Delays
- Embedded UX Designers
- The Three types of Usability Tests
- Usability Theater
- Ratatouille Principle
- Collaborative (Budget) Cutting
- Benevolent Cost Reductions
- Reasoned Objections
- Consent versus Consensus
- Change the System Using "No Blame"

Chapter 10

Linda – Shift Happens

STARTING WITH GRATITUDE

Linda arrived at the Product team meeting nearly ten minutes early. She wasn't alone. Evah, Jayson, and all of the Product Owners were already there, most likely just as eager as Linda to see what changes Angela had made. They seemed engrossed in a conversation, though, so Linda pulled her journal notebook out of her bag and flipped through the pages. Almost three-quarters of them were filled with writing. Her eyes lingered over a few of the passages as she flipped through, memories of days past and of old aspirations bubbling up in her brain.

Reviewing the past was one of her favorite ways to start a day. She had learned a long time ago that it was important to take some time to put everything into context. It was a good reminder that some things which seemed so important in the past could fade completely out of consciousness, even within the span of months. She looked over her notes from her 'early days' at Ares and found one about only scoring three fingers in a fist of five for an upcoming release. She looked at a note she had already scribbled to herself in the margins, *"You should have trusted yourself more. That turned out to be a disaster." "I'm getting better at that,"* she thought. She thought about all the support and encouragement she had received from Angela and others and smiled.

She flipped to the blank pages at the end. She was ready to write now. She had been using three prompts[1] recently to focus her journal entries. She copied them down at the top of page:

1. I am grateful for _____
2. What would make today great? _____
3. Daily affirmation: I am _____

"What am I grateful for today?" She asked herself. *"I am grateful that I have a job,"* she wrote. That felt trite, but she remembered from her time reading "The Artist's Way" book[2] that the point is to just start writing things. You have to get the words flowing. Don't judge the words. Just write.

---

1 From the Tim Ferris Morning Routine, *The Tim Ferriss Morning Routine – HumanWindow*

2 "The Artist's Way" by Julia Cameron, *The Artist's Way (theartistswaybook.com)*

So she just kept writing whatever came into her head, *"I am grateful that I get to work with smart people and tackle challenging problems. I am grateful that we're no longer under so much pressure. I am grateful that we're actually removing the obstacles in our way. I am grateful that we're now paying attention to how we're getting to our goals. I am grateful that we're starting to become methodical and scientific about solving our problems. The end does not justify the means."*

She paused, moved down to a new line, and wrote out the phrase again, *"The end does not justify the means. The means by which you pursue your end goal is the definition of your character."* Did she read that somewhere? Did someone famous say that? She couldn't tell, but it felt poignant.

She moved down another two lines in the notebook and gave it some space. She kept writing, *"HOW an organization chooses to pursue its goals is the definition of its culture."* She paused again.

She decided to let that sit and percolate in the back of her brain, so she moved on to the second prompt, *"What would make today great? Today would be great if the Product Owners and the Designers liked their pairings. Today would be great if everybody felt like they had a voice and that others were listening to them."*

She moved on to the last prompt, *"Daily affirmation: I am _____. I am a good listener. I am a good organizer, both of information and organizing the contributions of all people. I am a scientist. I am a leader."*

TEAM UNIFICATION

A cluster of animated voices started to fill her ears. She looked up to see Angela, Vera, and Zach entering the conference room, with several of the designers in tow. She smiled and put down her pen. They had obviously been having a lively discussion on the way over. She hoped that was a good sign of things to come. She closed her notebook and put it away in her bag.

Angela smiled and addressed the people already in the room, "I'm excited to see so many here already!" They exchanged greetings and pleasantries as everyone found seats.

When everyone was settled, Angela stood and addressed the room again, "Okay, I think everyone already knows that each team is getting a dedicated UX designer, and we're going to announce who was assigned to which team in just a few minutes. These were important decisions, so we wanted everyone to have a voice, and we agonized over the best way to do this. Ultimately we were inspired by a technique called STAR Voting[3]."

"Now, normally STAR Voting is for elections and choosing one or more people from a pool of candidates, but that didn't fit here. The core concepts were the same, but what we're doing is about alignment, alignment of perspectives, alignment of goals, and alignment of similar working styles. So we gave the product owners a list of designer names, and we gave the designers a list of the teams."

"Teams, good call!" Linda thought. The designers were joining an entire team, after all.

Angela went to the whiteboard to illustrate, "Here is the Likert scale. In the center is 'Neither Aligned Nor Unaligned'." She wrote those words on the board. "To the right," she added, "you have the options of 'Somewhat Aligned' and 'Very aligned', and to the left you have the options of 'Somewhat Unaligned' and 'Very unaligned'." She finished out the scale on the board.

Very Unaligned	Somewhat Unaligned	Neither Aligned Nor Unaligned	Somewhat Aligned	Very Aligned
○	○	○	○	○

"We tried to avoid the option of 'I don't know'," she added. "Instead we encouraged everyone to spend some time with each other, ask questions, look at work samples, and talk to friends, Linda, Jayson, Zach, or myself."

"I had never been interviewed by a Designer before," Venkat said out loud with a chuckle. "Usually I'm the one doing the interviews."

"I thought that went pretty well, though," responded Maxwell. Linda noticed a bunch of heads nodding around the room in agreement.

---

3 STAR Voting: *https://www.starvoting.org/*

Angela continued, "Then Zach, Vera, and I matched the scores between designers and teams. Now, before anyone asks, no, you cannot see the scores. And, I hope we all remember that not everyone is going to get their top pick, but everyone got someone that they were aligned to, and most importantly, nobody got anybody that they were unaligned with. Okay, is everybody ready?"

"Matchmaker, matchmaker, make me a match," Zach sung, unexpectedly.

Linda was already on the edge of her seat and burst out in a little flurry of clapping, "Good one, Zach!" She knew that song, from the musical "Fiddler on the Roof". Linda was impressed. She could tell from that small little snippet that Zach had a surprisingly good voice.

Angela added one more clarification, "Now, there is still room for negotiation, but I think we've made some wise decisions. Are you ready?"

"I am always ready!" Venkat called out.

"Wonderful!" Angela replied. "Okay, since Venkat is all in, let's start there."

Linda thought it sounded like a game show, so she started a drumroll on the table with her fingers.

Angela laughed and continued, "Venkat, the designer joining your team is..." Angela paused for dramatic effect before announcing, "Sandy!"

"What? Really?" blurted out Evah, probably unintentionally. She looked a little embarrassed after saying it.

Linda was also a bit surprised by that choice. *"Sandy wants to deal with Venkat?"* she thought to herself.

"Awesome!" Sandy confirmed. She stood up and addressed everyone, "As many of you know here, I am good friends with Geena on the Riverlands team. We are both very passionate about creating psychologically safe environments and since Riverlands chose 'Connecting as Humans' as one of their top problems to solve, we want to join forces with Venkat."

"Okay, let's do this," Venkat responded confidently, rubbing his hands together with perhaps a little bit of nervous anticipation. "The 'quick profile' view you did for me was just what I wanted."

"Well," Sandy replied, "you can expect more great designs with you, me, and Geena working together!"

Linda was so happy with the response that she applauded until she noticed that nobody else was applauding with her, so she stopped.

Some pairing announcements went smoother than others. Linda noticed some awkwardness in behavior from some of the Product Owners after their pairing announcements, but it looked like Angela and Zach noticed it too. They obviously had a system. She noticed them having private conversations with Product Owners when needed, glancing at their notes, and grabbing Vera and the designers for a quick chat also. But after some negotiation, and a little trading with Vera in the middle, the teams had all been worked out. None of the discussions had turned into a fight, which was a relief! Linda was reminded of that "Intrinsic Motivation" phrase that Angela kept throwing around.

After everybody had finished rearranging themselves, Angela allowed time for Product Owners and designers to chat before continuing with the session. Linda couldn't tell if they were entirely sincere, but everybody seemed to be at least curious if not fully excited about their new partnerships.

Linda walked over to Angela's side.

Angela smiled, "Yes, Linda?"

"I think I see what you're doing," Linda began. Then, noticing a raised eyebrow from Angela, immediately clarified, "Oh, nothing sinister! Sorry. I just mean that I'm noticing that every time there's a big decision to be made that affects a lot of people, instead of making the decision yourself, you facilitate. You gather the people affected most by the decision, and help *them* to make the decision for themselves!"

"Thank you for noticing!" Angela replied with a big smile.

Linda added, "I'm going to try to remember to do that myself going forward." Then she corrected herself, "No, I'm not going to try. I'm going to do it!" That instantly reminded her of Yoda from the Star Wars movies. She switched to a distinct resonating voice, imitating Yoda, "Do or do not. There is no try."

"That was pretty good!" Angela said encouragingly, laughing at Linda's impression.

"Thanks," Linda said a bit shyly, shaking her head to refocus. "Can I ask you another question?" Angela nodded her head yes. "Are you going to cover what we should expect from these pairings? Ooh, and how do we plan to check on the actual effectiveness of the pairings? After all, 'The means by which we pursue our goals is the definition of our character'."

Angela's eyes widened, "Oh yes! Good point! That's a great phrase! And a great question. How will we measure the effectiveness of these pairings? Let's answer your question with the group."

"Can we regroup again here for a little bit please?" She said aloud to the room. "Linda has a great question. Linda?"

Linda wasn't expecting to have to say it out loud but quickly recovered. "Yes, well, I was just wondering, how do we plan to check on the actual effectiveness of the new team changes? You know, to verify that this was the right change."

Evah was the first to offer a response, "Most importantly, we should be able to move faster, right? The expectation is for design work to be turned around faster due to the proximity of designers to their teams. We should be able to shorten our delivery times."

Vera jumped in, "But it's not about order taking." She clarified, "I agree that the goal is for us to move faster, but it's not just about 'turn around' times, right? The designers are to be fully integrated members of the team."

"Right you are," Angela confirmed. "It's vital that we all remember that designers should be fully integrated collaborators, especially in the very early stages of idea generation. Good catch on the use of the phrase 'turn around time', Vera. We probably will have some left-over language in our vocabulary based on how we have been working, but yes, this is definitely about moving faster!"

"Yeah, yeah, that's what I meant," Evah agreed.

Angela added, "Can I ask you all to jump in and graciously help us switch to new terminology the way that Vera did?"

Heads started nodding around the room gradually, including Linda's. It was a clever, two-part request. Angela wanted them to correct each other when using inaccurate words, but also to do it with graciousness. *"What great phrasing!"* Linda thought to herself, making a mental note to see where she could incorporate that prompt into her future work with the teams.

Evah nodded as well. A smile eased onto her face and she continued, "The data should be the same, though, regardless of what we call it, and we should be able to use our existing flow metrics. We already record the time from when we start working on a User Story until it is marked 'done'. If we compare times from before and after the change, the average time should shrink. I can track that data across several sprints."

Linda was impressed. Evah had it down!

"What do others think?" Zach asked, prompting further discussion.

Samuel spoke up, "There are many factors that can affect a whole sprint. How will we know whether this is due to embedded designers or other changes we recently adopted?"

Angela nodded slowly, "Yes, good question. How will we know whether this is working or not?"

Linda raised her hand vigorously, "Well, quantitative numbers like those are important but only half of the picture. As we saw in the Usability Theater, both qualitative and quantitative metrics matter."

"Wait," she paused and checked herself. "Did I use those right? Quantitative and qualitative sound so similar. I sometimes mix them up!" Several other people shook their heads in agreement.

Linda held one hand up in front of her and clarified, "Evah's suggestion effectively covers the *quantity* of data, the quan-ti-tative part," she said, slowly sounding it out. Then she held up her other hand. "For the people part, the quality part, the qual-i-tative data, maybe we can also ask the Product Owners, Designers, and the teams how they feel about the new arrangements at the same intervals?" People nodded their heads in agreement

"Yes!" Sam echoed. "So that means we'll need a survey every sprint."

Zach jumped in, "When collecting the quality data, the qualitative data, it's best to stay away from surveys. They're too impersonal. Linda, could we cover this during each team's sprint retro?"

"Yes," Linda responded, "that sounds like a splendid idea."

"Are you okay with owning that?" Zach clarified.

Linda smiled. "Of course!"

Angela asked this time, "Okay, is there anything else that is potentially unclear?"

Linda raised her hand again, but this time largely just to get people's attention then asked, "When should we check the data and make our pivot or persevere decision?"

"Another great question, Linda," Angela confirmed. "How much time do we think we need?"

Linda looked around. Most people were just shrugging their shoulders, and nobody was venturing an answer so she offered, "How about we have a cross-team review in one month? I'll find a space on the calendars and we can all get together. Evah can show us the data, and I can have each of the ScrumMasters report out about how it went from each of their two retros."

Angela smiled, "Thanks for that excellent offer, Linda! Then it's settled. Is there anything else?" The group remained quiet.

"Okay," Angela said, "let the unification begin!" She grasped her hands together, intertwining her fingers to emphasize the point. "Meeting adjourned!" People chuckled and started to collect their things.

UNEXPECTED EXPECTATIONS

"So you're saying," Jayson asked, "that after a month with the designers embedded in the teams, we didn't reduce the amount of time it takes to get a story done?!"

"No," Evah confirmed. "Well, technically, the average lead time for stories did go down slightly, but not as much as we thought it was going to."

Linda was also amazed and was chomping at the bit to explain it, but didn't want to interrupt Evah's part of the presentation. She waited, but she was jumping up and down with excitement inside.

"Does that mean we go back to the way things were?" asked Venkat rhetorically. "I'm not sure I want to do that. Do we have to?"

Linda smiled as she heard Venkat say that. She considered chiming in to tell Venkat to just wait until her part of the presentation, but Angela beat her to it.

"We still have more to go, Venkat," Angela offered. "We won't make any decisions until we've heard the whole story."

Venkat continued talking, only slightly pausing to hear Angela's response, "I mean, are we sure about this? It definitely seemed like Design was moving faster."

"And don't forget," Angela added, "to raise your hand and summarize your thoughts before you say it." Heads nodded in agreement.

"According to our metrics," Evah explained, "the average lead time from the point at which work started, to the point when it was tested and ready to go, only dropped by one day. Then if you dig down further, you find that the lead time for most of the stories didn't drop, but a few of the stories dropped by a huge amount, which resulted in a small average decrease."

Several hands went up.

"Evah," Angela said, urging her along, "why don't you take us down into the details first and see if it clarifies any questions, and then we'll come back and see if there are any remaining questions."

"Okay," Evah agreed. "When you look at the time spent in the first sprint, it started to look like it was going to get a lot shorter. We moved design to earlier in the process, during the refinement process instead of at the end of it. Almost immediately the first stories to get out of the design stage happened in less than one week. We weren't expecting that, so they actually just sat in the 'Ready for Development' stage for a week until the next sprint."

"There's a reason for that," Venkat interjected, "We had already committed to completing other stories that sprint, so they had to wait."

"A great example," Zach added, "of why you can't just look at 'Total Lead Time'. The 'Process Time' for design and refinement dropped a lot, but the 'Wait Time' increased by the same amount."

"Ooh, ooh, can I add something about our Kanban teams?" Linda asked, raising her hand eagerly in the air.

"Go for it, Linda," Angela said.

"Okay, well," Linda began, collecting her thoughts, "I saw something interesting with our Kanban teams. Their numbers were different since they weren't working in sprints. The designers were working from the top of the prioritized backlog, so when they were ready, the teams started implementing and they did get done faster."

"That's true," Evah agreed. "The Kanban teams saw a noticeable reduction in Total Lead Time for their stories, and that's part of what brought the average score down."

"Yes, Rafael?" Angela said, giving the floor to one of the developers.

"So does that mean that we all should go to Kanban?" he said, in a tone that sounded more like a suggestion than a question.

"No," Venkat insisted, raising his hand impatiently. Angela pointed his way, and he continued, "We prioritize our backlog too. The stories that were ready for development in that first sprint were the most important ones to work on next. Kanban wouldn't have made that better. And what we decided to do instead was to run some tests on the new designs during the second half of the sprint. We never had time to do that before."

Evah jumped in, "Oh, is that why some of the stories went back into the 'Design' stage after being marked as 'Ready'? I thought that was rework."

"No," explained Venkat, "not rework. We made them better... some of them, at least. I would call it 'new work' based on feedback."

"Is that the reason," continued Evah, "why the design stage numbers went back up in sprint two? After the design time dropped in half during the first sprint they returned to the same amount of time as before in the second sprint. You chose to spend more time on design?"

"For some of the stories, yes," Venkat clarified. "Some of the stories didn't need more time, but some of them did."

"And," Evah took over, "that would explain why some of the stories dropped by a lot while others didn't drop at all."

"Can I point out," Angela said, interrupting briefly, "that this is why the numbers don't tell the whole story, but you need the numbers in order to understand the whole story? As Linda would say, 'You need both the quantitative and the qualitative.'"

"Should we jump to my part?" Linda asked, a little apologetic for going out of turn. "This is what we discovered in the retrospectives too, and which I summarized as part of our qualitative research results."

"Not a bad idea," Angela agreed. "Are you okay with that, Evah?" Evah nodded in agreement.

"No good presentation survives first contact with the audience," Jayson added with a chuckle.

Linda chuckled at Jayson's joke[4] as she moved up to the front of the room and took over the remote control from Evah. She clicked forward a few slides.

"Okay, here we go," she said as she found the slide she wanted. "The nature of design evolved very quickly, and we discovered two main changes. First, looking backward, when the designers were involved after major architectural changes, their design changes caused a lot of rework. Architectures had to be adjusted and code rewritten. But by moving design earlier in the process, all of this rework went away, noticeably shortening the average lead time."

---

4 Helmuth von Moltke, 1880, "No good plan survives first contact with the enemy."

"But," continued Linda, "the people impact was even more important! When designers were included before architecture and coding, the developers became less frustrated with the designers, and vice versa! Which also showed up in the retrospectives. There was an increase in the number of contributions to 'What Went Well', and a decrease in 'What Didn't Go Well'." She looked around the room and saw a lot of nodding heads from the designers, Product Owners, and team members present.

Linda clicked to the next slide, but it wasn't the one she thought it was going to be. She clicked a few more times until she found it. "When I pull it all together," she summarized, "what I see is that while we were expecting to see design get faster, what really happened was that design *got better*. Now, not everything needed more design time, but when it was needed, the change allowed teams to spend more time on it without extending the overall timeline! ...And they had more fun doing it!"

"What a wonderful outcome!" said Angela enthusiastically. Then, turning to the room she asked, "Any more questions, or should we vote on whether or not to keep the change?"

"If we vote *not* to keep the change," Vera quickly inserted, "does that mean we have to go back to the way it was before?"

"No," Angela clarified, "we can make that a separate vote. We'll start with a temperature check. If we like the new way, we'll keep that as our new normal. But if it's not popular enough with a majority of us, then we'll start a new discussion about what to do next."

Heads nodded in agreement, so Angela opened the floor, "Thumbs up if you like the new design process and want to make it the new normal. Thumbs down if you don't like it. Thumbs sideways if you abstain, or you don't care."

Linda quickly tabulated the thumbs. It was an easy majority in favor of the new change. She smiled a warm smile that she felt all the way down into her heart.

GAME THEORY

A flurry of barking broke Linda out of her trance. Her two dogs, Jack and Max, were expressing their disapproval at the intruding delivery truck driver. It made Linda nearly tip over in her exercise bike. It even woke her cat, Smeraldina, who glared at her very disapprovingly.

"It's not my fault they woke you up!" Linda explained to the cat. "I'm with you!"

Smeraldina gave her a very disapproving stare anyway and settled back down in the beam of morning sunshine.

Linda checked the time on her smartwatch, and then her heart rate. Her virtual exercise class was over. She got off the bike and went into the kitchen to pour herself a glass of water. It felt cool and refreshing. She turned on the electric tea kettle and pulled out her special blend of mushroom coffee and took a deep inhale of the aroma. It was definitely an acquired taste, but she loved it. She grabbed a banana while she waited for the hot water to boil and tried to bring her mind back to what she had been piecing together in her brain while she was on the exercise bike.

Her brain was spinning around the review session they had the day before about the designers. Images of the data that she and Evah had been collecting started swirling through her mind's eye again. Each team had responded to integrating the designers differently. Some were focused on increased speed, others on increased quality, and a few teams also talked about quality of life in their retros. It was fascinating how many talked about how they didn't care about moving as fast as possible because they liked being more collaborative. They liked the sanity of having control over their day. While there were common themes, every team had responded differently, and those differences fascinated Linda.

The same thing was true of the Agile Mindset Mapping Index improvements. Even when teams had tackled the same categories in AMMI for improvement, they had each solved the problems in a unique way based on their unique personalities. It is a beautiful thing about human nature.

But she was worried that she was the only one to see it. Besides Angela and maybe Zach, she was the only one who got to visit all of the retros and hear their stories. It felt like a missed opportunity. It was not that everybody should attend everybody else's retrospective. That would be chaos... and overkill.

"Should I record them?" she thought briefly but then dismissed the thought just as quickly. Much of the retro was irrelevant to anybody who wasn't part of the team. But there were little nuggets of insight that should be shared.

"Ding!" Her phone notification called out for her attention. Her favorite video game wanted her to spend a little more time playing with it. It was relentless. Five minutes here, five minutes there, and she had to admit that it was easy to string several games together and quickly fill a half hour. The allure of closing out a section could be intoxicating.

It reminded her of the AMMI improvements actually. The teams had been tracking their AMMI scores in spreadsheets, and the more their scores rose, the teams had unexpectedly begun to become a little obsessed with scoring 100% in all the categories. It had almost become like a video game for them. They wanted to "complete the level" and "level up", two phrases that had started to become more and more common during retros.

"Should we?" Linda wondered. Each of the teams had vastly different criteria for what counted as 100% and they used different techniques in each category. *"Take Daily Collaboration as an example,"* she explained to herself. *"Some teams have Daily Standup Meetings, while others use Mob Programming. They all have daily collaborations, but it looks different in each team."*

But that was the same as in video games. Sure, some games required you to complete a predefined set of steps to "win" but others did not. Plus, even in those pre-defined games, everyone had their own unique style for getting through the level. Some raced to see who could complete the level the fastest, others liked to collect as many gems as possible, and a small contingent of game enthusiasts preferred to explore every inch of the game space looking for Easter eggs, hidden rewards, secret passageways, and even bugs and mistakes before clearing the level.

"How was that different from what just happened with the designer challenge?" she thought. "Wait," she said out loud to her dog Jack, "there is a book about the four components of all games. Where is that book?" Jack had long forgotten the delivery truck driver and had settled back down into a fluffy little ball on the rug. He perked up his head and watched as Linda crossed over to the bookshelf to find the book.

"Here it is!" she called out to Jack. "'Reality is Broken'[5] by Jane McGonigal." Jack looked excited to be included in the quest, but also really puzzled. Linda flipped through the pages looking for the passage she wanted. She found a bookmark that she had labeled as "the four traits"

---

5 "Reality is Broken" by Jane McGonigal, *Reality is Broken*

and read it out loud to Jack, "When you strip away the genre differences and the technological complexities, all games share four defining traits: a goal, rules, a feedback system, and voluntary participation."

Jack also found this fascinating, but at the same time didn't seem to understand why he was being consulted. Linda explained, "Don't you see? The teams have a goal. AMMI provides the rules. Angela established the requirement of voluntary participation. The only thing we don't have on this list is a feedback system!" Jack wagged his tail in shared excitement.

"And I think," added Linda, "that our designer integration review session is an example of a feedback system! Oh, I can't wait to run this by Angela!" One of those words caught the attention of her other dog, Max. It was probably the word "run", but he was all in now too, sitting at attention next to Jack, expectantly.

"What if," Linda asked the dogs, "each of the teams gave a quick summary presentation of how they chose to solve their chosen AMMI category, along with the data to back up their choices? We could then leave time for other teams to ask questions and discuss, and maybe even take a vote afterward to see if they qualify!"

Max barked in excitement. "You're right," replied Linda. "This isn't really a pass or fail kind of thing. Ooh! Everybody could vote on a scale of zero to four, and then we could average the scores!" Max barked again, excited by the new development. "Thanks, Max! Not a bad idea, buddy."

Jack just stared at them both, noncommittally. "Oh, you're right, Jack," Linda countered. "Why didn't I think of that? That's a fundamental maxim of science. What if the people voting don't understand that area? 'They may not know what they don't know', as Angela says. Their evaluation is subjective. How could we make it more objective?"

She thought for a few moments. "Well, there is 'The wisdom of crowds'. With a large enough sample, the natural diversity of experience will usually result in a better decision than any one person's opinion." Jack just continued to look unimpressed, staring up at her through his fluffy eyebrows. "You're right, Jack. This isn't a large enough sample size for that, and because we're all biased by the way we've been working in the past, we need to be more objective."

Max shuffled around and gave a series of barks. "Hmm, that's an interesting idea, Max. Only let the people who have already mastered that area vote?" Max barked again to confirm her understanding. "But what would we do in the beginning," she asked Max, "you know, when nobody has achieved mastery yet?" Max barked again. "The coaches? The leaders? Huh, that's not a bad idea, Max." Max smiled back at her. "In the beginning, Angela and any of the leaders who are experts in that area could vote on the first presentations. That could help set the standard."

This time Jack barked. "What are you trying to say, Jack?" Linda asked him. "Hmm. That's also a good point. What if people try to game the system?" Jack let out a plaintive whine to confirm his distress.

Linda petted him to soothe his concerns and continued exploring the thought, "I mean, I don't think they'll try to pay each other for false scores or anything." Max barked a couple of times. "Ah, good point, Max," she confirmed. "It may not be intentional. They might score somebody lower just because it's not the way they would have done it, or is missing some element that they use."

This time the cat meowed. "You have a thought, Smeraldina? What is it?" The cat just stared back, having already invested the maximum amount of energy that she intended. "Oh, great point, Smeraldina," Linda responded. "The whole process will actually be self-reinforcing. If somebody scores another team too harshly, they risk having that done to them as well. So we probably don't have to worry as much about biased low scores. Our main worry is probably going to be people giving scores that are too high. Maybe we need a Supreme Court?!"

Smeraldina just looked at her disapprovingly. "No, you're right, Smeraldina. Nobody appeals decisions that are better than they expected. They only appeal decisions that are worse than they expected." Linda thought a little more, then decided. "Maybe we need to give the coaches and the experts the ability to override a score, as long as they don't use it too often."

Linda walked over to her work bag and pulled out her notebook. She flipped to the empty pages at the back and wrote down all of the rules and details for the review sessions that she and her fur babies had figured out.

When she was done, she looked up at them and said, "Don't worry. I'll give you all full credit when I talk to Angela about these. Okay, who wants to go outside?!" Jack and Max jumped up in excitement, and Max did a couple of spins to accentuate how much he liked the idea. Smeraldina just got up and rotated enough to turn her back to them as she settled back in to enjoy her sunbath, now hopefully undisturbed.

THREE MONTHS LATER – AMMI COMMUNITY OF PRACTICE

"Okay," Linda said to the whole room, "it's time to vote! Rafael, put your fist down. Remember that we're not going to vote by holding up fingers like we did the last time. We're going to try Veni's new app this month."

"Hey," called out Logan, an automation engineer from the North team. "It says that I'm not allowed to vote. What gives?"

"Remember," Linda responded, "your team needs to score a four in order for you to be able to vote."

"I thought we didn't have to get a perfect score," Logan argued back.

Linda clarified, "You are remembering correctly that we're not looking for a perfect 100%, but you need to score at least 75%. A score of four means that you scored at least 75%, which doesn't have to be a perfect score, but your team got a three which means that you scored less than 75%. I'm sorry but you can't vote on this practice yet."

"Was I not supposed to talk during the discussions, then?" Logan asked again. "I'm so confused."

"It's okay," Linda reassured him. "You've only been here a few weeks. You'll get the hang of it. Everyone gets to talk. Always. You don't have to have voting rights to participate in the discussions, ask questions, or offer ideas."

Isabella jumped in this time, "But the Crownlands team can vote this week, right?"

"Yes," confirmed Linda. "We changed the rules this month. Last time we required teams to have fours across all of the practices in the category in order to vote, but this week the rule is that if your team scored a four on just this particular practice, you can vote. I'm sorry that we keep changing the rules, but I think this way is better."

"Totally agree!" Isabella responded. "Much better!"

"Okay, then," continued Linda. "Let's go ahead and get those scores in. I'll give you a few more minutes."

Linda was feeling good about the decision to allow more people to vote. The process worked better and was much more fun when more people got to vote. Requiring that teams complete all of the Design, Planning, or Implementation practices before they could vote on any of the individual practices had made logical sense... last month... but they quickly realized that some people in the room really did know the practice well, even though they hadn't mastered all of the other practices around it.

"Are we ready?" Linda asked the room again.

"Looks like all the eligible votes are in," Veni answered.

"Then click that button!" Linda ordered.

Veni clicked the button and the score appeared on the screen.

"Congratulations!" called out Linda. "You got an average score of 3.67! That rounds up to a four! Thank you for all your hard work! You all get to vote for this practice the next time it comes up!"

She checked her notes and then announced, "Next up will actually be three teams at once. The Riverlands, Westerlands, and The North teams. They all decided to do some Dependency Planning together in order to implement the new integrated Merchant login architecture."

"Taneesha will present for the team," Jayson announced.

"Great! Thanks, Taneesha," Linda replied. "Are you able to share that on the screen?"

"I'm good," Taneesha confirmed.

As Taneesha started her presentation, Linda started thinking back over the past couple of months since she had dreamed up the gamification for AMMI. It had taken off even better than she had hoped, though it wasn't without its hiccups. They had made some mistakes with the rules for voting, being too cautious and too restrictive in the early days.

Having more voters also meant that Angela and Zach didn't need to vote. It had turned out to be weird having Angela and Zach help the teams prepare their evidence and their presentations, and then turn around and vote on whether or not those presentations – that they had helped build – qualified or not. With more voters, Angela and Zach got to act exclusively as advocates for the teams, helping them to defend their scores. Angela affectionately referred to her and Zach now as Defense Attorneys, in addition to making sure that the teams didn't submit for evaluation before they truly qualified across all of the points of guidance. That prevented a lot of frustration with teams putting in all that work only to score a two or a three.

The other unexpected change was breaking off into three Communities of Practice in order to cover more ground. They kept running out of time to cover all of the presentations. They had been faced with the choice of either splitting into multiple Communities of Practice, or spending less time on discussions, and so they voted. They all really loved the discussions, so they decided to break off into multiple Communities of Practice.

The Developers were the first to break off, holding their own inaugural session immediately following the second main group session. Jayson and Ali sponsored a Technical Community of Practice to cover not only Architecture concerns but also the Implementation and Operations categories. They invited everyone to attend, but the Product Owners and Designers never showed up. Linda heard that they were happy to not have to listen to all of the technical details anymore.

As they entered their third month of sessions, Vera officially took over as Interim Product Manager. Angela still refused to take the job, and they were still struggling to hire a replacement for Naomi, but they felt like they needed someone in the role. One of Vera's first acts as the now-official, interim Product Manager was to launch her own Design Community of Practice, on a weekly basis. Linda suspected that it helped Vera feel like she still had the Designer Den, and the Designers loved it too.

That left Linda to run the original Community of Practice covering the People and Planning categories. The Scrum Masters always attended, and so did the Product Owners, most of the time, but not the designers. Linda missed having the designers there. The rules were that anybody could attend any Community of Practice, but attendance was never mandatory. People eventually figured out their favorites and stopped going to the rest. After all, there was only so much time in the day. The only major exception was when a whole team went to support their teammates during presentations, which happened frequently enough. Evah was one of the few people besides Linda who tried to attend all three.

Linda was jolted out of her reminiscing by a few raised voices.

"But Linda just told me that everyone's allowed to talk!" Logan was saying, a little too emphatically.

"Yes," Taneesha countered, "you are allowed to talk, but not until I'm done presenting."

Logan pushed back, "But I didn't agree to do that story in that sprint. It was the next sprint. That's all I'm saying. The Dependency Board is wrong."

"It doesn't matter," Taneesha said again, "if the board is right or wrong. We're just presenting how we created the board and the process that we used. We can fix it later!"

"It matters to me," Logan insisted.

"Logan," Linda interrupted, "yes you are allowed to talk, but at the designated point in the process. We use the Double Aces approach for this meeting, remember? Step one is listening to the entire presentation; if you have thoughts you write them down on sticky notes or in your notebook; step two is Appreciations and Acknowledgements only; step three is Clarifying or Confirming questions; and step four is when you can introduce Enhancements or Evolutions."

That seemed to work, as she saw Logan settle back into his seat. She felt fortunate that she knew that he was on the autistic spectrum, although she wasn't going to share that fact with others until he was ready to share it. She also felt fortunate that he was a stickler for rules. It was what made him an exceptional architect. It also meant that once he understood the rules, he was highly likely to follow them, to the letter.

And he wasn't the only new hire. With the replacement for the new account workflow in place, they were no longer losing market share, and actually starting to pull ahead of Intuition Bank again. Customers were happy again – or at least happier – and that extra income had translated into more budget for new hires, in addition to a huge reduction in stress.

Angela was right. Helping people solve their own problems through a new system was more fruitful than trying to solve problems for them. And Tim was right. They were beating Intuition not by copying Intuition but by listening to their customers and removing their obstacles. She smiled to herself and went back to listening to Taneesha's presentation.

She was so proud of all her teams!

A MONUMENTAL SHIFT

A week later, the entire Ares Innovation Center was back in American Banking's main auditorium.

"And now it is my pleasure," Tim announced to the entire Ares Innovation Center, "to introduce the CEO of American Banking Systems, who will present our last series of rewards! Everyone, please welcome Ahmed!" The audience clapped enthusiastically from their dinner tables as Ahmed made his way to the front of the room and accepted the mic from Tim.

This was the moment that Linda had been waiting for. Her stomach was tied in knots. She had not been allowed to tell anyone else about the decision yet, and keeping the secret was killing her. Only the leadership team knew about it so far.

"Thank you, Tim," began Ahmed. "It has been a real rollercoaster hasn't it?" he asked the audience. A knowing chuckle reverberated throughout the ballroom. "Less than three years ago, Tim approached me with an idea – an innovative, bold idea. An idea that worked! We sailed off into new waters under a blue sky, king of our domain, only to find ourselves quickly surrounded by pirates, trying to steal what was ours. And they almost did." He paused for effect, and Linda could hear a few people hissing their disapproval of Intuition Bank.

"In truth," he continued, "we almost let them. I don't know if you know this, but I've been a user of Breeze since the very beginning. But I also started using Cynch shortly after they launched, because one of my golf buddies coerced me. We had made a friendly wager, and I won. I think that's why he did it, because he was a poor loser, and he forced me to use Cynch to accept his money!" More hissing from the audience. A couple of people even openly booed.

"Right?" he asked the audience, egging them on. "The gaul! But what annoyed me even more was that Cynch really was a cinch. It was better than our app. That was a dark day for me... and then we started losing market share." The unexpected turn in the story brought a hush to the room.

"We almost shut you down!"

The frank statement from Ahmed shook Linda. Tim also. Linda could see Tim edging forward, looking like he wanted to interrupt Ahmed, but not sure if he should.

Ahmed continued his thought, "We're here to make money, right?" He smiled a knowing smile, but nobody smiled with him. "I mean, we expected you to operate at a loss in the beginning, but it didn't look like it was ever going to turn around. When I told Tim that we were going to shut the project down, by god did he fight for you all! He told me that you were on the cusp of change, an 'inflection point' as he called it. It would take a little while longer to pay off, but it would pay off. Seriously, the faith he has in this team is amazing! The board promised to give him one more quarter. Actually, we decided to give him two more quarters, but we only told him that he had one more quarter!" Ahmed laughed heartily at the inside joke, but no one else joined in.

"And one of the things that is so amazing about Tim is that he is consistently able to see what other people can't see! Let's raise a glass to Tim!" He held up his champagne flute. "Here's to Tim, the visionary, the innovator, the advocate, and the fortune teller! ...In more ways than one," he added with a sly chuckle and a wink.

Linda raised her glass and turned to clink glasses with Angela, Zach, and Evah. They all smiled and returned her look of relief that Ahmed's speech had been able to turn the corner and come back towards the positive.

"And the numbers speak for themselves," Ahmed continued. "We have regained the upper hand against Cynch over the last three months, and we have increased customer retention by 83%! As a result, Ares Innovation has increased our gross revenue by a rocketing 20% this quarter with over 40% growth rate in just the past year! This is incredible, but just the beginning, because you have successfully delivered a sustainable business model. My friend at the club even commended me on Breeze's progress. That makes me very happy, so thank you for all your hard work!" He started applauding, and the whole room joined in.

"Can I see one of those trophies you were just handing out?" Ahmed asked Tim. Linda handed hers to Ahmed for him to inspect. "I like how they're each different themes," Ahmed commented. "Clever. There's a cash register for Merchant Services, golden pyramids of value for our foundation teams, a boxer for the support team, and did I even see one with a bull on it? Classic! My favorite, though, is probably that golden cornucopia with gold coins dribbling out of it!"

"Those were Evah's ideas," Linda called out.

"Oh?" Ahmed confirmed. "Great idea, Evah."

"I just said they should all be unique," Evah called back from her seat. "Linda, Zach, Angela, Jayson, and Vera all contributed to the ideas."

"Alright," Ahmed commented. "Well, good work to all of you. I guess I'm going to be boring in comparison," he said, switching gears.

"My award for everyone in the room is just a measly... thousand-dollar bonus!" The room was caught off guard but erupted in excitement.

"And let's not forget your amazing leadership team! You will all have a little extra in your next paycheck as well," he said, turning around to gesture at their tables, leading the ballroom in another round of applause.

"But a shift like this doesn't happen on its own," he added as the applause began to die down. "From what I hear, the woman at the center of it all was Angela! Let's give her a round of applause!" The room broke out into warm applause.

"Angela, come up here." Angela scooted her chair back and walked up to join Ahmed. "I hear that you're an avid traveler like Tim here," Ahmed said to Angela.

"Guilty as charged," Angela said.

"Well," Ahmed responded, "as our thanks to you, we are giving you a trip to Costa Rica, with airfare and hotel accommodations! Courtesy of one of our Merchant Services partners, Island Breeze Vacations."

Angela stepped forward, with excitement, to shake Ahmed's hand, and accept the envelope he was offering. The audience clapped enthusiastically.

Ahmed kept going, "And now for the biggest news of the night. With the recent success of the Innovation Center, the board of American Banking Systems has agreed to go all in on Ares Innovation! We want to integrate what you have done here into our core banking services. With your help and insight we're going to turn all of ABS into an adaptive organization!"

"And to lead the way we have asked Linda and Zach to become Directors of Agile Management within ABS Core Banking Services! Congratulations, Linda and Zach, on your promotions!!"

The whole room erupted in applause. As it started to die down, Linda heard someone call out from the back, "Mom, you're leaving us?!"

"Yeah, we'll miss you, Linda!" shouted out another unrecognizable voice from one of the far tables. A bunch of other voices joined in.

"You too, Zach!" someone else added. "Congratulations! But we're sorry to see you go." More voices of agreement joined in.

"Can I borrow the microphone for just a moment?" Linda asked Ahmed apologetically.

"Sure, here you go," he agreed.

"Don't worry," Linda said to the crowd, "you're still going to see us. Yes, we're going to be spending more time with the teams in our parent company, to help them choose their own Agile adventures... but we're coaches for all of ABS, and that includes you! We're not leaving you and we still expect to see everyone at the Communities of Practice!"

"We'll be there!" someone replied.

"Congratulations!" added another, and it evolved into a bunch more callouts that easily transitioned into another round of applause.

Linda handed the microphone to Zach, who just said, "Thank you everyone!" and handed the microphone back to Ahmed.

Ahmed gave the closing words, "Finally, one more award to the entire Ares Innovation Center. This is a tribute to everyone who not only survived but thrived and grew through these difficult times. Tomorrow will be a paid day off for the Innovation Center!" The room erupted in cheers again. "With that, thank you, and ***le-e-e-e-e-e-et's PARTY!***"

The scene exploded in festivity. Champagne bottles popped, and people started lining up for the buffet tables.

FINAL REFLECTIONS

Hours passed by quickly, fueled by plenty of laughter and excitement.

"What a gala!" Linda thought. She took a moment and sat back down at her table. She reached into her purse and pulled out her notebook. She had one more exercise that she liked to do at the end of every day, and she was inspired to do it right then.

She flipped to an open page and wrote out the first prompt, *"Three amazing things that happened today."*

She paused for a moment to focus her thoughts and wrote, *"1. I helped save over 200 jobs."* She didn't realize how close they had been to being shut down. That was scary.

She shook off the feeling and moved on to the second thought that had struck her that evening. *"2. Today, I was seen. I got a promotion, and I didn't have to change jobs to get recognized for my achievements."*

She moved to the next line and wrote the number three. She didn't have a third one right away but pushed herself to think of one. Then it came to her, *"3. I helped over 200 other people feel seen tonight."*

She moved down a line and wrote her second favorite prompt for the end of the day, *"How could I have made today better?"*

She didn't have to think about this one. She wrote the word, *"NOTHING"* in big letters, closed the notebook, put it back in her purse, grabbed her champagne glass, and went to rejoin the festivities with a big smile on her face and a warm feeling of love in her heart.

Key Points of Learning

- Journaling
- Game Theory
- Agile Mindset Mapping Index (AMMI)
- Communities of Practice

Epilogue

Naomi – Shifting the Unmovable

“Congratulations, Tim,” Naomi said with a twinge of regret that she tried her best to cover.

“It was a nice event,” Tim admitted, “but I do honestly wish that you could have been there. I still consider you a big part of what we were celebrating.”

“That’s very nice of you to say,” Naomi said sincerely.

“So,” asked Tim, changing the subject, “are you still liking the new job?”

Naomi sighed, “You ask that each time we meet for coffee, and the answer is still yes.” Tim gave her a look of doubt so she added, “It’s not splashy and fun, but it’s dependable. We’re not winning any industry awards, but my team is solid, and I’m the queen of my domain. It’s what I need right now.”

Naomi redirected the conversation, “Okay, Tim, what’s the latest struggle?”

“Ready to switch gears?” Tim asked. “No problem. I’ve got a doozie this time.”

“Hit me with your best shot!” Naomi urged him on. Naomi was never going to admit it, but she actually liked talking about Breeze with Tim, despite how she left. It helped her feel connected with the innovation center that she had helped build, and it helped her feel valuable that Tim wanted to brainstorm on strategy. Plus she didn’t have to worry about getting blamed if anything didn’t work. Best of both worlds!

“Fair enough,” Tim agreed. “So, as I mentioned last time, all of the teams have direct customer interaction now.”

“And they really haven’t scared off a single customer yet?” Naomi interrupted.

“Nope,” Tim replied. “The customers seem to really love the attention. The merchant services team in particular. They can’t stop raving about the new one-step account creation process.”

“Two steps,” Naomi corrected.

“What?” asked Tim.

Naomi clarified, “They go to their nested bank login page and then are directed back. That’s technically two steps.”

“Ok,” agreed Tim. “They love the new two-step account creation process.”

“And Ali’s fine with having competing account creation architectures?” Naomi inquired.

Tim countered, "You can't argue with a four hundred percent increase in transactions."

"Fair enough," Naomi agreed. "That really is an amazing accomplishment."

"Thanks," Tim replied, "and I'm not trying to say 'I told you so' here, but it is just a strong reminder for me personally that copying Cynch would not have worked here. It really was listening directly to our customers describe their own troubles in their own words that led to that discovery."

Naomi held her tongue. She was sure that she would have come up with a different alternative eventually that didn't require two architectures, but that wasn't her problem anymore.

Tim continued, "So the new problem that they've expressed is that they keep having to switch between their ABS bank account and the Breeze merchant app. This was never a problem before. I guess now that they're no longer complaining about the new account process, this has become the topic 'du jour'."

Tim looked at Naomi, "Okay, so now that you have the big picture, what do you think is the problem?"

Naomi stared at Tim and said, nonchalantly, "Maybe you aren't looking at it from a long-term perspective."

Tim looked confused, "We do look at the long-term perspective. We have an overall set of company guidelines for growth..."

Naomi interrupted him, mid-sentence, "What does Angela have to say?"

Tim chuckled and said, "She said that this is why she never had any intention of taking over as Product Manager. 'Agile coaching is not a substituteforgoodproductmanagement', Ithinkthatwaswhatshesaid. Her answeristoleadtheProductOwnersthroughsomebrainstormingsessions."

Naomi rolled her eyes. Tim must have noticed because he switched gears, "That's what I like about Angela. She recognizes when she is in over her head, and admits it. As she's fond of joking, 'Damnit, Tim! I'm a coach, not a banker!' That's far better than wasting time pretending to have an answer and discovering later that you never did. Bad decisions do not get better over time."

"Maybe Angela doesn't have a savior complex after all," Naomi thought. She felt the tug of wanting to dive back in but held back.

"What's Vera's take?" she said instead.

But before Tim could answer, Naomi's phone rang, again. She couldn't help but glance down, and saw her new boss's name on the screen.

"Oh, I'm sorry, Tim," she said, "I hate to interrupt you, but this is the third time that my boss has called me since we got here. I should probably take this. Do you mind?"

"No," replied Tim, "of course not. It sounds urgent. Go for it."

Naomi stepped away a distance and answered the call, "Hello, Naomi here."

"Naomi, where are you?" the voice on the other end said urgently and insistently.

"Just grabbing coffee," she answered, leaving out the part about it being with her old boss. "Why? What's up?"

"We just got word from on high," her boss answered. "They're cutting 25% of the workforce. I need you back here to tell me who's dead weight on the teams so I can make a list of cuts before this hits the papers! Get back here now!"

Her boss hung up the phone and Naomi's mind just started racing. "Why is it never easy?" she thought. Her brain started jumping back and forth between different members of her new teams. *"There are a few obvious people that aren't pulling their weight,"* she thought, *"but I'm just starting to build a rapport with the others. This is really going to damage all of those connections."* The easiest decisions were probably the newest hires. That seemed only fair.

"Wait!" A new thought entered Naomi's head, vying for first place in her attention. *"What about me? I'm the newest hire among the management staff. Is anyone having the same discussion about me?"* Now her mind was thinking about Sam and the kids. It had taken her so long to find this job, and the stress that had put on the family! She couldn't go through that again. The job-hunting. The searching. The interviews. The months of back-to-back rejections.

"Naomi, are you alright?" It took a few seconds before Tim's words registered in Naomi's mind. "Naomi? Should I call somebody?"

"What?" said Naomi, finally. She noticed that she was still holding her mobile phone, but that it had drifted down away from her ear. The call was clearly over.

"Ok. Whew! " said Tim. "You're back. Are you alright? I was worried that this might be a repeat... you know... of what happened before."

"Sorry," apologized Naomi, "what have I been doing?"

"Well," explained Tim, "you ended the call with 'I understand' and 'Thank you very much' then just stopped as if frozen for the last minute or so!"

"Oh wow. I did?" Naomi asked, a flush racing to her cheeks. "My apologies, Tim! You must think I'm crazy."

"Not at all," Tim insisted.

Naomi continued without stopping. "It's just that I have to get back to the office. We just got the word about budget cuts. We have to cut 25% of the staff before it hits the papers."

"Oh, lord, I get it," Tim said in commiseration. "We had a similar scare."

"Wait, you did?" Naomi asked, caught for a moment by surprise. "I heard about your budget cuts, but I don't remember hearing about staff cuts at Ares."

"Oh, we found another way," Tim explained. "We got together and figured out a way to not have to fire anybody. I hope you're going to be alright?"

"Yeah, sure," Naomi lied. "Probably. I mean, who are they going to get to replace me with, right?" She smiled and laughed, regaining her composure.

"You are irreplaceable," Tim agreed. "God knows I've tried," he said with a jovial smile.

"I'm sorry to cut our coffee short," Naomi apologized.

"Of course," Tim agreed.

"The answer to your problem, though, is bank accounts," she tossed off as she gathered her things.

"Bank accounts?" Tim asked.

"Yes, bank accounts," Naomi confirmed. "It was something I had been exploring but never got to launch. Yeah, we started off as a mobile app, but we are a bank after all. You are," she corrected herself. "You are still part of ABS Bank. You have access to their infrastructure. Allow merchants to manage their ABS bank accounts from within the app. Do it by default. Make it easier to bank with Breeze than to transfer their money to a third-party bank, which would also increase deposits, which increases your cash on hand, and makes more funds available to act as securities for loans. Ahmed will love that."

"Now I really have to run," she said, winding up the visit.

"How do I have the answers to Tim's problems so easily," she thought, *"but not my own?"* It infuriated her, but she decided to turn that fury into energy. She had to go into fight mode now, for herself, Sam, and the kids. It was time to show her worth and fight for her job.

"I'll pay for the drinks," she heard Tim say. "Thank you! And good luck!"

"Thank you, Tim! Let's do this again soon, but preferably some time when the sky isn't falling," she added with lighthearted ease.

She didn't feel lighthearted, but as she had learned a long time ago from a commercial when she was a kid,

"Never let them see you sweat."

THE END...
OF THE BEGINNING

Author's note by Michael Dougherty

This book started due to a shared training event in Herndon, Virginia where Pete Oliver-Krueger and I teamed up to do Leading SAFe at Lithespeed to people at Fannie May in January of 2020.

Pete Oliver-Krueger and I had previously met a few times at Agile Conferences since I knew the CEO and co-founder, Sanjiv Augustine, who taught me the certified Scrum Master training all the way back in 2010, eight years after I had started doing Scrum (but not "being Agile") at Halliburton/KBR.

Pete and I really hit it off during the training and talked during the end of the first day when he popped up the desire to write a book. Having that same desire and failing once writing a technical book on Documentum, I thought this was a wonderful opportunity.

We came in full of excitement and optimism, expecting the book would be done in a year, maybe two years if we really went slow.

Well over four years later we finally have our book. There were definitely some major setbacks along the way. Surprisingly, COVID was not one of them and even perhaps an accelerator.

However, our book wasn't written like a typical guide. Instead, we wrote a true novel in third person past tense changing the main perspective each chapter.

Unfortunately, when writing a true novel, we grimly discovered in the summer of 2022 how bad it can be to have a major plot change mid-way in the book causing so many splits that felt like a moment from the Time Variance Authority (TVA) within the Marvel series, "Loki".

Pete and I had a good system. I'd write from nothing, and then he would refine what I wrote with his perspective. However, at our peak,

I got six chapters ahead of him with my raw content and so when we hit that major plot change, all six of those chapters basically had to be scrapped, affectionately known as "The Cutting Room Floor".

Yes, we are guilty of waterfalling the book and you would think we would have not fallen prey to that. We had a flow issue and I needed to throttle back my work to match Pete's capacity and pace.

After that very grueling summer where rework was king and demotivation was queen, we then realized that we did not have one book in front of us, but instead at least three books! The next year was primarily spent reducing the book and that became yet another exercise in tedium!

Our other two books have the following operative titles:

- Shift 2: From Products to Problems
- Shift 3: From Enterprises to Adaptive Organizations

This would be the full series, but further books may result, just in another timeline. Our rough schedule would be to have Shift 2 and Shift 3 released in the next two to three years each. Of course, we do not follow a specific schedule, but more of "when the book is ready, it is ready", so we flex on scope, not schedule, just like in Agile!

However, we will certainly share with our readers early versions along the way so you can help influence the direction of our upcoming books as well so let's keep the continuous feedback loop open and thank you for reading our book! It is a dream come true!

Author's note by Pete Oliver-Krueger

The inkling of the idea for this book stemmed from necessity and frustration. Michael and I kept seeing clients making the same mistakes over and over again. They thought they "were Agile" but they didn't know what they didn't know. There is a whole world of new techniques that we both love to teach, but that organizations can't even begin to explore until they have fixed the fundamentals. So this book is about fixing those fundamentals and building a strong foundation on which to build the future of your organization.

Roy, the Data Scientist in the story, actually represents this frustration in the book. He definitely lacks in the social graces, but from the beginning, he was ready to operate at a higher level of performance, but was unwilling to put in the work to rebuild the company's foundations. Our challenge was how to more quickly allow companies to see the cracks in their foundations. As coaches we can only work with one or two organizations per year. So instead we decided to tell the story of what a year is like with coaching in this new way of thinking. All we had to do was figure out the best format for telling this story to an unpredictable number of people across a dozen tightly integrated disciplines.

When we kicked this project off, I had recently finished reading George R. R. Martin's Game of Thrones book series, and the entire Expanse novel series by James S. A. Corey. I was enamored with their "Rotating Third Person Limited" style of writing. I personally struggle with third-person omniscient books because knowing everyone's thoughts feels unnatural to me. Conversely, first-person limited perspective books are great when you are only following one character through their life, but that was never going to be sufficient for a book on collaboration and integrating multiple perspectives. Rotating the narrator every chapter and looking at an organization from multiple directions quickly emerged as the perfect antidote.

Now, when I say "reading" Game of Thrones and The Expanse, what I really mean is that I was listening to them. I discovered late in life that I am dyslexic, which explains why I can (almost) never finish a printed book. I can, however, quickly knock out a good audiobook, which I have done for decades, going all the way back to having a real, honest-to-God, books-on-tape subscription at a physical audiobooks store. I was also a very early subscriber on my Palm Treo to Audible, way before Amazon bought them, which is now going to totally give away my age.

So I was never going to be able to be the author of a "normal" book, which is why I was so pleased that Michael was willing to explore this world building project with me. I don't read (or write) books, I hear them. As a former actor and director I also used to act them out and build entire worlds from stories on stage. The implication was that it took us a while to settle on a style for this book. In our early drafts I was writing screenplays, and Michael was writing a book. That meant that we had to meet somewhere in the middle, but happily we found that center.

It was also personally important to me that the characters not be shadows and reflections of Michael and me, but distinct real people, so I called on the power of the Enneagram. If you have never heard of the Enneagram, you should definitely go check it out! As a former actor and director, I spent a lot of time collecting what I called "Character Shortcuts" – ways to understand the backstories, thought patterns, aspirations, and the decision making of different characters. I needed a way to contrast the character against myself, so that I was acting out the character's life, not always my own. I collected many models for character development, but none of them were as fast, as powerful, or as clear and distinct as the Enneagram. But I digress.

Each of the characters in this book are based on different iterations of the nine Enneagram personality types. Michael and I thought about people from our professional pasts who matched each Enneagram type and mashed them all together to protect anonymity. It quickly became our organizing principle for keeping all of the characters straight. We will address the Enneagram in future books, so I won't reveal here which characters were assigned to which types. I will leave that for you as the reader to puzzle out for yourselves. I love stories with hidden gems, a la easter eggs from movies and video games.

Easter eggs and leaving hints about the future were a principle of the book from the start, but also became even more necessary when we realized that we hadn't written one book. We had written three... literally. It's another reason that it took us four years to write this book. We wrote two books worth of content, thinking that it was one book. We just didn't realize it until our publisher finally asked us to count the total pages. At that point we had to cut the book in segments and rewrite the story arc using only one third of the original content.

SPOILER ALERT: If you haven't finished the story yet, skip this paragraph or skip forward one minute (if you're listening on audiobook). One example of a significant change that happened as a result of the split is that in our original story line, Naomi returned halfway through the book and helped build a new operating model for Ares Innovation in collaboration with Angela. When we chopped the book in half, we had to break that story arc. Naomi didn't get to return to Ares in book one. You'll have to check out book two to learn what we decided to do instead.

So you can expect to see a second book. We have already written most of it, but we will have to reorganize it to accommodate the splitting. As such, it will also have to happen further off in the future in the evolution of Ares Innovation Center. In this second book we will address all of those topics that can't be done without the foundations found in this book: Leadership by Intent, Lean Startup, Customer Discovery, Minimum Viable Products, Design Thinking, the Scientific Method, Metrics-Based Decision making, the Role of Architects in and Agile organization, and many more!

After that, book three will probably be about a complete Agile Operating Model for organizations from top to bottom, as this is what we are researching right now.

NOTES